THE EXPERIENCE
OF THE
FOREIGN

SUNY Series, Intersections:
Philosophy and Critical Theory

Rodolphe Gasché and Mark C. Taylor, Editors

Antoine Berman

THE EXPERIENCE
OF THE
FOREIGN

*Culture and Translation in
Romantic Germany*

*Translated by
S. Heyvaert*

10·02

State University of New York Press

Originally published as *L'Épreuve de l'étranger*
© Editions Gallimard, 1984

Published by
State University of New York Press, Albany

For information, address State University of New York
Press, State University Plaza, Albany, N.Y., 12246

Production by Dana Foote
Marketing by Fran Keneston

Library of Congress Cataloging in Publication Data

Berman, Antoine.
    [Épreuve de l'étranger. English]
    The experience of the foreign : culture and translation in
romantic Germany / Antoine Berman : translated by S. Heyvaert.
      p. cm. — (Intersections)
    Translation of: L'Épreuve de l'étranger.
    Includes bibliographical references and index.
    ISBN 0-7914-0875-2 (CH : acid-free). — ISBN 0-7914-0876-0 (PB :
acid-free)
    1. Translating and interpreting—Germany—History—19th century.
2. Romanticism—Germany. I. Title. II. series: Intersections
(Albany, N.Y.)
    P306.8.G3B4713 1992
    418'.02'0904309034—dc20   90-28938
                                            CIP

10 9 8 7 6 5 4 3 2 1

CONTENTS

A Note on the Translation

Translating a book which includes some pages on the "ethics of translation" and which concludes with a somewhat polemical exhortation to create a new science of translation, should give any translator pause. In this note, I shall justify a few choices I necessarily had to make in order to serve both masters in a way, I hope, acceptable to both.

The most important choice is the very title of the book. The French, *L'Épreuve de l'étranger,* is itself the translation of a phrase by Heidegger writing on Hölderlin: *Die Erfahrung des Fremden.* The French *épreuve* has much richer connotations than the rather bland *experience.* There is a tinge of violence, of struggle, in it (captured best in the English *ordeal*), which makes it perfect as a rendering of Heidegger's *Erfahrung.* In the essay "The Essence of Language" (*Das Wesen der Sprache*), Heidegger writes that "to have an experience with something, be it a thing, a human being, or a god, means that it goes against us [*uns widerfährt*], that it affects us, comes over us, throws us over and changes us."[1] The problem is that, in French, the word *experience* is also very frequent, in exactly the same sense as its English cognate, and that Berman uses it as well. Though at times it would seem that he uses both terms indiscriminately, I have chosen to add *épreuve* in brackets each time he uses this term. Whenever this happens, the reader should read *experience* as the kind of *Erfahrung* Heidegger means.

Still connected with the title, there is the word *l'étranger,* which is set up in an oppositional relation to *le propre*—another borrowing from Hölderlin.[2] The first one did not pose any problem: It has been rendered as "the foreign." The second one does not allow for a one-word translation ("the own" would not be accepted by English readers); therefore, I have had to resort to the rather inelegant phrase "what is one's own," which then, for reasons of symmetry connected with the oppositional scheme mentioned above, has forced me to sometimes render *l'étranger* as "what is foreign." I have preferred these somewhat elaborate phrasings over more simple words like "identity," or "specificity," both of which would be correct translations of *le propre* in another

context. In this book, which is devoted largely to the Jena Romantics and
Hölderlin, "what is one's own" does indeed touch upon an "identity"
and certainly refers to what is most specific to a people or an individual,
but it is not quite the same thing: Its static quality denies the dialectical
relationship with "the foreign."

Since Berman quotes frequently from other sources (mostly German),
either using existing French translations or providing his own, a word
has to be said on these translations as well. I have adopted the following
policy. Whenever they were available to me, I have used existing English
translations of Berman's sources. When English translations were not
available, I modeled my own translation from the source after Berman's,
even though he sometimes translates rather loosely himself. In each
case, I have checked the translations (whether by Berman, other French
translators, or English translators) against the originals,[3] and silently
modified them when necessary. Thus, I sometimes modified the existing English translations to accommodate Berman's own interpretations
of German texts, or to correct mistakes not made by the French translators.

A final remark: Berman wrote this book ten years ago, in France,
where there was (and still is) much less of an awareness about gender-
biased language than in the USA today. Consequently, the reader will
sometimes find *he, him,* and *man* used to refer to people (translators,
writers, readers) in general. I apologize to all those who might be
offended by my failure to substitute *s/he, him/her,* and *person* in the
appropriate cases. I believe Berman's unrelenting emphasis on the necessity of an experience [*épreuve*] with the foreign suffices to clear him
of any exclusionary prejudice.

Notes

1. Martin Heidegger, *Unterwegs zur Sprache* (*Gesamtausgabe*, vol.
12), Frankfurt am Main: Klostermann, 1985, 149.

2. *Das Fremde* and *das Eigene,* elaborated in the famous letter to
Boehlendorff, which is quoted by Berman in chapter 11 (see p. 000).

3. Except for the very few quotations from Russian (Bakhtin), Spanish (Borges), and Portuguese, since I have no competence to speak of in
these languages.

The art of translation has been pushed further in Germany than in any other European dialect. Voss has rendered the Greek and Latin poets in his language with surprising accuracy; William Schlegel the English, Italian, and Spanish poets with a variety of colors for which no example can be found before him. . . .

—Madame de Staël, *De l'Allemagne*

Any translator must inevitably encounter one of the following obstacles: he will cleave with too much accuracy either to the original, at the expense of his people's language and taste, or to the originality of his people, at the expense of the work to be translated. . . .

—Wilhelm von Humboldt, Letter to Schlegel, 23 July 1796

THE MANIFESTATION OF TRANSLATION

The domain of translation has always been the site of a curious contradiction. On the one hand, translation is considered to be a purely intuitive practice—in part technical, in part literary—which, at bottom, does not require any specific theory or form of reflection. On the other hand, there has been—at least since Cicero, Horace, and Saint Jerome—an abundance of writings on translation of a religious, philosophical, literary, methodological or, more recently, scientific nature. Now, though numerous translators have written on their discipline, it is undeniable that until recently the bulk of these writings has come from non-translators. The definition of the "problems" of translation has been undertaken by theologians, philosophers, linguists, or critics. This has had at least three consequences. First, translation has remained an underground, hidden activity because it did not express itself independently. Second, translation as such has largely remained "unthought," because those who dealt with it tended to assimilate it to something else: (sub-)literature, (sub-)criticism, "applied linguistics." Finally, the analyses produced almost exclusively by non-translators, whatever their qualities may be, inevitably contain numerous "blind spots" and irrelevancies.

Our century has witnessed the gradual transformation of this situation and the constitution of a vast corpus of texts by translators. In addition, the reflection on translation has become an *internal necessity* of translation itself, as was in part the case in classical and romantic Germany. This reflection does not quite take the form of a "theory," as can be seen from Valery Larbaud's *Sous l'invocation de saint Jerôme*. But in any case, it indicates the will of translation to become an autonomous practice, capable of defining and situating itself, and consequently to be communicated, shared, and taught.

History of Translation

The construction of a history of translation is the first task of a *modern* theory of translation. What characterizes modernity is not an infatuation

1

with the past, but a movement of retrospection which is an infatuation
with itself. Thus the poet-critic-translator Pound meditated simultaneously on the history of poetry, of criticism, and of translation. Thus the
great *re-translations* of our century (Dante, the Bible, Shakespeare, the
Greeks, etc.) are necessarily accompanied by a reflection on previous
translations.[1] This reflection must be extended and deepened. We can
no longer be satisfied with the uncertain periodizations concerning the
Western history of translation edified by George Steiner in *After Babel*.
It is impossible to separate the history of translation from the history of
languages, of cultures, and of literatures—even of religions and of
nations. To be sure, this is not a question of mixing everything up, but
of showing how in each period or in each given historical setting the
practice of translation *is articulated* in relation to the practice of literature, of languages, of the several intercultural and interlinguistic exchanges. To take an example, Leonard Forster has shown that European
poets at the end of the Middle Ages and in the Renaissance were often
multilingual.[2] They wrote in several languages for an audience which
was itself polyglot. No less frequently did they translate themselves.
Such is the moving case of the Dutch poet Hooft who, on the occasion
of the death of his beloved wife, composed a whole series of epitaphs, at
first in Dutch, then in Latin, then in Italian, then—somewhat later—
again in Dutch. As if he needed to pass through a whole series of
languages and self-translations in order to arrive at the right expression
of his grief in his mother tongue. Reading Forster, it seems clear that the
poets of that period worked—be it in cultivated or popular spheres—
in an infinitely more multilingual environment than our own period
(which is also multilingual, but in a different way). There were the
learned languages—the "queen" languages, as Cervantes put it: Latin,
Greek, and Hebrew; there were different written national languages
(French, English, Spanish, Italian), and a mass of regional languages and
dialects, etc. A person walking along the streets of Paris or Antwerp must
have heard more languages than are heard today in New York City: His
language was only one among many, which relativized the meaning of
the mother tongue. In such an environment writing tended to be, at
least in part, multilingual, and the medieval rule that assigned certain
poetic genres to certain languages—for example, from the thirteenth to
the fifteenth century, among the troubadours in the north of Italy, lyrical
poetry was assigned to Provencal while epic, or narrative, poetry was
assigned to French—was in part prolonged. Thus Milton wrote his love
poems in Italian because, as he explained in one of them to the Italian
lady to whom they were addressed, "*questa è lingua di cui si vanta
Amore.*" It goes without saying that the said lady also knew English, but
that was not the language of love. For men like Hooft and Milton, the

conception of translation must have been different from ours, as was their conception of literature. For us, self-translations are exceptions, as are the cases where a writer chooses a language other than his own— think of Conrad or Beckett. We even think that multilingualism or diglossia make translation difficult. In short, the entire relation to the mother tongue, toward foreign languages, toward literature, toward expression and translation is structured differently today.

To write the history of translation is to patiently rediscover the infinitely complex and devious network in which translation is caught up in each period or in different settings. And it is to turn the historical knowledge acquired from this activity into an opening of our *present*.

An Ancillary Condition

In the final instance, the issue is to know what translation must mean in our cultural setting today. This problem is accompanied by another one, of an almost painful intensity. I am referring here to something that cannot not be mentioned—the obscured, repressed, reprieved, and *ancillary* condition of translation, which reflects upon the condition of the translator to such an extent that it is hardly possible these days to make an autonomous discipline of this practice.

The condition of translation is not only ancillary; it is, in the eyes of the public as well as in the eyes of the translators themselves, suspect. After so many successful accomplishments, masterpieces, the overcoming of so many alleged impossibilities, how could the Italian adage *traduttore traditore* still remain in place as the last judgment on translation? And yet, it is true that in this domain, *fidelity* and *treason* are incessantly at issue. Translating, as Franz Rosenzweig wrote, "is to serve two masters"; this is the ancillary metaphor. The work, the author, the foreign language (first master) have to be served, as well as the public and one's own language (second master). Here emerges what may be called the drama of the translator.

If the translator chooses the author, the work, and the foreign language as exclusive masters, aiming to impose them on his own cultural realm in their pure foreign form, he runs the risk of appearing to be a foreigner, a traitor in the eyes of his kin. And the translator cannot be sure that this radical attempt—in Schleiermacher's words, "to lead the reader to the author"—will not turn against him and produce a text leaning toward the unintelligible. But if the attempt is successful and the accomplishment perhaps recognized, the translator cannot be sure that the other culture will not feel "robbed," deprived of a work it considered irreducibly its own. Here we touch upon the hyperdelicate domain of the relations between the translator and "his" authors.

On the other hand, if the translator settles for a conventional adaptation of the foreign work—in Schleiermacher's words, "leading the author to the reader"—he will have satisfied the least demanding part of the public, sure enough, but he will have irrevocably betrayed the foreign work as well as, of course, the very essence of translation.

Nevertheless, this impossible situation is not the inescapable reality of translation: It is, rather, based on a number of ideological presuppositions. The lettered public of the sixteenth century, mentioned by Forster, rejoiced in reading a work in its different linguistic variants; it ignored the issue of fidelity and treason because it did not hold its mother tongue sacred. Perhaps this very sacralization is the source of the Italian adage and of all the "problems" of translation. Our lettered public, for its part, demands that translation be imprisoned in a dimension in which it must be suspect. Hence—though this is by no means the only reason—the effacement of the translator who seeks "to make himself very small," to be a humble mediator of foreign works, and always a traitor even as he portrays himself as fidelity incarnate.

Time has come to meditate on this repression of translation and on the "resistances" that underlie it. We may formulate the issue as follows: Every culture resists translation, even if it has an essential need for it. The very aim of translation—to open up in writing a certain relation with the Other, to fertilize what is one's Own through the mediation of what is Foreign—is diametrically opposed to the ethnocentric structure of every culture, that species of narcissism by which every society wants to be a pure and unadulterated Whole. There is a tinge of the violence of cross-breeding in translation. Herder was well aware of this when he compared a language that has not yet been translated to a young virgin. It is another matter that in reality a virgin language or culture is as fictitious as a pure race. We are dealing here with unconscious wishes. Every culture wants to be self-sufficient and use this imaginary self-sufficiency in order to shine forth on the others and appropriate their patrimony. Ancient Roman culture, classical French culture, and modern North-American culture are striking examples of this.

Here, translation occupies an ambiguous position. On the one hand, it heeds this appropriationary and reductionary injunction, and constitutes itself as one of its agents. This results in ethnocentric translations, or what we may call "bad" translations. But, on the other hand, the *ethical aim* of translating is by its very nature opposed to this injunction: The essence of translation is to be an opening, a dialogue, a cross-breeding, a decentering. Translation is "a putting in touch with," or it is *nothing*.

The contradiction between the reductionist aim of culture and the ethical aim of translating can be found on all levels—on the level of theories and methods of translation (as, for example, in the perennial opposition between the champions of the "letter" and the champions of the "spirit"), as well as on the level of the translating practice and the psychic being of the translator. At this point, in order for translation to gain access to its own being, an *ethics* and an *analytic* are required.

Ethics of Translation

On the theoretical level, the *ethics of translation* consists of bringing out, affirming, and defending the pure aim of translation as such. It consists of defining what "fidelity" is. Translation cannot be defined solely in terms of communication, of the transmission of messages, or of extended *rewording*. Nor is translation a purely literary/esthetical activity, even when it is intimately connected with the literary practice of a given cultural realm. To be sure, translation is writing and transmitting. But this writing and this transmission get their true sense only from the ethical aim by which they are governed. In this sense, translation is closer to science than to art—at least to those who maintain that art is ethically irresponsible.

Defining this ethical aim more precisely, and thereby liberating translation from its ideological ghetto, is one of the tasks of a theory of translation.

But this positive ethics in turn supposes two things: first, a *negative ethics*, that is, a theory of those ideological and literary values that tend to turn translation away from its pure aim. The theory of non-ethnocentric translation is also a theory of ethnocentric translation, which is to say of *bad translation*. A bad translation I call the translation which, generally under the guise of transmissibility, carries out a systematic negation of the strangeness of the foreign work.

Analytic of Translation

Second, this negative ethics must be complemented by an *analytic of translation and of translating*. Cultural resistance produces a systematics of deformations that operates on the linguistic and literary levels, and that conditions the translator, whether he wants it or not, whether he knows it or not. The reversible dialectic of fidelity and treason is present in the translator, even in his position as a writer: The pure translator is the one who needs to write starting from a foreign work, a foreign language, and a foreign author—a notable detour. On the psychic level, the translator is ambivalent, wanting to force two things: to force his own language to adorn itself with strangeness, and to force the other language to trans-port itself into his mother tongue.[3] He presents himself as a writer, but is only a re-writer. He is an author, but never The Author. The translated work is a work, but it is not The Work. This network of ambivalences tends to deform the pure aim of translation and to graft itself onto the ideological deformation discussed above. And to strengthen it.

If the pure aim of translation is to be more than a pious wish or a "categorical imperative," an analytic of translation should be added to the ethics of translation. The translator has to "subject himself to analysis," to localize the systems of deformation that threaten his practice and operate unconsciously on the level of his linguistic and literary choices—systems that depend simultaneously on the registers of language, of ideology, of literature, and of the translator's mental make-up. One could almost call this a *psychoanalysis of translation*, similar to Bachelard's *psychoanalysis of the scientific spirit*: it involves the same ascetic, the same self-scrutinizing operation. This analytic can be verified, carried out by global and restricted analyses. Dealing with a novel, for instance, one might study the system of translation that has been used. In the case of an ethnocentric translation, this system tends to destroy the system of the original. Every translator can observe within himself the redoubtable reality of this unconscious system. By its nature, like every analytic procedure, this analytic should be plural. Thus one would be on the way toward an open, no longer solitary, practice of translation. And toward the establishment of a *criticism of translation*, parallel and complementary to the criticism of texts. Furthermore, a textual analysis, carried out against the background of translation, should be added to this analytic of the translating practice: Every text to be translated presents its own systematicity, encountered, confronted, and revealed by the translation. In this sense, it was possible for Pound to say that translation is a *sui generis* form of criticism in that it lays bare the hidden structures of a text. This system-of-the-work presents the fiercest resistance to translation, while simultaneously making it possible and giving it meaning.

The Other Side of the Text

In this framework there will also be room to analyze the system of "gains" and "losses" manifested in all translations, even successful ones—what is called the "approximating" character of translation. Affirming, at least implicitly, that the translation "potentiates" the original, Novalis has contributed to our understanding that gains and losses are not situated on the same level. That is to say, in a translation there is not only a certain percentage of gains and losses; alongside this—

undeniable—level, there is another level where something of the original *appears* that does not appear in the source language. The translation turns the original around, reveals another *side* of it. What is the other side? This is what needs to be discerned more clearly. In that sense, the analytic of translation should teach us something about the work, about its relation to its language and to language in general. Something that neither a mere reading nor criticism can unveil. By reproducing the system-of-the-work into its language, the translation tilts it, which is, unquestionably, again a "potentiation." Goethe had the same intuition when he talked about "regeneration." The translated work is sometimes "regenerated"; not only on the cultural or social level, but in its own *speaking*. To this, in addition, corresponds an awakening in the target language of still latent possibilities by the translation, which it alone, in a different way than literature, has the power to awaken. The poet Hölderlin opens up the possibilities of the German language, homologous but not identical to those he opened up as a translator.

Metaphysical Aim and the Drive of Translating

Presently, I should like to examine briefly how the pure ethical aim of translation is articulated along with another aim—the *metaphysical aim of translation* and, correlatively, with what may be called the *drive of translating*. By the latter I mean that *desire* for translating that constitutes the translator as translator, which can be designated by the Freudian term *drive* since it has, as Valery Larbaud emphasized, something "sexual" in the broad sense of the term.

What is the metaphysical aim of translation? In a text that has become almost canonical, Walter Benjamin speaks of the *task of the translator*. This would consist of a search, beyond the buzz of empirical languages, for the "pure language" which each language carries within itself as its messianic echo. Such an aim, which has nothing to do with the ethical aim, is rigorously metaphysical in the sense that it platonically searches a "truth" beyond natural languages. The German Romantics, whom Benjamin mentions in his essay, and most notably Novalis, have been the purest incarnation of this aim. It is the translation *against Babel*, against the reign of differences, against the empirical. Curiously, this is also looked for, in its wild state as it were, by the pure drive of translating such as it is manifested, for instance, in A.W. Schlegel or Armand Robin. The desire to translate everything, to be a poly- or omnitranslator, is accompanied in Schlegel and Robin by a problematic, even antagonistic, relation to their mother tongue. For Schlegel, German is clumsy, stiff; capable, to be sure, of being put to "work," but not to "play." For him, the aim of polytranslation is precisely to make the "mother tongue" play. In one instance, this aim merges with the ethical aim, as it is expressed by someone like Humboldt, for whom translation should "expand" the German language. In reality, however, the translating drive leaves any humanist project far behind. Polytranslation becomes an end in itself, the essence of which is to radically *denaturalize* the mother tongue. The translating drive always starts off with a refusal of what Schleiermacher has called *das heimische Wohlbefinden der Sprache*—the indigenous well-being of language. The translating drive always posits an *other* language as ontologically *superior* to the translator's own language. Indeed, is it not among the first experiences of any translator to find his language deprived, as it were, poor in the face of the linguistic wealth of the foreign work? The difference among languages—other languages and one's own language—is *hierarchized* here. Thus, for example, English or Spanish would be more "flexible," more "concrete," "richer" than French! This hierarchization has nothing to do with an objective statement of fact: The translator takes off from it, hits upon it in his practice, reaffirms it incessantly. Armand Robin's case clearly proves this "hatred" of the mother tongue, which sets in motion the translating drive. Robin had, as it were, two native languages: Fissel, a Breton dialect, and French. His polytranslational activity obviously springs from the hatred of his "second" mother tongue, which he considers to be severely deficient:

> All the more I loved foreign languages, to me pure, at such a distance: in my French language (my second language) there had been all forms of treason.
> In it, one could say yes to infamy!

It is obvious that, in this case, the metaphysical purpose of surpassing the finitude of empirical languages and of one's own language in a messianic momentum towards pure speech—in Robin's words, "to be the Word, not words"—is linked to the pure translational drive which seeks to transform the native language through a confrontation with non-native, and therefore superior, languages—more "flexible," more "playful," or more "pure."

One might say that the metaphysical purpose of translation is a bad sublimation of the translational drive, whereas the ethical purpose is the surpassing of it. Indeed, the translational drive is the psychic foundation of the ethical aim; without it, the latter would be nothing but an impotent imperative. The translational mimesis is necessarily of the nature of a drive. At the same time, however, it surpasses the drive, precisely because it no longer seeks this secret destruction/transformation of the native language which is wished for by the translational drive and the metaphysical aim. Through the surpassing represented by the metaphysical aim, another desire is manifested: the desire to establish a *dialogic relation* between foreign language and native language.

> *History of Translation*
> *Ethics of Translation*
> *Analytic of Translation*

These, then, are the three axes along which we can define a *modern* reflection on translation and translating.

Translation and Transtextuality

A fourth axis should be added, dealing with the domain of literary theory and of transtextuality. A truly literary work is always developed against the background of translation. *Don Quixote* is the most striking example of this. In his novel, Cervantes explains that the manuscript containing his hero's adventures was allegedly written by a Moor, Cid Hamet Bengeli. This is not all: several times Don Quixote and the priest engage in scholarly discussions concerning the translation, and most of the novels that have upset the hero's spirit are also translations. There is a fabulous irony in the fact that the greatest Spanish novel should have been presented by its author as a translation from the Arabic, which had been the dominant language in the Peninsula for centuries. To be sure, this could teach us something about the Spanish cultural consciousness. But also about the connection between literature and translation. This connection can be witnessed throughout the centuries: from the fifteenth- and sixteenth-century poets through Hölderlin, Nerval, Baudelaire, Mallarmé, George, Rilke, Benjamin, Pound, Joyce, Beckett.

This is a fruitful field of research for the theory of translation, provided it goes beyond the narrow framework of transtextuality, and is connected to research on languages and cultures in general—a multidisciplinary field within which translators could collaborate fruitfully with writers, literary theorists, psychoanalysts, and linguists.

Paris, May 1981

INTRODUCTION

The present essay is devoted to an examination of the theories of translation by the German Romantics—from Novalis, Friedrich Schlegel, and A. W. Schlegel to Schleiermacher. These theories will be compared briefly with the contemporary ones by Herder, Goethe, Humboldt, and Hölderlin. It is well known that the German Romantics, at least those associated with the journal *Athenäum*, produced a series of great translations which have turned out to be a durable asset to the German patrimony: A. W. Schlegel (together with Ludwig Tieck) translated Shakespeare, Cervantes, Calderón, Petrarch, as well as numerous other Spanish, Italian, and Portuguese works. Schleiermacher, for his part, translated Plato. This is an enterprise of systematic and highly selective translation. Translations by Goethe, Humboldt, and Hölderlin are also highly selective, but their orientation is considerably different.

All these translations, carried out at the dawn of the nineteenth century, refer historically to an event that has been decisive for German culture, language, and identity: Luther's sixteenth-century translation of the Bible. In effect, this translation marked the beginning of a tradition in which translation henceforth, and up to the present century, has been considered an integral part of cultural existence and, furthermore, as a constitutive moment of Germanity (*Deutschheit*). This has not escaped the attention of a plethora of great German thinkers, poets, and translators from the seventeenth to the twentieth centuries:
Leibniz:

> I cannot believe that it would be possible to translate the Holy Scriptures into other languages as gracefully as we possess them in German.[1]

Goethe:

> Independently of our own production, we have already achieved a high degree of culture (*Bildung*) thanks to the full appropriation of what is foreign to us. Soon other nations will learn German, because they will realize that in this way they can to a large extent save themselves the apprenticeship of almost all other languages. Indeed, from

11

what languages do we not possess the best works in the most eminent translations?

For a long time now the Germans have contributed to a mutual mediation and recognition. He who understands German finds himself on the market place where all nations present their merchandise.

The force of a language is not to reject the foreign, but to devour it.[2]

A. W. Schlegel:

Only a manifold receptivity for a foreign national poetry, which, if possible, must ripen and grow into universality, makes progress in the faithful reproduction of poems possible. I believe we are on the way to invent the true art of poetic translation; this glory has been reserved for the Germans.[3]

Novalis:

Apart from the Romans, we are the only nation to have felt the impulse of translation so irresistibly, and to owe to it so infinitely in culture (*Bildung*). . . . This impulse is an indication of the very elevated and original character of the German people. Germanity is a cosmopolitanism mixed with the most vigorous individualism. Only for us have translations become expansions.[4]

Schleiermacher:

An internal necessity, in which a peculiar calling of our people is clearly expressed, has driven us to translating on a grand scale.[5]

Humboldt:

Just as the understanding of a language increases, likewise the understanding of a nation widens.[6]

In Germany, as an activity that has generated an identity, translation from Luther until the present has been the object of a reflection for which an equivalent could probably hardly be found. The translating practice here is accompanied by a reflection, sometimes purely empirical or methodological, sometimes cultural and social, sometimes outright speculative, on the meaning of the act of translation, on its linguistic, literary, metaphysical, religious, and historical implications, on the relation among languages, between same and other, between what is one's own and what is foreign. In itself, Luther's Bible is the self-affirmation of the German language against the Latin of "Rome," as Luther himself emphasized in his *Letter on Translation*. Nevertheless, in the eighteenth century, after the rich blossoming of baroque translations, and until Herder and Voss, the influence of French classicism brought along a trend of purely formal translations conforming to "good taste" as defined by the Enlightenment. Such is Wieland's case, whose translations of Shakespeare, as Gundolf tells us, "start from the public" instead of "starting from the poet."[7] This tendency, termed *gallicizing* by the contemporary Germans themselves, is victoriously defeated by the penetration into Germany of English literature and the beginning of a return to the "sources" (folk poetry, medieval poetry, the philosophy of Jakob Boehme, etc.), as well as by an increasingly "manifold" (A. W. Schlegel's term) opening onto different world literatures. This is also the age, first with Lessing, then with Herder and Goethe, in which their *own* literature becomes an issue (not quite national, even less nationalist, as with late Romanticism), a literature which could clearly define its relation with French classicism, the Encyclopedists, the Spanish Golden Age, Italian renaissance poetry, Elizabethan drama, the eighteenth-century English novel and, finally and essentially, Graeco-Roman Antiquity, in the framework of the old battle between Ancient and Modern, revived by Winckelmann. In this respect, the issue is whether Greeks or Romans should be given prominence—an issue that was of the utmost importance to the *Athenäum* Romantics and which will retain its actuality through Nietzsche.

In this global self-definition, this *situation* within the space of European literature, translation plays a decisive role, largely because it is the *transmission of forms*. The revival, from Herder to Grimm, of folk tales and folk poetry, of medieval songs and epics, points in the same direction: It is an intratranslation of sorts, through which German literature acquires a vast treasury of *forms*, even more than a repository of themes and contents. Philology, comparative grammar, textual criticism, and hermeneutics, which are inaugurated in Germany at the turn of the eighteenth century, have a functionally analogous role in this enterprise: A. W. Schlegel is at the same time critic, translator, literary theorist, philologer, and comparatist. Humboldt is at the same time translator and theoretician of language. Schleiermacher is "hermeneuticist," translator, and theologian. Hence the close connection, the meaning of which will be seen later, between criticism, hermeneutics, and translation.

Within this cultural field, which the Germans were beginning to call *Bildung* (culture and education), the enterprises of the Romantics, Goethe, Humboldt and Hölderlin, will be developed. The translations of the Romantics, which take on the conscious form of a *program*, simultaneously correspond to a concrete need of the age (to enrich the poetic and theatrical forms), and of a vision peculiar to them, marked by the Idealism defined by Kant, Fichte, and Schelling. Friedrich Schlegel, Novalis, and Schleiermacher themselves take an active part in this speculative process. For Goethe, less of a theorist, translation is integrated into the context of *Weltliteratur* (world literature), for which the purest medium might well be the German language, as is suggested by the passages quoted above. Translation is one of the instruments for the constitution of a universality—a view belonging to German classicism, of which he, with Schiller and Humboldt, is the prime representative. For the Romantics of the *Athenäum*, translation on a "grand" scale is an essential moment, together with criticism, of the constitution of a "universal progressive poetry"—that is to say, of the affirmation of poetry as absolute. As a programmatic practice, it found its executors in A. W. Schlegel, L. Tieck, and its theorists in F. Schlegel and Novalis. To be sure, in the latter two one does not find a systematic exposition of the theory of translation any more than a systematic exposition of criticism, the fragment, literature, or art in general. Nevertheless, in the mass of romantic texts, there is a reflection on translation, closely connected to the more fully developed reflections on literature and criticism. The issue for us, then, is to *reconstruct* this reflection by situating it in the labyrinth of their theories—a labyrinth which, in its structure, will turn out to be concerned with translation and translatability. When Novalis writes to A. W. Schlegel, "In the final analysis, all poetry is translation,"[8] he places the concept of *Dichtung* (supreme with him) and that of *Übersetzung* in an unfathomable essential proximity. When F. Schlegel writes to his brother, "The power to penetrate into the most intimate singularity of a great spirit, for which you have often ill-humoredly rebuked me, calling it 'the talent of the translator',"[9] he places *criticism*, *understanding*, and *translation* within the same essential proximity, though in a psychological way. One may be tempted to hear in this an echo of Hamann's words in *Esthetica in nuce*:

> *Speaking* is *translating*—from an *angelic language* into a *human language*, that is to say, transposing *thoughts* into *words*—*things* into *names*—*images* into *signs*.[10]

But it is obvious that, in their reflection on the connection of translation and poetry, Novalis and F. Schlegel have something more specific in mind than the affirmation that all thought and all discourse are "translations." While they do adhere to this traditional point of view, they envisage a more essential connection between poetry and translation. We will have to show that, for them, translation is a structural double of *criticism* (in the strict sense that this notion carries for the *Athenäum*), and that translatability is the very means of realizing knowledge, of the *Encyclopedia*. In both cases translating is a "romanticizing" operation, the essence of spiritual life which Novalis termed "infinite versability."[11] In the framework of such a—purely speculative— theory, how does it stand with languages, with the concrete practice of translation? Some idea of what happens when translation sets out to work on "the translatability of everything into everything" may be gathered from the following remark by Rudolf Pannwitz, according to which A. W. Schlegel's translation would have "italianized" rather than "germanized" Shakespeare:

> A. W. Schlegel's translation of Shakespeare has been overestimated. Schlegel was too soft and too much immersed in Romance and Goethean verse to capture the majestic barbariousness of Shakespearean verse; his verses are more Italian verses than English verses.[12]

Pannwitz's obviously polemic contention refers in the first place to the historical fact that the Romantics have "appropriated Romance artistic forms to German literature."[13] It can hardly be forgotten that *Romanticism* derives from *Romance*, dealing both with "Romance" and "novelistic" [*romanesque*] forms. But also, and more profoundly, it refers to the "versatile" relation the Romantics held with languages in general, as if it were possible for them to inhabit them all. As Armel Guerne observed quite poignantly, Novalis has a curious relation to Latin and French (as well as to the expressions of Romance origin existing in German):

> Novalis' language . . . is curiously gallicized or latinized even down to its vocabulary.[14]

It can be said that, to a certain extent, Romantic translation seeks to play with languages and their literatures, to make them "fall into" one another at all levels (especially the level of meter, which motivates Pannwitz's remark: sometimes in his translation of Shakespeare, A. W. Schlegel had recourse to "Italian rhyme"), just as the *Encyclopedia* aimed at making the different categories of the sciences fall into each other:

> A science can only be truly represented by an other science.[15]

> *Encyclopedistic.* There is a *Doctrine* of philosophical, critical, mathematical, poetical, chemical, historical, *Science*.[16]

> But to transport oneself arbitrarily now in this, now in that sphere, as if into another world, not merely with the understanding and the imagination, but with one's whole soul; to freely relinquish first one and then another part of one's being and to confine oneself entirely to a third; to seek and find now in this, now in that individual the be-all and end-all of existence and intentionally forget everyone else: of this only a spirit is capable that contains within itself, in some sense, a plurality of spirits and a whole system of persons.[17]

Encyclopedia and *universal progressive poetry* play the same game. And this game is not futile, it is not only the psychological expression of a "translator talent": it is the reflection, or rather the symbol, of the game of Spirit with itself. For Novalis, language plays such a game, as he states in his famous "Monologue":

> One can't help but be astonished at the absurd, wholly erroneous assumption people make—that their talk is about things. No one knows what is most distinctive about language, namely, that it is concerned solely with itself. This is why it is such a marvelous and fertile mystery—that when someone speaks just in order to speak, precisely then does he pronounce the most magnificent and original truths. . . . If one could only make clear to them [people] that it is with language as with mathematical formulas—they constitute a world by themselves, they play only among themselves . . . and for that very reason they are so expressive and mirror the singular interplay of things. It is only through their freedom that they are parts of nature, and only in their free movement does the world soul express itself and make them into a delicate measure and outline of things. So it is too with language.[18]

One can see clearly that the conquest of foreign meters, Novalis' gallicization of language, depends on a certain game with language and with languages. But, in such a game, what of the *untranslatability*, that is to say, of that which in the difference of languages purports to be the irreducible, at a level which need not be that of linguistics, and which every translator encounters as the very horizon of the "impossibility" of his practice—an impossibility which he, nevertheless, has to confront and live with? We will have to inquire into the status (or non-status) accorded to it by the Romantics—a status closely connected to the notions of criticability and uncriticability. We will see that translatability and untranslatability are, as it were, determined *a priori* by the very nature of the works—a paradox which we may formulate as follows: that which has not already translated itself, is not translatable, nor is it worth being translated.

It is striking to notice that the speculative theory of translation nowhere really encounters the problem of language and languages as Goethe, Humboldt, and Hölderlin did. Being integrated into the theory of literature and of the work as medium for the poetic absolute, translation loses its cultural and concrete linguistic dimension, except with A. W. Schlegel, where the almost technical reflections on the introduction of metrics into German are concerned. Even so, language, in this context, does not appear as a dimension, but as the docile or stubborn instrument of a certain poetic play. A. W. Schlegel writes:

> I am convinced that language is not capable of anything without the will, the zeal, and the sensibility (*Sinn*) of those who use it. . . . Our language is stubborn; we are all the more pliant; our language is harsh and rude; we do everything to select soft and pleasant sounds; if

necessary, we are even skilled in playing on words, something for which the German language is extremely ill-suited because it always wants to work, never play. Where, then, are those highly celebrated qualities which would make our language in itself the only one to be called upon to translate all others? A certain wealth of vocabulary, which is not such as to not make its poverty felt often in translation; its capacity to compound, and occasionally to derive; a slightly more free word order than some other modern languages; and, finally, a certain metrical flexibility. As far as the latter is concerned, it is entirely natural, because since the Provencal age our poetry has generally followed foreign models. I have shown elsewhere that the success of the introduction of ancient metrics . . . must be attributed rather to the zeal and the sensibility of certain poets than to the structure of the language itself.[19]

It seems that the whole point would be to make the language play at a game—the game of flexibility—for which it is never naturally prepared. In the same text, A. W. Schlegel compares this operation to those of the Romans, who also "civilized" their language by an immense effort of translation.

With respect to the practical and theoretical attempts of the *Athenäum*, the reflections by Schleiermacher and Humboldt represent the moment when translation enters into the horizon of hermeneutics and the science of language. It is characteristic to note that both thinkers are confronted immediately with the problem of language and the problem *of the relation between man and language*—as that which man can never dominate from the position of an absolute subject. Novalis, most often, had thought language as the instrument of a thinking subject:

Language also is a product of the impulse towards formation (*Bildungstrieb*). Just as the latter always forms the same things in the most diverse circumstances, so does language, through culture and through an increasing development and enlivening, become the profound expression of the idea of organisation, of the system of philosophy. The whole of language is a postulate. It is of a positive, free origin.[20]

Postulate and *positive* refer here to the fact that language is posited, instituted by spirit as its mode of expression. In such a conception, language can never be thought as the unmasterable dimension of human being, which confronts it with the multiplicity, simultaneously empirical and "transcendental," of languages: the opaque being-Babel of natural language. Humboldt and Schleiermacher, for their part, approach this reality of language, though without recognizing it as such. But their undertaking, above all, is no longer speculative, as was that of the *Athenäum*. It inaugurates, starting with Weimar classicism for Humboldt, with Jena Romanticism for Schleiermacher, a new phase in the reflection on translation, which will be taken up again in Germany by such minds as Rosenzweig and Schadewaldt, when the time has come—after a whole period of *re-translations* of great literary and religious texts of the past. Rudolf Pannwitz takes complete stock of this turning of the time when he declares:

> Our versions, even the best ones, start out from a false principle—they want to germanize Sanskrit, Greek, English, instead of sanskritizing, hellenizing, anglicizing German. . . . The fundamental error of the translator is to preserve the contingent state of his own language rather than submit it to the violent motion of the foreign language. . . . One does not imagine to what extent the thing is possible, to what degree a language may transform itself; from language to language there is hardly a greater distance than from dialect to dialect, though certainly not when they are taken too lightly, much rather when they are taken seriously enough.[21]

It is at this point that Hölderlin's translations, precisely because they do submit themselves to the "violent motion of the foreign language," move to center stage, and with them the relation of languages, relations of *coupling* and *differentiation*, of *confrontation* and *hybridization*—to be more precise: The relation of the mother tongue to other languages as it is enacted in translation, and *as it determines the relation of the mother tongue to itself.* This development belongs to us, or should be ours, and gradually establishes itself along with that which linguistics, modern criticism, and psychoanalysis, among others, teach us about language and languages in general.

The Romantic theory of translation, poetical and speculative, constitutes the basis of a certain modern consciousness of literature and translation in quite a few respects. Here, the aim of our study is double: on the one hand to *reveal* the still underestimated role of this theory in the economy of Romantic thought but, also, on the other hand, to *question* the postulates, and thus to contribute to a critique of our modernity. The "speculative" theory of translation and the "intransitive" or "monologic" theory of literature are related.[22] Striking twentieth-century examples may be found in Blanchot, Steiner, or Serres. This evolution, begun by the *Athenäum*, is now in its repetitive and epigonal phase: What is at stake today is a liberation from it so as to prepare a new domain of literature, criticism, and translation.

The "speculative" theory of translation and the "intransitive" theory of poetry are, in a profound sense, "things of the past," whatever may be the "modern" finery with which they adorn themselves. They block the way of the historical, cultural, and linguistic dimension of translation and poetry. And it is this dimension which is beginning to reveal itself at the present day.

As for us, our critical work on the theories of translation from the classical and romantic age in Germany has originated from a twofold experience.

In the first place, it originates from a long and almost symbiotic familiarity with German Romanticism.[23] As many others, among them Breton, Béguin, Benjamin, Blanchot, Guerne, Jacottet, we have sought in it the *fascinating origin* of our literary consciousness. What is more fascinating, that is to say, more invested by the imagination, than German Romanticism? It is even more fascinating because it is adorned by the double prestige of the *theoretical* and the *fantastic*, and because we believe to find in it the union (itself imaginary) of the poetic and the philosophical. Romanticism is one of our myths.

A literary and intellectual trajectory, all the more starved for self-affirmation and absoluteness in proportion as it progressively cut itself off from any historical and linguistic ground, thought it had found in it its own image—more and more bloodless and deprived of life. Not all is monologue and self-reflection in modern poetry and literature.[24] But it certainly constitutes a dominant tendency. One may recognize oneself perfectly in it. It is also possible, and this is our position, to refuse it in the name of the experience of another literary dimension—the one which we find in European poetry and theater prior to the seventeenth century, in the novelistic tradition, and which has evidently never disappeared. German Romanticism has certainly known this dimension, since it made it the privileged field of its translations and of its literary criticism. But it simultaneously remained separate from it by an unbridgeable abyss (as will be seen with A. W. Schlegel).

And it is this dimension which has opened itself to us when, having translated some German Romantics, we have been led to translate some modern Latin-American novels. Like the authors of sixteenth-century Europe, Roa Bastos, Guimaraes Rosa, J.-M. Arguedas—to name only the greatest—write from an oral and popular tradition.[25] Hence the problem they pose for translation: how to render texts rooted in an oral culture into a language like our own, which has followed the reverse historical, cultural, and literary trajectory? One may look at this as a purely technical, sectorial problem, and leave it at that. But in fact it constitutes a challenge that puts the meaning and the power of translation at stake. The work to be done on modern French, in order to make it capable of welcoming that literary domain authentically—that is to say, without ethnocentrism—shows quite clearly that we are concerned here, in and through translation, with a participation in this movement of decentering and change that our literature (our culture) needs if it wants to find again an image and an experience of itself which it has partly (though, certainly, not completely!) lost since classicism—even though *French* Romanticism had the ambition of finding them again. Translation, if it wants to be capable of participating in such a movement, must *reflect on itself* and on its powers. Inevitably, such a reflecton is a *self-affirmation*. And this, we must repeat, is historically and culturally located: It is at the service of a certain *turn* in literature. The problems posed by Latin-American translations are by no means sectorial; they may easily be found in other domains of translation. No "theory" of translation should be necessary if there were not something to be changed in the practice of translation. The Germany of the Romantics—of Goethe, Humboldt, Hölderlin, and Schleiermacher—has, in its way, known an analogous problematic. That is the reason why we have been led to attempt to write—even if partially—a chapter in the history of European translation and a chapter in German cultural history—a chapter particularly heavy in meaning, since we recognize in it choices that have been our own, even though our cultural field has changed.[26] This "historical" work itself serves a certain *cultural battle* in which the specificity of translation as well as the refusal of a certain modern literary tradition have to be affirmed. Translation would deserve its secular ancillary status if eventually it did not itself become an act of creative decentering conscious of itself.

All that remains is to indicate those studies to which the present essay is most indebted. To our knowledge there is no study on the translations and the theory of translation of the Romantics. At best one finds some monographs devoted to the translations by L. Tieck and A. W. Schlegel. Some German doctoral dissertations study the relation between one Romantic and a foreign literature, though they never directly tackle the question of the nature, the purpose, and the meaning of the translations this Romantic was able to make from that foreign language.[27] The scant publications in Germany devoted to the Romantic theory of language note its importance for translation but do not offer an analysis of it beyond the level of paraphrase. The same is true for Goethe. Hölderlin's translations, on the other hand, have been carefully studied (at least those from the Greek) by F. Beissner and W. Schadewaldt.

Walter Benjamin, in *The Concept of Art Criticism in German Romanticism*—perhaps the most perspicacious work on the *Athenäum* ever written—remains the only author who has fully measured the importance of the subject and who has situated it in the larger context of a reflection on Romanticism:

> Apart from the translation of Shakespeare, the durable poetic work of the Romantics is the annexation of Romance artistic forms for German literature. Their efforts were consciously directed to the appropriation, development, and purification of these forms. But their relation to them was entirely different from that of the preceding generations.

Unlike the *Aufklärung*, the Romantics did not conceive of form as an aesthetic rule for art, the following of which was a necessary precondition for the pleasurable or edifying effect of the work. For them, form was neither a rule, nor did it depend on rules. This conception, without which A. W. Schlegel's truly significant translations from the Italian, the Spanish, and the Portuguese would be unthinkable, was developed philosophically by his brother.[28]

Elsewhere, in "The Task of the Translator," Benjamin also mentions the Romantics:

> They, more than any others, were gifted with an insight into the life of literary works which has its highest testimony in translation. To be sure, they hardly recognized translation in this sense, but devoted their attention to criticism, another, if a lesser, factor in the continued life of literary works. But even though the Romantics virtually ignored translation in their theoretical writing, their own great translations testify to their sense of the essential nature and the dignity of this literary mode.[29]

Even if Benjamin underestimates the value of those rare texts which the Romantics devoted to translation, it still remains that he has circumscribed exactly the space it occupies with them. Furthermore, his own view of translation may be considered as a radicalization of Novalis's and F. Schlegel's intuitions.

We have also used the works on Romantic thought by P. Szondi, B. Allemann, M. Thalmann, and P. Lacoue-Labarthe and J.-L. Nancy. As far as Novalis and F. Schlegel are concerned, we have relied in part on reflections from our previous study, "Lettres à Fouad El-Etr sur le Romantisme allemand."

Among the works devoted to the problematic of translation, we recognize a particular affinity with those by Mikhaïl Bakhtin. George Steiner's *After Babel*, by its magnitude and the abundance of its information, is a fundamental basic work, even if one does not share his theoretical conclusions. Finally, the collection published by H. J. Störig, *Das Problem des Übersetzens*, offers an excellent overall view of the theories of translation in Germany since Luther.[30]

Within the primarily theoretical framework of our study, we have had to renounce, a few exceptions notwithstanding, a concrete analysis of translations by the Romantics and their contemporaries. In order to be pertinent, such an analysis would have required more space than we have available here.

1

LUTHER:
TRANSLATION AS FOUNDATION

The masterpiece of German prose is
therefore, fairly enough, the masterpiece
of its greatest preacher: the Bible has so
far been the best German book.

—F. Nietzsche, *Beyond Good and Evil*

In his "Notes and Essays for a Better Understanding of the West-Eastern Divan", Goethe writes:

> Since the German continually moves ahead of the East by way of translations of all kinds, we find occasion to put forward here some remarks that are well known, but that cannot be repeated too often.
>
> There are three kinds of translation. The first acquaints us with the foreign on our own terms; a simple prosaic translation is best in this respect. For since prose totally cancels all peculiarities of any kind of poetic art and since prose itself pulls poetic enthusiasm down to a common water-level, it does the greatest service in the beginning, by surprising us with foreign excellence in the midst of our own national homeliness, our everyday existence; it offers us a higher mood and real edification while we do not realize what is happening to us. Luther's Bible translation will produce this kind of effect at any time.[1]

This observation is echoed accurately by a passage from *Dichtung und Wahrheit*:

> For the circumstance that this excellent man [Luther] handed down a
> work, composed in the most different styles, and gave us its poetical,
> historical, commanding, didactic tone in our mother-tongue, as if all
> were cast in one mould, has done more to advance religion than if he
> had attempted to imitate, in detail, the peculiarities of the original. In
> vain has been the subsequent endeavour to make Job, the Psalms, and
> other lyrical books, capable of affording enjoyment in their poetical
> form. For the multitude, upon whom the effect is to be produced, a
> plain translation always remains the best. Those critical translations,
> which vie with the original, really only seem to amuse the learned
> among themselves.[2]

Goethe's judgment, largely shared by the entire German tradition,
concerns first and foremost the historical significance of the Lutheran
translation. Renouncing the production of a "critical translation" closely
tied to the "particularities of the original," Luther managed to create a
work accessible to the German people, capable of providing a solid
base for the new religious sensibility of the Reformation. This was
obviously the issue in the case of the Bible. To what extent does this
evaluation correspond to the reality of Luther's work?

From 1521 to 1534, Luther and a team of scholars work on the
translation, having recourse simultaneously to the Latin and Greek versions, as well as occasionally to the Hebrew original. There were at the
time other German translations of the Bible—the first one published in
1475—, but they were swarming with Latinisms. Luther, for his part,
aims at the Germanization, *Verdeutschung*, of the sacred texts from the
outset. This aim is explicitly pronounced in a polemical text, "On Translating: An Open Letter," in which he defends his translations and his
principles against those who alleged that

> in many places the text [of the Bible] has been modified or even
> falsified, whereby many simple Christians, even among the learned
> who do not know the Greek and Hebrew languages, have been star-
> tled and shocked.[3]

Concerning a detail—the addition of an *only* in a text by St. Paul,
which is found in neither the Latin version nor the Greek text—Luther
states:

> I wanted to speak German, not Latin or Greek, since it was German I
> had undertaken to speak in the translation. But it is the nature of our
> German language that in speaking of two things, one of which is
> affirmed and the other denied, we use the word *solum* (*allein*) [alone
> or only] along with the word *nicht* [not] or *kein* [no]. . . . There are
> innumerable cases of this kind in daily use.[4]

This discussion refers to a more general purpose: to offer the
community of believers a text in good German. But what is, in Luther's

age, *good* German? Certainly not a German that would obey rules and predetermined canons. It can only be the German of the dialects, the *Mundarten*. Further on in the same text, Luther is very clear on this subject:

> We do not have to inquire of the literal Latin, how we are to speak German, as these asses do. Rather we must inquire about this of the mother in the home, the children on the street, the common man in the marketplace. We must be guided by their language, and do our translating accordingly. That way they will understand it and recognize that we are speaking German with them.[5]

To translate, then, with an ear for popular, everyday speech, so that the Bible may be heard and understood. Good German is that of the people. But the people speak an infinity of Germans. What is at stake, then, is to translate into a German that in a certain way rises above the multiplicity of *Mundarten* [dialects] without denying or crushing them in the process. Hence Luther's twofold attempt: to translate into a German that *a priori* can only be local—his German—*Hochdeutsch*, but to raise this local German in the very process of translation to the level of a common German, a *lingua franca*. In order not to become in turn a language cut off from the people, this German must conserve within it something of the *Mundarten* and the general modes of expression of popular speech. One would have, then, the constant and deliberate use of a very oral language, charged with images, locutions, phrases, together with a work of purification, of dedialectization of this language. Thus, for instance, Luther translates Christ's words "*ex abundantia cordis os loquitur*" (Matth. 12:34) not as "out of the abundance of the heart the mouth speaks," because "no German could say that," but as "what fills the heart overflows the mouth." "The mother in the home and the common man say this." Not Latin, nor a pure dialect, but a generalized popular speech. A difficult operation, as Luther admits:

> For the literal Latin is a great hindrance to speaking good German.[6]

Difficult, but apparently successful: as soon as it appeared, the Lutheran Bible was a sensation, despite all the criticism. One re-edition follows another. Very soon the people to whom it was destined learn passages from it by heart and integrate it into their patrimony. From the start, it becomes the cornerstone of the Reformation in Germany, as Goethe very well observed. But it is even more than that: By transforming the *Hochdeutsch* into a *lingua franca*, it makes it into the medium of *written* German for centuries. In the Lutheran translation, a first and decisive self-affirmation of *literary* German is played out. A great "reformer," Luther is henceforth considered a great writer, a creator of language, and it is in this capacity that he is celebrated by Herder and Klopstock.

Let us have a closer look at what is at stake in the *Verdeutschung*, since this may shed some light on the problematics of translation that will culminate at the end of the eighteenth century in the theories of Goethe, the Romantics, and above all with Hölderlin's translations from the Greek. What Luther violently pushes aside is *Latin* as the official medium of the Roman Church and, more generally, of writing. We are presented here with a phenomenon peculiar to the sixteenth century (to the Reformation and the Renaissance), which Bakhtin has excellently described in his work on Rabelais:

> An intense interorientation, interaction, and mutual clarification of languages took place during that period. The two languages frankly and intensely peered into each other's faces, and each became more aware of itself, its potentialities and limitations, in the light of the other. This line drawn between the languages was seen in relation to each object, each concept, and each point of view.[7]

In the present case, the delimitation Bakhtin mentions is, of course, concerned with the confrontation of German and Latin. But at the same time it is concerned with

> the sphere of national folk idioms. A single national language did not exist as yet, it was slowly formed. The process of transforming the whole of philosophy to the vernacular and of creating a new system of literary media led to an intense interorientation of dialects within this vernacular. . . . However, the process was not limited to the inter-orientation of dialects. The national language, having become the medium of ideology and literature, inevitably entered into contact with other national languages.[8]

Here, quite logically, Bakhtin emphasizes

> the immense importance of translations in the above mutual clarification of languages. We know that translation played a considerable role in the linguistic and literary life of the sixteenth century. . . . These works had to be translated into a language that had not been finally developed and formed. Indeed it had to be shaped in the very process of translation. . . .[9]

Which is precisely what happens with Luther's Bible. As a matter of fact, the space Bakhtin describes is European, even though his book deals with French literature. But no French translation of that period— as the relatively secondary role assigned to translation in Du Bellay's *Défense et illustration de la langue française* clearly shows—could assume the foundational role of the Lutheran Bible, because there does not exist in France a work that could, by itself, play the role of a foundation of national and literary French. We do not have a *Divine Comedy*. If Luther's Bible plays this role, it is because it claims to be a *Verdeutschung* of the Scriptures, connected historically to a vast movement of reformulation of the faith, of a renovation of the relation to sacred texts, of a radical reinterpretation of the Testaments, as well as to a national religious affirmation against the "imperialism" of Rome. Conversely, this movement only acquires its strength from the actual existence of a "germanized" Bible accessible to all. We have here a decisive historical and cultural conjunction that establishes a real rupture in Germany: Henceforth, there is a *before* and an *after Luther*, not only religiously and politically, but *literarily*.[10] The rediscovery of a pre-Lutheran literary past by Herder and the Romantics will not question this rupture, and Goethe is perfectly well aware of it in the text cited above: In order to read the *Nibelungen* or Meister Eckhart, the Germans have to resort to intratranslations, not needed by the Italians to read Dante, who is nevertheless a contemporary of Meister Eckhart.

The fact that the foundation and the formation of common literary German should have happened by means of a translation is what allows us to understand why there will exist in Germany a *tradition of translation* that regards translation as the creation, transmission, and expansion of the language, the foundation of a *Sprachraum*, of a linguistic space of its own. And it is by no means a coincidence that the Romantics will link their theories of literature, criticism, and translation to a theory of the Bible, to a "universal method of biblification."[11]

Franz Rosenzweig, who collaborated with Martin Buber on a new *Verdeutschung* of the Bible, conforming to the needs of the faith in the twentieth century, has brought out the meaning of Luther's translation for German culture, language, and literature in a remarkable way. We quote at length from his essay "Die Schrift und Luther":

> Languages may be accompanied by writing for centuries without the emergence of what is designated with the peculiar expression of "written language." . . . At one time in the life of a people the moment comes when writing, once its servant, becomes the master of language. This moment arrives when a content embracing the entire life of the people is poured into writing; that is, when for the first time there is a book "that everyone must have read." From this moment on, language can no longer proceed unaffected. . . . And truly, from then on the tempo of the development of the language is heavier than before. Today, we still largely understand Luther's German if we modernize the spelling. . . . On the other hand, it would be very difficult for us to read the literature contemporaneous with Luther to the extent that it has not already been influenced by him. . . .
>
> To be sure, the domination of a book over a language does not

mean that the latter's development has ended. Nevertheless, it is tre-
mendously slowed down. . . .

The problematic of the classic, foundational book is intensified by
the fact that it is a translation. Because for translations there holds a
law of unicity, connected here with that unicity of the classic moment
of the history of the language. The history of translation has a very
typical course. In the beginning, unassuming interlinear translations,
which want to be no more than aides for reading the original, coexist
with free adaptations—reformulations wanting to convey in some way
to the reader the meaning of the original or what they consider to be
its meaning. . . . Then, one day the miracle of the marriage of the two
spirits of language happens. This does not happen without prepara-
tion. Only when the receiving people, out of their own longing and by
their own expression, go out to encounter . . . the foreign work, that
is when its reception no longer follows from curiosity, interest, cultural impulse [*Bildungsdrang*], or even aesthetic pleasure, but in the
broadness of a historical movement, only then has the time for such a
hieros gamos, such a sacred wedding, arrived. Thus for Schlegel's
Shakespeare only at the time when Schiller creates for the Germans a
theater of their own; thus for Voss' Homer only when Goethe approaches the antique form. . . . Then the foreign book becomes one's
own. . . . This tremendous step in the unification of the Babel of the
peoples does not owe its existence to a single translator; it is a fruit
ripened by the life of the people under the constellation of an entirely
unique historical moment. A moment that cannot be repeated. The
moment of the history of the people does not return because it has no
need to return; within the limits which alone enter into consideration
here—the limits of the horizon of a momentaneous national
presence—it is immortal. As long as the connection of this present
with the past is not catastrophically broken . . . that which Voss made
of Homer remains Homeric for the German people, and that which
Luther made of the Bible remains biblical. No new attempt at translation can attain this national significance. . . . To be sure, the new
translation of Homer may be much better than Voss' translations, but it
cannot constitute a world historic event; it can only seek to obtain the
laurels bestowed upon it by the spirit of its own people, not those
bestowed by the world spirit, which can be bestowed only once because the world tournament can be played only once, unlike the
training games of peoples and people which are played every year and
every day.[12]

This important text raises many questions. Rosenzweig links the
historical unicity of a translation—in this case Luther's—to the vaguely
Hegelian notion of *world spirit*. In Luther's case, undoubtedly there is
no need to resort to this speculative notion: The historicity of his translation is obviously linked to precise religious, national, and linguistic
factors. But Rosenzweig's text has the merit of raising the problem of the

historicity of translation in general. Indeed, if not evident, the historicity of a *work* is at least undisputed. Homer's work is historic in the sense that Greek history (not only Greek literary history) is unthinkable without it. The same goes for a Dante. Still, at stake here is the historicity of a certain national linguistic or cultural space. But these works are equally historic at the level of the Western space as a whole, and beyond: They constitute what is called "universal literature"—which they certainly could not have been without the mediation of translation. But two points have to be made here. First, it is because they were already *potentially* universal that they have been universally translated. Which is to say that they already carried within themselves, at the level of their form and their content, their own translatability. The work of someone like Kafka, in the twentieth century, has a universal value, and it has been translated almost everywhere. But—and this is the second point—this does not mean that all the translations of those works have an historic value. For instance, Kafka's influence in France did not depend on a translation that drew attention in and of itself, that is, as a *work* properly speaking. The same may be said of the translation of a Joyce or a Dostoevsky. In these circumstances, a translation should be called *historic* if it has been *epoch-making as a translation*, a translation which appears *as such*, and in that way, strangely, attains the rank of a work and is no longer confined to be a humble mediation of an historic text. In other words: The translation of an essential text, a text heavy with history, is not itself necessarily historic. Thus, it is necessary to distinguish the *general historicity* of translation, its role of unassuming mediation which obviously contributes to the movement of history, from those relatively rare translations which, by their own effect, turn out to be heavy with history. Indeed, as Rosenzweig says, these are the unique translations—which do not prevent the existence of other translations (unique or not) of the same originals. In Germany, Luther's Bible, Voss' Homer, Hölderlin's Sophocles and Pindar, A. W. Schlegel's Shakespeare, and Tieck's *Don Quixote*, clearly belong to this type of translation. But one cannot simply state that these translations "came at their time" (it was not the case for Hölderlin), because the translations that only mediate can also only "come at their time"—by virtue of that selectivity belonging to cultures which makes possible all omnitranslation. Moreover, in the case of the German translations we mentioned, it is interesting to note that they are all *re-translations*: there were already numerous translations of these works, often of an excellent quality. To be sure, the new translations emerge from an historically precise soil: The reformulation of the relation to the Bible and revealed faith (Luther), the deepening of the relation to the Greeks (Voss, Hölderlin), an opening to English and Iberian literatures (A. W. Schlegel and Tieck). They could only exist on such a soil. The deepening of the already existing relation to foreign works demanded new translations. But this is a somewhat determinist view, because we can also consider these translations as that *unforeseeable and incalculable novelty* which is the essence of a truly historic event. It seems that these translations could only emerge as retranslations: going beyond the framework of simple intercultural communication carried out by mediating translations, they manifest *the pure historic power of translation as such*, which is not to be confounded with the historical power of translation in general. At a given moment, it is as if the historical relation with another culture or another work could only be established abruptly by means of translation. It does not necessarily happen like this; for instance (and we shall come back to this), the profound relation to Antiquity maintained by classicist France does presuppose a great many translations—those made in the sixteenth and seventeenth centuries—but by no means one translation in particular; not even Amyot's Plutarch. The peculiarity of German culture is perhaps to have experienced this unique power of translation several times. And it emerged for the first time with Luther.

In this respect, an examination of the limits of Luther's *Verdeutschung*, specifically with regard to the Hebrew text, may have seemed of secondary importance. Besides, these limits have only become evident in the twentieth century, together with the reinterpretations, rereadings, and retranslations of the Gospels and the Old Testament. As Rosenzweig emphasizes—but this is already indicated by the example of Luther's translation quoted above—Luther, even though he certainly referred back to the Hebrew text, in the final analysis worked from the Latin version:

> Even as he studied the Hebrew text, he did not think in Hebrew, but in Latin.[13]

Which was inevitable, since it was Latin and not Hebrew that constituted the linguistic, religious, and cultural background of Luther's thought. Nevertheless, by bringing about the delimitation of German and Latin, the *Verdeutschung* did not proceed to a simple germanization in the sense in which we would speak depreciatingly of the "gallicization" of a foreign text today. This is all the more impossible inasmuch as, in the case of a religious translation like that of the Bible and of a return to the "sources" like Protestantism, the Hebrew original could not be simply left aside. Here, the appeal to Hebrew functioned rather to reinforce the efficiency of the "Reform" movement. Even though it was by no means the determining factor in the entire Lutheran undertaking, Hebrew inflected the *Verdeutschung* and lent it a supplementary originality. Luther knew very well that opening the Biblical word to the community of believers was at the same time giving them this word in the language of the "woman in the home," of the "children in the street," and of the "common man in the market place," and *transmitting to them the Bible's own speaking*, that is to say, the Hebrew speech, which requires that the framework of the German be sometimes pushed aside:

> On the other hand I have not just . . . disregarded altogether the exact wording of the original. Rather with my helpers I have been very careful to see that where everything turns on a single passage, I have kept to the original quite literally, and have not lightly departed from it. For example, in John 6 [:27] Christ says, "Him has God the Father sealed [*versiegelt*]." It would have been better German to say, "Him has God the Father signified [*gezeichent*]," or, "He it is whom God the Father means [*meinet*]." But I preferred to do violence to the German language rather than to depart from the word. Ah, translating is not everyman's skill as the mad saints imagine. It requires a right, devout, honest, sincere, God-fearing, Christian, trained, informed, and experienced heart. Therefore I hold that no false Christian or factitious spirit can be a decent translator.[14]

Elsewhere, Luther writes of his translation of the Psalms:

> On the other hand we have at times also translated quite literally— even though we could have rendered the meaning more clearly another way. . . . Therefore . . . we should keep such words, accustom ourselves to them, and so give place to the Hebrew language where it does a better job than our German.[15]

In the same text, he broaches the problem of the "meaning" and of the "letter" in a more general way, stating he has translated

> at times retaining the words quite literally, at times rendering only the meaning.[16]

This is a direct allusion to Saint Jerome, translator of the *Vulgate*, for whom the translation of the Scriptures was only a rendering of meaning. As he says in his "Letter to Pammachius," this is a rule already well-instituted by Cicero and the Latin poets:

> I do not only admit but recognize clearly that in translating the Holy Scriptures from the Greek . . . I have not translated word for word, but meaning for meaning.[17]

St. Jerome and his translation remain the background for the Lutheran Bible, but the latter nevertheless intends to leave "some room" to the Hebrew language. Thus, the *Verdeutschung* seems to oscillate between several modes of translation. And we must use the term *mode* here, because in Luther there is no concern with a set of empirical rules—as is the case in Estienne Dolet's *La manière de bien traduire d'une langue en aultre*—nor of a method in the sense of a systematic definition of types of translation, as in Schleiermacher's "On the Different Methods of Translating."[18] Not to choose between literalness and freedom, between the "meaning" and the "letter," between Latin and Hebrew, does not signify a methodological wavering but a perception of the fundamental aporias of translation and an intuition of what can and must be done at a given historical moment.

As such, Luther's translation opens a double horizon: an historical-cultural one, which we have mentioned above, and the more limited one of future German translations and their meaning. Since Luther, no translation from a foreign work and a foreign language can be made without some reference to his translation of the Bible, even if it is only to put his principles aside and to attempt to go beyond them. Voss, Goethe, and Hölderlin will take precise stock of this. If the Lutheran Bible establishes a rupture in the history of the German language, culture, and literature, it also establishes one in the domain of translations. *Moreover, it suggests that the formulation and the development of a national culture of its own can and must proceed by way of translation, that is, by an intensive and deliberate relation to the foreign.*[19]

This affirmation may appear, and in part is, of the utmost triviality. At least it is our custom to consider it such. But it is one thing to think that, for one's own development of whatever order, it is good "to rub one's brains with another" (Montaigne); it is another to think that any relation to oneself and to what is one's "own" passes radically through this relation to the other and to the foreign, so much so that it is by such an *alienation*, in the strictest sense of the word, that a relation to oneself is possible. There lies, on the psychological level, the mental operation of many translators, an operation André Gide once formulated in a conversation with Walter Benjamin:

> It is precisely the fact that I removed myself from my mother tongue that provided me with the necessary momentum to master a foreign language. What matters most for the learning of languages is not to learn, but to abandon one's own language. Only in that way does one eventually fully understand it. . . . It is only in leaving a thing that we name it.[20]

But things become more complicated when this law leaves the psychological sphere and is applied on the historical-cultural level. In addition, the disproportion of the passage through the foreign makes the threat of the loss of one's own identity hover perpetually over the level of the individual as well as that of a people and a history. What is at stake here is not so much this law as it is the point where it crosses its

own limits without, for all that, transforming itself into a genuine relation to the Other. And this is what sometimes seems to happen in
German culture: When the "flexibility," so highly praised by Goethe and
A. W. Schlegel (by the former for the German language, by the latter for
the German character), is transformed into the *unified and protean
power to fall into alterity*. At the outset of the nineteenth century, this
power is attested to by the prodigious development of philology, literary criticism, comparative studies, hermeneutics, and, of course, translation. In the literary sense, authors like Tieck, Jean Paul, and Goethe
show the same dangerous "flexibility" (in the vocabulary of the time
versatility is readily used to designate this mental and cultural agility,
without a pejorative meaning). This movement, very productive culturally, starts from the paradox, apparent or not, that a community has
better access to itself in proportion as it opens itself to what it is not. In
his *Untimely Meditations*, Nietzsche will regard what he summarizes by
the expression *historical sense* as a genuine disaster—the disaster of the
European nineteenth century.[21]

Obviously, a spirit as "versatile" as F. Schlegel's was perfectly well
aware of the nature of this relation. In his fragments, he mentions two
nations of translators—the Romans and the Arabs—and what sets them
apart in this respect. The Romans made a language and a literature for
themselves on the basis of a tremendous work of translation from the
Greek, a work of symbiosis and annexation—think of an author like
Plautus. According to Schlegel, the Arabs proceeded in a different manner:

> Their fondness for destroying or throwing away the originals when the
> translations are finished characterizes the spirit of their philosophy.
> Precisely for that reason it may be that they were ultimately more
> cultivated but, with all their culture, more purely barbaric than the
> Europeans of the Middle Ages. For barbarism is defined as what is at
> once anti-classical and anti-progressive.[22]

Indeed, to burn the originals—an act of an immeasurable, almost
mythical complexity—has a twofold effect: It suppresses any relation to
a literature considered to be an historical model (the "anti-classical")
and it makes impossible any re-translation (whereas each translation
implies its re-translation, that is, a "progressivity").

In that way, starting from the historical precedent of Luther's translation of the Bible, a whole set of questions is posed to German culture,
questions that concern its very essence: What are we if we are a nation
of translators? What is translation, and what is a good translation, for the
people we are? Also, to what extent does this hypertrophic and disproportionate relation not constitute for us a radical threat? Should we

not rather turn to that which, in our culture, has *become* foreign to us, though it actually constitutes our innermost nature—our past? What is *Deutschheit*, if it is the site of all these questions? Herder, Goethe, the Romantics, Schleiermacher, Humboldt, and Hölderlin, each in their own way, attempt to confront these questions that situate translation in a cultural problematic extending far beyond all "methodology." In the nineteenth century, Nietzsche and philological positivism will take them up again, followed in the twentieth century by thinkers as diverse as Lukács, Benjamin, Rosenzweig, Reinhardt, Schadewaldt, and Heidegger.

2

HERDER:
FIDELITY AND EXPANSION

This chapter, devoted to Herder and the problematic of translation established in Germany in the second half of the eighteenth century, could be placed under the aegis of two notions that recur frequently in texts of that period: *Erweiterung* and *Treue*. *Erweiterung* means expansion, amplification. We have already encountered this word in Novalis, when he states that only in Germany have translations become "expansions." *Treue* means fidelity. The word carries great weight in German culture at the time and stands for a cardinal virtue in the affective sphere as well as in translation and national culture. In this respect, to state that a translation must be faithful is not as trivial as it may seem at first sight. For, as Rosenzweig says, to translate is "to serve two masters":[1] the foreign work and the foreign language; one's own public and one's own language. A double fidelity is needed, then, incessantly threatened by the specter of a double treason. But fidelity, for that matter, is by no means an historical constant. At the time when, in Germany, fidelity is being celebrated with almost marital overtones by Breitinger, Voss, and Herder, France translates without the least concern for fidelity and continues its never-abandoned tradition of "embellishing" and "poeticizing" translations. The German theory of translation consciously positions itself against these translations "after the French manner." At the close of this period, A. W. Schlegel expressed this view in very vigorous terms:

Other nations have adopted a totally conventional phraseology in poetry, so that it is totally impossible to make a poetic translation of
anything whatsoever into their language—French is an example. . . .
It is as if they wanted every foreigner among them to behave and to
dress according to the customs of the land, and that explains why they
never really get to know the foreign.[2]

This way of translating is in perfect conformity with the dominant
position of French culture at the time, a culture which did not need to
go through the law of the foreign to affirm its own identity. French, far
from opening itself to the influx of foreign languages, rather tended to
replace these as a means of communication in the European intellectual
and political sphere. In these circumstances, there is no room for any
consciousness of fidelity. The position of eighteenth-century German
only acquires more weight in the process. It refers to a cultural problematic which, as it were, is the *reverse* of the French.[3]

This problematic could be formulated at first in the following way:
the German language lacks "culture," and to acquire it, it must go
through a certain *expansion*, which presupposes translations marked
by fidelity. For in what respect could a translation that mirrors the
"French manner" expand the horizon of the language and the culture?
Such is the general argument for Breitinger, Leibniz, Voss, and Herder.
To be sure, in order to triumph, this argument has to struggle against
the French influence as well as against a certain pragmatism born from
the most mediocre tendencies of the Enlightenment. Schadewaldt has
characterized this situation very aptly:

> Frankly, there are certain ways of translating that are entirely non-
> problematic: those that do not want to be, in the strict sense of the
> word, faithful to the original or, in any case, do not consider fidelity to
> the essence of the original an obligatory requirement. When, in Ger-
> many before the beginning of the eighteenth century, translation was
> practiced as a formal-rhetorical exercise in the manner of Cicero and
> Quintillian . . . it did not make a difference if prose was translated
> into poetry or poetry into prose. . . . For original here means: "stylistic
> model," and fidelity is submitted to the arbitrariness of an uncultivated
> or deformed sense of taste. Later on, when a foreign work is ap-
> proached with the intention to lay hold of its material and objective
> content and to make it accessible to one's contemporaries, one is
> considered as faithful if one feels obliged to the transmitting of con-
> tent. Here, translations are "writings" (and I quote a definition by the
> *Aufklärer* Venzky, published in 1734 in Gottsched's *Critical Contribu-
> tions*) "which render a matter or a learned work into another . . .
> language, so that those who do not know the original language . . .
> may read those matters and that work with greater advantage and
> pleasure." And if such a translation has "clearly and completely ex-

pressed the understanding of an original writing, it is as good as the original." Because here, the original is the sum of facts that are useful and worth knowing. Therefore, it is perfectly compatible with the idea of fidelity to correct and complement the original, to add notes, clarify obscurities. . . . Nevertheless, the actual translation in this case is an essentially negative task: the translator is concerned with the overcoming of the intolerable situation introduced into the world by the Babylonian confusion of tongues.[4]

Still, these rationalist and empirical trends, which do not even have the superb ease of the classical French "non-translations," are not peculiar to the dominant tendencies of German translation in the eighteenth century; they rather represent a phenomenon—almost ahistorical in its constancy—of negation of the meaning of translation.

Leibniz, who had a keen interest in the problems of translation and of his own language, took a position concerning the expansion of German language and culture in two texts that are not very original but that already announce Herder:

> The real touchstone of the wealth or poverty of a language appears when translating good books from other languages. Then it becomes clear what is lacking and what is available.

> I do certainly not believe that there exists a language in the world that could render the words of other languages with equal force and equivalent words. . . . But the richest and most convenient language is the one best suited to word for word translations, translations which follow the original foot by foot.[5]

Here, the power of language lies in its capacity for literalness, and translation is the mirror in which language perceives its own limits.

In his *Critische Dichtung*, the Swiss critic Breitinger also defends literalness:

> One demands of a translator that he should translate the concepts and ideas discovered in an eminent model according to the same order, the same type of connection and composition . . . so that the representation of thoughts makes the same impression on the reader's sensibility. A translation . . . deserves all the more praise in proportion as it is faithful to the original. Which is why the translator must submit to the severe law that prohibits him to stray from the original, neither from the point of view of thoughts, nor from that of form. These must remain unchanged, retain the same degree of light and force.[6]

This prescription of fidelity, not further specified, is a good indication of the general tendency of the reflections of the time, in spite of its very rationalist language.

But it is with Herder and the *Literaturbriefe*[7] that the problematic of expansion and fidelity will be tied together. It is well known that Herder developed an entire philosophy of culture, history, and language in which such notions as *genius, people, popular poetry, myth*, and *nation* acquired their patent of nobility. He himself translated poetry, notably Spanish "romances." Because of his manifold poetic, philosophical, and linguistic interests, he was well placed to gauge the importance of the relation to the foreign that manifested itself in Germany with increasing force, specifically under the influence of English literature and Graeco-Roman antiquity. At the same time, a return to the "sources," that is, a return to popular poetry and the prestigious medieval past, was inaugurated. Herder, with his *Volkslieder*, played a leading role in this movement. His reflection, centered essentially on language and history, represents the first version of German classicism. We shall briefly comment here on a series of Herder's texts which clearly outline the new space of German culture.[8] These are sometimes quotations from the *Literaturbriefe* commented upon by the thinker.

The problems of translation, as far as they affect the relation of the mother tongue to foreign languages, often have an immediate intensity for Herder, which is expressed in almost amorous and sexual terms. Thus,

> It is not to unlearn my language that I learn other languages; it is not to exchange the habits of my education that I travel among foreign peoples; it is not to lose the citizenship of my fatherland that I become a naturalized foreigner; if I were to act in this way, I would lose more than I would gain. But I walk through foreign gardens to pick flowers for my language, as the betrothed of my manner of thinking: I observe foreign manners in order to sacrifice mine to the genius of my fatherland, like fruits ripened under a foreign sun.[9]

The relation of what is one's own and what is foreign is expressed in images, but the specter of a possible treason lurks behind the very choice of the comparisons and the apologetic and defensive tone of the text. Predominance of the foreign: loss of what is one's own. Transformation of the foreign into the simple pretext of the enrichment of what is one's own: treason of the very experience of strangeness.

In the face of the imbalances inherent in any relation to the foreign—imbalances which have their immediate projection in the domain of translation—the temptation to refuse this relation altogether is great. Klopstock, more than Herder, has experienced this temptation, not so much on the level of translation as on the level of interlingual relations, like the borrowing of foreign words. He was preoccupied by this problem as a poet and as a grammarian, to the extent that he considered German a purer language than English (afflicted by an unsettling mass of Latin words) and freer than French (prisoner of its classicism). As for Herder, the mother tongue was for him "a sort of reservoir of the most original concept of the people."[10] As such, it had to delimit itself in relation to other languages and affirm its own territory. Hence the dream, for him and Herder, of a *virgin language*, protected against any foreign blemishes, in particular the blemish that translation runs the risk of being. Again, Herder's language takes on a curious sexual coloring:

> Even though there are many reasons to recommend *translations* for the formation (*Bildung*) of the language, language nevertheless has greater advantages in protecting itself from all translation. Before translation, a language resembles a young virgin that has not yet had intercourse with a man, and therefore could not have conceived the fruit of the mingling of their blood. It is still pure and in a state of innocence, the faithful image of the character of its people. Even if it would be nothing but poverty, caprice, and irregularity, it is the original national language.[11]

A text disturbing in its utopian naïveté, in the kind of profoundness which it possesses nonetheless, deriving from the image of the young virgin applied to the mother tongue as well as the—obviously vertiginous—myth of a language closed onto itself, not "knowing," in the biblical sense, any other languages. Utopia is the right term here, since the destiny of the virgin is to become a woman, just like, to draw from the stock of vegetal images with which German classicism and Romanticism are so well endowed, it is the destiny of the bud to become a flower and then fruit. The very choice of Herder's image, even if one takes into account the Christian or perhaps Rousseauian valorization of virginity, shows that the relation to the foreign cannot and should not be avoided.

For a culture and a language threatened too much by this relation, there remains the temptation of a pure closure onto itself, just like in late Romanticism we encounter the temptation of the ineffable, the unspeakable, and, as we shall see, the untranslatable: *Not only not to translate any more, but to become untranslatable itself, this is perhaps the most complete expression of a closed language.* A regressive temptation, if it is true that the relation to the foreign is also, and above all, a relation of *differentiation*, of *dialectic*, or however else one wants to call that movement of the constitution of the self by the experience [*épreuve*] of the non-self, which, as we shall see, is the very essence of *culture* for German classicism and idealism.

Trying, like Goethe, to maintain a balance between this temptation and the inverse temptation of a pure being-outside-oneself (of which examples may be found in certain Romantics), and starting from the reflections of certain collaborators to the *Literaturbriefe*, Herder defines the nature, the role, and the options of the translator—which are all closely linked to the expansion of language and culture. Thus, he quotes Thomas Abbt in his *Fragments*:

> The genuine translator has a higher purpose than to make foreign books comprehensible to the reader; a purpose which elevates him to the rank of an author and which transforms the small vendor into a merchant who really enriches the state. . . . These translators could become our *classic* writers.[12]

> Homer, Aeschylus, and Sophocles created their masterpieces out of a language that did not yet possess any cultivated prose. Their translator must implant their masterpieces into a language which remains prose . . . even in hexameters, so as to lose as little as possible. They clothed thoughts in words and images; the translator himself must be a creative genius if he wants to satisfy both the original and his own language.[13]

Regarding another *Literaturbrief*, Herder goes further:

> A second, higher degree: if translators could be found who not only study the author in order to translate the meaning of the original into our language, but also to find its individual tone, who put themselves in the character of its writing style and express correctly for us the genuine distinctive traits, the expression, and the tone of the foreign original, its dominant character, its genius and the nature of its poetic genre. Frankly, this is very much, but not yet enough for my ideal translator. . . . If someone translated for us the father of poetry, Homer: an eternal work for German literature, a very useful work for geniuses, a precious work for the muse of antiquity and our language. . . . All this can become a Homeric translation if it raises itself above the level of the *attempt*, if it becomes, as it were, *the whole life of a scholar* and shows us Homer as he is, and as he could be *for us*. . . . So far for the introduction; and the translation? It should in no way be embellished. . . . The French, who are too proud of their national taste, draw everything close to it, instead of adapting themselves to the taste of another epoch. . . . We poor Germans, on the other hand, still almost without public and without country, still without the tyrant of a national taste, we want to see this epoch as it is. And in Homer's case the best translation cannot accomplish this without the notes and explanations of an eminent critical spirit.[14]

The great translations of the German classical and romantic age, all of them, are announced in this text. The notion of fidelity here receives a less rational definition than with Breitinger: the translator, who is also writer, creative genius, scholar, and critic, must capture the uniqueness of the original, itself defined as its "expression," its "form," its "character," its "genius," and its "nature." To be sure, all these are terms that are more appropriate for an individual than for a work: *but the work is now defined as an individual*—a point of view that will be radicalized by the Romantics in the light of Fichte's philosophy. It is this work-individual that the genius-translator must render, in a centrifugal moment which Herder, logically, opposes to the centripetal movement of the French, and that should not contain any *embellishment*: this, in effect, would annul the entire meaning of such a capturing. The work must be shown "such as it is," and such as it may be "for us" (which is less clear). A movement in which criticism, history, and philology are implied. The fidelity to the individuality of the work is the direct productive agent of linguistic and cultural expansion.

From Luther to Herder there is a progression which the French influence and the rationalism of the Enlightenment have at most only hindered: At the time of the constitution of a *literature* and a *theater* that would form, as it were, the two center pieces of German culture (and this is, indeed, the central preoccupation of Herder and Lessing), translation is called upon *for the second time* to play a central role. To be sure, it shares this role—and in this Herder announces the Romantics— with *criticism*. Regarding the text we have just commented upon, we may speak, for that matter, of *critical translation*. But from Herder's perspective, translation, so to speak, plays a more immediate role because it deals directly with language; which is a point that Jean Paul, in his *School for Aesthetics*, has well perceived—at a time, to be sure, when the translations Herder had wished for were already historic:

> In Schlegel's Shakespeare and in Voss' translations, language lets its artful fountains play, and *both* works give weight to the wish of the author of the present work: that translators in general might know how much they have done for the sonority, the plenitude, the purity of the language, often more than the writer himself, because language, precisely, is their subject matter, whereas the writer sometimes forgets language to the benefit of the subject matter.[15]

More specifically, what remains to be asked is: To what extent does German culture, as it is defined in the second half of the eighteenth century with Lessing and Herder, then Goethe and the Romantics, *specifically* imply translation as an essential moment of its constitution? And further: Once it has been stated that the essence of translation is the *fidelity to the spirit of the works* which opens a culture to the foreign and thus enables it to expand, what are the preferred *domains of translation* that must be opened to the German *Bildung*? In other words, having answered the questions *why translate?* and *how to translate?*, one must answer the question: *what should be translated?* These three questions are at the very center of any *historical* theory of translation.

3

BILDUNG AND THE
DEMAND OF TRANSLATION

The concept of *Bildung* is one of the central concepts of German culture at the end of the eighteenth century. It can be found everywhere: in Herder, in Goethe and Schiller, in the Romantics, in Hegel, in Fichte, etc. *Bildung* generally means "culture," and it may be considered the German counterpart of *Kultur*, which is of Latin stock. But because of the lexical family to which it belongs,[1] it means much more and it is applied to many more registers: thus it is possible to speak of the *Bildung* of an artwork, the degree of its "formation." Likewise, *Bildung* has a very strong pedagogical and educational connotation: the process of formation.

It is no exaggeration to state that the concept summarizes the conception which the German culture of the time formed of itself, *the way in which the culture interprets its mode of unfolding*. We shall attempt to show that translation (as the mode of relation to the foreign) is structurally inscribed in *Bildung*. And, in a subsequent chapter, we shall see that, though it is common to all writers and thinkers of the age, *Bildung* receives its canonical form with Goethe.

We do not pretend to proceed here to a semantic-historical analysis of the concept of *Bildung*, but to present some sort of ideal profile of it, based on the different meanings it takes on, notably in Herder, Goethe, Hegel, and the Romantics.

What, then, is *Bildung*? It is a process, as well as its result. Through *Bildung* an individual, a people, a nation, but also a language, a literature, a work of art in general are formed and thus acquire a form, a *Bild*. *Bildung* is always a movement toward a form, *one's own form*—which is to say that, in the beginning, every being is deprived of *its* form. In the speculative language of German Idealism, the beginning may be the particularity which lacks the determination of the universal, the unity from which the moment of scission and opposition is absent, the panic indifference lacking all articulation, the thesis without its antithesis or synthesis, the unmediated immediate, the chaos which has not yet become world, the position deprived of the moment of reflection, the unlimited which must be limited (or vice versa), the affirmation which must go through negation, etc. These abstract formulations also have a concrete and metaphorical side: the child that must become adult, the virgin that must become woman, the bud that must become flower and then fruit. The almost constant use of organic images to characterize *Bildung* indicates that the concept deals with a necessary process. But at the same time, this process is an unfolding of freedom.

Because *Bildung* is a temporal, and therefore historical, process, it is articulated in periods, stages, moments, ages. Thus there are "epochs" of humanity, of culture, of history, of thought, of language, of art, and of individuals. These epochs are often dual, but most frequently triadic. At bottom, all *Bildung* is triadic—which is to say that its structure is essentially homologous to what Heidegger defined as

> the principle of unconditioned subjectivity of the German absolute metaphysics of Hegel and Schelling, according to whose teaching the being-with-itself of spirit requires a return to itself which, in turn, requires a being-outside-itself.[2]

Of course, the interpretation of this principle varies from author to author. But it may be said that it provides the *speculative basis for the concept of* Bildung, or that the latter provides it with *its historical-cultural base*.

In this sense, *Bildung* is a *process of self-formation* concerned with a "same" unfolding itself to attain its full dimension. And probably the highest concept German thinking of the age created to interpret this process is that of *experience*, which Hegel extracted from the narrow meaning assigned to it by Kant. For experience is the only notion capable of embracing all others, it is a broadening and an identification, a passage from the particular to the universal, the experience [*épreuve*] of scission, of the finite, of the conditioned. It is voyage (*Reise*) and migration (*Wanderung*). Its essence is to throw the "same" into a dimension that will transform it. It is the movement of the "same" which, changing, finds itself to be "other." "Die and become," Goethe said.

But as voyage, it is also the experience of the *alterity of the world*: in order to have access to that which, in the guise of a becoming-other, is in truth a becoming-itself, the same must experience *that which is not itself*, or at least what *appears* as such. For Idealism, the accomplished experience is the becoming-itself of the other and the becoming-other of the same:

> He lifted the veil of the Goddess at Saïs. But what did he see? He saw—miracle of miracles—himself.[3]

Thus Novalis in *The Disciples at Saïs*. But experience would only be a false pretense if it was not also the experience of *apparent radical alterity*. "Consciousness" must live the alterity as absolute and then, at another stage, discover its relativity. Which is why experience is always the "crossing of appearances," in proportion as it discovers that appearances are not only other than they are, but that alterity is not as radical as it seems. As the experience [*épreuve*] of alterity, the formation of self through the experience [*épreuve*] of alterity, experience must finally emerge as reunion, identity, unity, supreme though delayed moment, since the truth of this experience [*épreuve*] is situated somewhere between its closure and its infinity.

As the way of the same to itself, as experience, *Bildung* takes on the form of a *novel*:

> Every human being who is cultivated and who cultivates himself contains a novel within himself.[4]

> Nothing is more romantic than what is commonly called the world and destiny. We live in a colossal novel.[5]

> Life should not be a novel given to us, but a novel we have made ourselves.[6]

The novel is the experience of the apparent strangeness of the world and of the apparent strangeness of the same to itself. Proceeding towards a point where both strangenesses will be canceled, the novel has a "transcendental" structure. Hence the polarities, in Goethe and the Romantics, which define the novel: the everyday and the miraculous (one of the faces of strangeness), the near and the far, the known and the unknown, the finite and the infinite, etc.

This experience, which proceeds toward the point where all the initially hostile polarities will become one, is necessarily *progressive*:

> Here . . . all is in constant progress and nothing can get lost. Which is why no stage can be omitted, the present one is necessarily connected to the previous as well as the following one, and what may have seemed obsolete for centuries will be reanimated with a new youthful

vigor when the time has come for spirit to remember itself and to return to itself.[7]

And it belongs to the nature of this progression to be, in a certain way, *passive*. Novalis: "passive nature of the novelistic hero";[8] "One does not do, one does what can be done."[9] This passivity, for that matter, is implied by the organicist imagery of *Bildung*. And culturally it is not without consequences. The precedence of passivity in the movement of experience entails that the *relation of the same to the other cannot be a relation of appropriation*. To be sure, Novalis, well before Hegel and Nietzsche, developed a theory of appropriation, of *Zueignung*.[10] He even assimilates thinking and eating. But this mode of oral appropriation, to the extent that it is a becoming-same of the foreign as well as a becoming-foreign of the same, has nothing in common with a theory of radical appropriation as it is developed by Nietzsche.[11] Romantic agility and Goethean curiosity are not Will to Power.

This brief and schematic characterization of *Bildung* shows immediately that *it is closely connected with the movement of translation*— for translation, indeed, starts from what is one's own, the same (the known, the quotidian, the familiar), in order to go towards the foreign, the other (the unknown, the miraculous, the *Unheimliche*), and, starting from this experience, *to return to its point of departure*. In a movement governed by the law of appropriation, there could never be an *experience* of the foreign, but simply an *annexation* or *reduction* of the other to the same. Which is precisely how Nietzsche, evoking Roman antiquity, interprets the act of translation and culture as such:

> The degree of the historical sense of any age may be inferred from the manner in which this age makes *translations* and tries to absorb former ages and books. . . . And Roman antiquity itself: how forcibly and at the same time how naively, it took hold of everything good and lofty of Greek antiquity, which was more ancient! How they translated things into the Roman present! . . . As poets, they had no sympathy for the antiquarian inquisitiveness that precedes the historical sense; as poets, they had no time for all those very personal things and names and whatever might be considered the costume and mask of a city, a coast, or a century, and quickly substituted their own Roman actuality for it. . . . They did not know the delights of the historical sense; what was past and foreign was an embarrassment for them, and being Romans, they saw it as an incentive for a Roman conquest. Indeed, translation was a form of conquest. Not only did one omit what was historical; no, one also added allusions to the present and, above all, struck out the name of the poet and replaced it with one's own—not with any sense of theft, but with the very best conscience of the *imperium Romanum*.[12]

Words which, consciously or not, echo those of Saint Jerome, when he says of one of his Latin predecessors that he has "led the meanings captive, as it were, into his own language with the right of a conqueror."[13] Here, the movement of the imperial expansion of culture is strictly equivalent with the movement which brings the meanings to itself as captives. But this conquering coming and going has nothing to do with the cyclical movement of experience as it was expressed by F. Schlegel:

> Which is why, since he is certain to always find himself again, man incessantly goes outside of himself, in order to find the complement of his innermost being in that of another. The play of communication and of bringing together is the occupation and the force of life.[14]

> The essence of spirit is to determine itself and, in a perpetual alternation, to go outside of itself and return to itself.[15]

> The true middle is only the one to which one always *returns* from the most excentric paths of enthusiasm and energy, not the middle one never leaves.[16]

This circular, cyclical, and alternating nature of Bildung *implies in itself something like trans-lation,* Über-Setzung, *a positing of oneself beyond oneself.*[17]

The importance of translation for German culture at the end of the eighteenth century, then, is profoundly connected to the conception it has of itself, that is to say of *experience*—a conception opposed in every respect to those of ancient Rome or classicist France. One may surely see in the "eccentric" *Bildung* an internal weakness—which is how Nietzsche interprets it. It may be seen as the incapacity to be one's own center to oneself, and that is the whole problem of *mediation* which constitutes a fundamental problem in Novalis, F. Schlegel, and Schleiermacher. The latter was perfectly aware of the "mediating nature" of *Bildung*.[18] Goethe's *Wilhelm Meister* is the story of the education of the young hero, a formation which passes through a series of mediations and mediators, one of whom is significantly called the "Foreigner." *Because the foreign has a mediating function, translation can become one of the agents of* Bildung—a function it shares with a series of other "trans-lations" which constitute as many critical relations to the self and the foreign.[19] Thus the age of Voss, Hölderlin, Schleiermacher, and A. W. Schlegel witnesses the rise of folklore, of great national dictionaries, of literary and art criticism; even the memorable travels of Alexander von Humboldt, Wilhelm's brother, take place in this dimension.[20] In all of these trans-lations, the essence of *Bildung* affirms itself.

But in order for this multiple opening to the foreign not to fall into a total symbiosis with it, its horizon must be delimited. *Bildung* is also, and essentially, limitation (*Begrenzung*). Such is the wisdom of *Wilhelm Meister*; such is also—though stained with ambiguity—the conviction of the Romantics.

Friedrich Schlegel:

> Without delimitation, no *Bildung* is possible.[21]

And Novalis:

> The possibility of self-limitation is the possibility of all synthesis—of all miracle. And the world started with a miracle.
>
> There are no limits to our intellectual progress, but we must posit for ourselves transitional limits *ad hunc actum*—to be simultaneously limited and unlimited.[22]

In a text to which we shall return, F. Schlegel gave a very precise formulation of this relation of the limited and the unlimited in the literary work and in *Bildung* in general:

> A work is cultivated (*gebildet*) when it is everywhere sharply de-limited, but within those limits limitless and inexhaustible; when it is completely faithful to itself, entirely homogeneous, and nonetheless exalted above itself. Like the education of young Englishmen, the most important thing is *le grand tour*. It should have traveled through all three or four continents of humanity, not in order to round off the edges of individuality, but to broaden its vision and give its spirit more freedom and inner versatility; and thereby greater independence and self-sufficiency.[23]

Limitation is what distinguishes the experience of *Bildung* from the purely erratic and chaotic adventure where one loses oneself.[24] The *grand tour* does not consist of going just anywhere, but there where one can form and educate oneself, and progress towards oneself.

But if Bildung *is accomplished by an essentially cyclical and de-limited translation, what should it translate towards? More precisely, which translations, which domains of translation can function as mediation here?*

By virtue of its experiential nature, *Bildung* can never be the simple imitation of the foreign. Nevertheless, it maintains an essential connection with what is called in German *Urbild* (original, archetype) and *Vorbild*, the model of which it can be the reproduction (*Nachbild*). This also refers to its experiential nature: he who seeks himself in foreign parts is confronted with figures which function initially as *models*, then as *mediations*. Such are the people Wilhelm Meister encounters during the years of his apprenticeship: first he attempts to identify with them, but they eventually teach him to find himself.

The *Vorbild*, a manifestation and exemplification of the *Urbild*, gathers within it that perfection and completion which make it into a "classic." It is the form, if not the norm, to which *Bildung* must refer without being obliged to copy it. Thus A. W. Schlegel speaks of that genuine imitation which is not "the aping of a man's outer manners, but the appropriation of the maxims of his actions."[25]

Regarding culture and literature, starting with Winckelmann the entire antiquity becomes *Urbild* and *Vorbild* for the Germans:

> The first among us . . . to recognize and, with divine enthusiasm, re-
> veal the archetype of accomplished humanity in the forms of art and
> antiquity was the holy Winckelmann.[26]

Henceforth, antiquity may be said to function as *Vorbild* and *Urbild* of *Bildung* itself—to the extent that the history of ancient culture, literature, and language appears as "an eternal history of taste and art." From there on, the relation to this model becomes a burning issue: "the necessity of the return to the ancients," as that which is both *originary* and *classical*. No other culture, neither past nor present, possesses this precedence. Compared to antiquity, modernity is still in the phase of looking for itself in the rending of unfinished reflection. For German classicism, the creation of a modern *Bildung* is first of all determined by the relation to antiquity as a model. This means that it must strive to attain a degree of culture equivalent to that of the ancients, notably by appropriating their poetic *forms*. The study of these forms—philology—henceforth acquires a leading role:

> To live classically and to realize antiquity practically within oneself is
> the summit and the goal of philology.[27]

As far as translations are concerned, they must be devoted to the ancients first and foremost, which is why Herder demands a translation of Homer, the "father of poetry." Voss responds to this wish by translating the *Odyssee* in 1781, and the *Iliad* in 1793. His translations aim at translating the Greeks as faithfully as possible, but also at submitting the still "unformed" German language to the "beneficial" yoke of Greek metrical forms. Though disputed, Voss's work rapidly acquires an exemplary historic significance, similar to Luther's translation.

Goethe:
> Voss, who will never be praised enough. . . . But whoever can now see
> what has happened, what versatility has come to the Germans, what
> rhetorical, rhythmical, metrical advantages are at the disposal of the
> talented and knowledgeable youngster . . . may hope that literary his-
> tory will plainly state who was the first to take this road in spite of so
> many obstacles.[28]

F. Schlegel:
> Even though the poetry of Voss has long since lost its importance, his

merit as translator and language artist will . . . shine all the more brightly.[29]

Humboldt:

> Voss, who may be said to have introduced classical antiquity into the German language.[30]

Which is an extremely important process, leading to the graecization of the poetical German language—the *Griechischung der deutschen Sprache* mentioned by Hofmannsthal—of which Hölderlin is the foremost example.

Nevertheless, once this precedence of the relation to the ancients is established, a question arises which will stir German culture, more or less surreptitiously, from Romanticism to Nietzsche: *Which is nearest to us, the Greeks or the Romans*? It goes without saying that this question is never asked as such—on the one hand, because Winckelmann taught that antiquity should be viewed as a "whole," thus amalgamating Greeks and Romans; on the other hand, because from the point of view of originality and *Vorbildlichkeit* (the capacity of being a model) the Greeks are far superior.[31] Greece is the native soil of poetry and its genres, the birthplace of philosophy, rhetoric, history, grammar, etc. Accordingly, its cultural precedence is total. But at the same time, Greece seems to conceal something that is profoundly foreign to modern culture, and which probably refers to its relation to *myth*. If Greek *Bildung* formally constitutes a model, its *ground* cannot but manifest its *strangeness* as soon as one ventures to recognize it for what it is. F. Schlegel and Nietzsche, both philologers by training, have felt this instinctively.

F. Schlegel:

> We are closer to the Romans and can understand them better than the Greeks.[32]

> To believe in the Greeks is only another fashion of the age. People are rather fond of listening to declamations about the Greeks. But if someone were to come and say, here are some, then nobody is at home.[33]

Nietzsche:

> One does not *learn* from the Greeks—their manner is too foreign, and too fluid, to have an imperative, a "classical" effect.[34]

Conversely, the Romans may seem to be closer because of the derivative, mixed, cross-bred character of their culture. To Nietzsche as well as to the Romantics, it is clear that the mixing of genres, parody, satire, the recourse to masks, the indefinite play with matter and form that characterizes Alexandrian literature and Latin poetry are at bottom infinitely more attractive than the Greek purity, whether it is considered from the point of view of "classical perfection" (Goethe) or perceived in its archaic originality (Hölderlin). F. Schlegel does not fail to mention this irresistible affinity of Romanticism with Latin eclecticism:

> The fondness of Alexandrian and Roman poets for difficult and un-poetical themes is really a result of their grand thought that all should be poeticized; not as a conscious artistic intention, but as a historical tendency of their work. And behind the mixing of all the artistic genres by the poetical eclectics of late antiquity there lies the demand that there should be One Poetry as well as One Philosophy.[35]

Which is exactly the program of the *Athenäum*. Hence, probably, the taste for syncretism and the profusion of "synactivities" advocated by Novalis and F. Schlegel (sympoetry, symphilosophy, syncriticism), where the dialogic element is less important than the *plural practice of mixing*.

But under these circumstances the beautiful unity of the concept of antiquity falls to pieces: an abyss opens between Greeks and Romans as well as between Greeks and Moderns. Or rather, two models are proposed to *Bildung* simultaneously: Latin syncretism, carrier of an "increasing perfection," and Greek completeness, the pure image of a "natural cycle."[36]

But there is more: Roman eclecticism has its historical extension in the modern literature which begins with the troubadours, the medieval cycles—everything we call old Romance literature—and comes to bloom with Dante, Petrarch, Ariosto, Tasso, Boccaccio, Calderón, Cervantes, Lope de Vega, Shakespeare, etc. So much so that a certain filiation appears: romanity—Romance cultures—novelistic [*romanesque*] forms—romanticism.[37] F. Schlegel and Novalis were perfectly aware of this:

> Our ancient nationality was, it seems to me, authentically Roman. . . . Germany is Rome, as a country. . . . The universal politics and the instinctive tendency of the Romans are to be found as well in the German people.[38]

> Romantic philosophy. *Lingua romana*.[39]

Rome/the novel [*Roman/roman*]: this is precisely the Romantic field of action, that of their critiques and their translations, the starting-point of their theories of the new literature.

Conversely, the classics (Goethe, Schiller) and Hölderlin principally translate the Greeks, the former because these are models for them, the latter because the Greeks, in their cultural trajectory, represent the reverse of the "modern," the "foreign," and because, Hölderlin says, this must be learned together with what is our "own."[40]

Here, we see taking form, with a precision that derives directly from divergent cultural choices, *the horizon of German translation at the end of the eighteenth century, together with the always-central place reserved for it in the cultural field conceived as* Bildung. Starting from this it would be possible to draw a *map* of the German translations of the time, a differential, selective, hierarchical and, as it were, disjunctive map, in which the "Greek" and the "Roman/novel,"[41] the "pure" and the "mixed," the "cyclical" and the "progressive" are in some way mutually exclusive.[42] Moreover, this position refers to the battle of the Ancients and the Moderns, to the conflict of the classical and the Romantic, to the discussions on poetic genres and the respective roles of theater, music, and literature in German culture—discussions that will stir this culture throughout the nineteenth century and beyond. One needs only to think of Wagner, Nietzsche, and Thomas Mann.

Before going on to the Romantic theory of *Bildung* and of translation, we have to inquire how, with Goethe, the whole of this problematic found its most classical figure.

4

GOETHE: TRANSLATION AND WORLD LITERATURE

*Translators are like busy matchmakers
who praise a half-veiled beauty as being
very lovely: they arouse an irrepressible
desire for the original.*

—Goethe, *Maxims and Reflections*

In the age of German Idealism no one has lived with such intensity the multiplicity of translations implied by *Bildung* than Goethe; none has contributed more to a harmonious, living and accomplished image of *Bildung* than he has. Whereas the lives of the Romantics and Hölderlin seem devoured by speculative and poetic fever, Goethe's life leaves a considerable part to what might be called natural existence, which in his case included numerous love affairs, a family life, his unrelenting activity in Weimar, as well as his travels, his correspondence, and his conversations. Schiller characterized him as "the most communicable of men."[1] His work bears the stamp of the same rich and vital diversity: He practiced all poetic and literary genres, produced works he judged to be strictly scientific, wrote diaries and memoirs, animated periodicals and newspapers. True, *criticism* and *speculation* are absent from this ample palet, even though he wrote numerous critical articles and texts of a theoretical appearance. Translations, on the other hand, to which a

volume of his *Complete Works* is devoted, were with him from beginning to end: Benvenuto Cellini, Diderot, Voltaire, Euripides, Racine,
Corneille, as well as numerous translations of Italian, English, Spanish,
and Greek poems. To be sure, these translations do not distinguish
themselves by any particular importance. Goethe is not Voss, not Hölderlin, not A. W. Schlegel. But they are witness to an almost constant
practice (to which he was disposed by a knowledge of languages developed from early childhood), a practice accompanied by a mass of ex-
ceptionally rich reflections, scattered through his articles, book reviews,
introductions, dialogues, diaries, and correspondence, and which
found their most famous expression in *Dichtung und Wahrheit, Noten
und Abhandlungen zur besseren Verständnis des West-Ostlichen Divans,*
and "Zu brüderlichen Andenken Wielands". Furthermore, Goethe in-
serted fragments of translations in two of his other works, *Werther* and
Wilhelm Meister, which is by no means a coincidence. Nor is this all: He
is a translator-poet who also, and very soon, became a translated poet.
And in him, *being translated* nourished an absolutely fascinating reflection. The fact that he devoted a poem—"Ein Gleichnis"—to having
been able to read himself in another language, and that, from 1799 on,
he dreamed of publishing a comparative edition of the Danish, English,
and French translations of *Hermann and Dorothea,* shows that he lived
the fact of being translated as an *experience* and never, it would seem, as
the narcissistic satisfaction of a writer. Goethe's statements on translation, which are of a great diversity, are never gathered together in the
form of a theory, but they possess their own coherence deriving from
his view of natural, human, social, and cultural reality—a view itself
based on an interpretation of *Nature* as a process of interaction, participation, reflection, exchange, and metamorphosis. It is impossible to
offer an exhaustive study of this interpretation here. Rather, we have
chosen to approach Goethe's reflection on translation starting from a
concept that arises fairly late in his work (1827), and which he has given
its patent of nobility: that of *Weltliteratur,* world literature. In effect, this
reflection is almost entirely integrated into a certain view of intercultural and international exchanges. Translation is the action *sui generis* that incarnates, illustrates, and also makes possible these exchanges,
without, to be sure, having a monopoly on them. There is a multiplicity
of acts of translation that assure the plenitude of vital and natural interactions among individuals, peoples, and nations, interactions in which
they construct their own identity and their relations to the foreign.
Goethe's interest proceeds from this vital and originary phenomenon of
exchange to its concrete manifestations. Generally speaking, his thinking tends to remain on the level of these concrete manifestations, even
if he always uncovers "the Eternal One-ness, which manifests itself in

many ways."[2] Goethe rests his view on the double principle of interaction and, within and through interaction, revelation of the "general" and the "substantial." In 1783, he already writes about Nature:

> Each of her works has its own being, each of her phenomena its separate idea, and yet all create a single whole.[3]

Also very early, he copied the following text by Kant for his own use:

> Principle of simultaneity according to the law of reciprocal action or community. All substances, to the extent that they can be perceived as simultaneous in space, are in continual interaction.[4]

Elsewhere he states:

> Man is not a teaching, but a living, acting, and working being. Only in effect and countereffect do we find pleasure.[5]

To this view of the *co-acting present*, the perception of *unicity in diversity* must be added:

> In every particular, whether it be historical, mythological, fabulous, more or less arbitrarily invented, one will always see . . . this general quality becoming more and more apparent.[6]

The same principle governs his search for the "originary Man," the "originary Plant," or, more profoundly, that of the "originary Phenomenon" (*Urphänomen*). Translation and *Weltliteratur* are thought in this twofold dimension.

What, then, is world literature? Not the totality of past and present literatures accessible to the encyclopedic gaze, nor the more limited totality of works—like those of Homer, Cervantes, Shakespeare—that have attained universal status and have become the patrimony of "cultivated" humanity. Goethe's notion of *Weltliteratur* is an historical concept concerning the *modern* situation of the relation among diverse national or regional literatures. In that sense, it would be better to speak of the *age of world literature*—which is the age in which literatures are no longer satisfied with interacting (a phenomenon that has always more or less existed), but explicitly conceive their existence and their unfolding in the framework of an incessantly intensified interaction. The appearance of world literature is contemporaneous with the appearance of a *Weltmarkt*, a world market for material goods. As Strich observes:

> It is an intellectual barter, a traffic in ideas between peoples, a literary world market to which the nations bring their spiritual treasures for exchange. To illustrate his idea Goethe himself was particularly fond of using such images taken from the world of trade and commerce.[7]

The appearance of world literature does not signify the disappearance of national literatures: It is the latter's entrance into a space-time where they act upon one another and seek to mutually clarify their images. Between 1820 and 1830, Goethe has expressed himself clearly on this matter:

> National literature is now rather an unmeaning term; the epoch of world literature is at hand, and each must strive to hasten its approach.[8]

> In venturing to announce a European, indeed a world literature, we did not mean merely to say that the different nations should inform themselves about one another and about each other's works. . . . No! It is rather a matter of living . . . men of letters getting to know each other and, through their own inclination and sense of community, to find occasion to act socially (*gesellschaftlich*).[9]

Thus, world literature is the active coexistence of all *contemporary* literatures. This contemporaneity, or simultaneity, is absolutely essential for the concept of *Weltliteratur*.

Strich:

> World literature is the spiritual space in which contemporaries, whatever their nationality, encounter each other, come together, and act communally.[10]

Goethe writes further:

> If we go back in history, we find personalities everywhere with whom we would agree and others with whom we could certainly be in conflict. *But the most important element, after all, is the contemporaneous, because it is reflected most clearly in us and we in it.*[11]

The active and conscious coexistence of contemporary literatures implies a modification of the relation to the self and the other. Though it does not entail the effacement of differences, it requires their intensified interaction. Such, for Goethe, is the essence of *modernity*.

In the new space announced here, translations play a primordial role. In 1828, Goethe writes to Carlyle concerning the English translation of his *Torquato Tasso*:

> I should like to have your opinion on how this *Tasso* can be considered English. You would greatly oblige me by enlightening me on this matter; for it is just these connections between original and translation that express most clearly the relationship of nation to nation and that one must above all understand if one wishes to encourage a . . . world literature.[12]

Which is to make of translation, if not the model, at least the touchstone of world literature. Goethe's thought here oscillates between two poles: *to promote a generalized intertranslation, or to consider German language and culture as the privileged medium of world literature*. In both cases, the task of the translator remains primordial:

He who understands and studies German language finds himself on the market where all nations offer their merchandise, he plays the interpreter in proportion as he enriches himself. And thus every translator should be considered a mediator striving to promote this universal spiritual exchange and taking it upon himself to make this generalized trade go forward. For whatever may be said of the inadequacy of translation, it remains one of the most essential and most worthy activities in the general traffic of the world. The Koran says: God has given to each people a prophet in their own language. In this way each translator is a prophet to his people.[13]

Elsewhere he writes:

For it is the destiny of the German to raise himself to the state of representative for all world citizens.[14]

According to the latter line of thought, the German cultural space, because translation has always opened it more to foreign cultural spaces, could become the "exchange market" par excellence of *Weltliteratur*. It may be said without exaggerating that the German language, for Goethe, sometimes became the *language-of-translation*. Which is precisely what is expressed in one of his conversations with Eckermann. Goethe's words here have a certain flatness, which suggests that he did not totally believe in what he said:

It cannot be denied . . . that when someone understands German well, he may do without many other languages. I am not speaking here of French—that is the language of conversation, and particularly indispensable when traveling, because everyone understands it, and it can be used in every country in lieu of an interpreter. But as far as Greek, Latin, Italian, and Spanish are concerned, we can read the best works of these nations in German translations of such outstanding quality that there is no further reason . . . to lose time over the painful learning of languages.[15]

The motto introducing this chapter may usefully—and ironically— correct the quotation above. Nevertheless, Goethe is aware of the primordial role of translation for German culture: In the same way France formed its language to be the "language of the world" (of intellectual and diplomatic, even aristocratic, exchanges), the Germans have educated their language to become the language in which other languages may make their works' own voice resound. And this is a process which, for Goethe, is practically finished in 1830, a process which he saw accomplished in the course of his life. But this historical statement— which can be found in Schleiermacher, Humboldt, and Novalis—does not necessarily entail the idea that there should be a unique medium of *Weltliteratur*, a kind of "chosen people" of world literature and translation. *Weltliteratur* is rather the age of generalized intertranslation, in which all languages learn, in their own way, to be languages-of-translation and to live the experience of translation—a process Goethe saw emerge in the years 1820–1830 in France and England with, precisely, the translation of German literature (beginning with himself, Schiller, and Herder), and to which he devoted the most acute attention.

This implies above all that translation be everywhere considered an essential, dignified task, and, in fact, *belonging to the literature of a nation*. That Goethe considered it as such is attested by a fairly striking anecdote. In 1808, in the middle of Napoleon's domination, certain intellectuals wanted to compose a collection of the best German poetry for the use of the "people." The nationalist intention of the project was not denied.[16] The authors of the future collection consulted Goethe about the choice of poems. The only advice he gave them was to include German translations of foreign poems *as well*, first of all because German poetry was indebted to the foreign for the essence of its forms—and this since its beginning—and second, because in his eyes these translations were creations belonging authentically to the national literature.

Once the rights, the dignity, and the status of translation were assured, Goethe could give what would come closest to a theory of translation, in the form of a reflection on the *ages* or the *modes* of translation, a reflection that, as we shall see, runs absolutely parallel to the thinking he devoted to the "epochs" of *Bildung*. If *Bildung* is the process in which the relation to the self becomes firmer through the relation to the foreign and produces a balance of both relations by the gradual passage from the infertile closure upon oneself to living interaction, translation, being an exemplification of this relation, is marked by stages, stages which may be regarded as historical periods or as moments and modes destined to repeat themselves indefinitely in the history of a culture:

> There are three kinds of translation. The first kind acquaints us with the foreign on our own terms; a simple prosaic translation is best in this respect. . . .
>
> A second epoch follows in which [the translator] only tries to appropriate foreign content and to reproduce it in his own sense, even though he tries to transport himself into foreign situations. I would call this kind of epoch the *parodistic* one, in the fullest sense of that word. . . . The French use this method in their translations of all poetic works. . . . Just as the French adapt foreign words to their pronunciation, just so do they treat feelings, thoughts, even objects; for every foreign fruit they demand a counterfeit grown on their own soil. . . .
>
> Since it is impossible to linger either in the perfect or the imperfect and one change must of necessity follow, we experienced the

third epoch, which is to be called the highest and the final one, namely the one in which the aim is to make the translation identical with the original, sò that the one can be valued not instead (*anstatt des andern*) but in the place of the other (*an der Stelle des andern*).

This kind had to overcome the greatest resistance originally; for the translator who attaches himself closely to his original more or less abandons the originality of his nation, and so a third comes into existence, and the taste of the multitude must first be shaped towards it. . . .

But since these three epochs are repeated and inverted in every literature; since, indeed, these three methods can be applied simultaneously, a translation into prose of the *Shàh-náma* and the works of Nizami's is still in order. . . .

But it is about time now for someone to offer us a translation of the third type, which would correspond to the different dialects as well as to the rhythmical, metrical, and prosaic ways of speech in the original, and which would allow us to enjoy that poem anew in all its idiosyncrasy. . . .

It remains to explain in a few words why we called the third epoch the final one. A translation which attempts to identify itself with the original in the end comes close to an interlinear version and greatly enhances our understanding of the original; this in turn leads us, compels us as it were, to the source text, and so the circle is closed at last: in it the coming together of the foreign and the native, the unknown approximation and the known keep moving toward each other.[17]

This famous text provides the most advanced expression of the *classical* German thought on translation. Neither Schleiermacher nor Humboldt have been able to go beyond it. Some comment is called for. From the outset, Goethe presents the three modes of translation as *historical* modes, each connected with a certain relation to the foreign. Even though the third mode is called the "highest" and the "final," it does not therefore simply constitute a mode dialectically superior to the two others, particularly the second. It is rather the "highest" because it constitutes an *ultimate possibility of translating* (the interlinear version conscious of itself) and because with it the inflection of the circle begins, by which everything returns to the starting point. From mode one to mode three, the entire trans-lation of what is one's own to what is foreign has been completed, and for Goethe it is evident that no other modes are possible. Furthermore, depending on the different domains of translation, these modes may coexist: The translation of oriental texts, for instance, did not take place at the same time as the translations of the Greeks or of Shakespeare. But what keeps Goethe from privileging the third mode, as we would tend to do in the twentieth century, are two points not approached by the text of the *Divan* but mentioned else-

where. The first is the relation of translation to the *untranslatable*; in
1828, he writes to Chancellor von Müller:

> In translation one should not engage in a direct struggle with the
> foreign language. One must attain the untranslatable and respect it; for
> it is precisely there that the value and the character of each language
> lie.[18]

The same remark is found in *Maximen und Reflexionen*:

> In translation, one must attain the untranslatable; only then does one
> become aware of the foreign nation and the foreign language.[19]

The third mode of translation of the *Divan* would well seem to
engage in an immediate struggle with the foreign language and tend,
precisely, to translate the untranslatable, in a struggle reminiscent of
Rimbaud's "spiritual battle." *The untranslatable, in reality, is not anything particular, but the totality of the foreign language in its strangeness and its difference.* Goethe intends to respect this difference (which
is the meaning of his humanism), but also to relativize it to the extent
that, even though it constitues the value and the originality of the foreign language, it is not necessarily what is *essential* to it. Along this line
he judged the contemporary attempts—notably by A. W. Schlegel—of
translations in verse, and not in prose, of foreign poetry, attempts whose
legitimacy may seem evident to us but at the time seemed revolutionary:
A. W. Schlegel's entire translator's gospel is based on this. Now, these
attempts are based on an absolute valorization of *poetic form*, a valorization Goethe rejects, first because he does not want to separate form and
content, but above all *because he assigns an almost transcendental
value to content*—granting that content here is not that which could
simply be grasped beyond the form in a work, but something more
mysterious. It might be said that content is to form what Nature is to its
manifestations. Two of Goethe's texts, in *Dichtung und Wahrheit*, make
his position on the subject explicit:

> I value both rhythm and rhyme, whereby poetry first becomes poetry,
> but the part that is really, deeply, and fundamentally effective, that
> which is truly formative and furthering, is what remains of the poet
> when he is translated into prose. Then remains the *pure, perfect sub-
> stance [Gehalt]*.[20]

To be sure, in the rest of this text Goethe presents the prose translation of poetry as a first stage, and cites the Lutheran Bible translation as
an example. But it is true that by putting forth the "pure and perfect
content" as the "acting" and "formative" principle, he has amply justified
this type of translation. In another passage of *Dichtung und Wahrheit*—
in which Luther and the Bible are also under consideration—he develops his view of the "content" of the work:

What matters most in all that is handed down to us, particularly in writing, is the ground, the inner being, the meaning, the direction of the work; for there lies what is original, divine, efficient, untouchable, indestructible, and neither time nor outside influences could affect this primal inner being [*Urwesen*], not any more than a disease of the body can affect a well-built soul. Thus, language, dialect, idiosyncracies, style, and finally writing, should be regarded as the body of any work of the spirit. . . .

Therefore, to research the inner, authentic being of a work that particularly pleases us is everyone's business, and what should be weighed above all is how it is related to our own inner being and to what extent its vital force excites and fertilizes our own; on the other hand, the exterior which does not affect us or whose effect is doubtful, should be relegated to criticism, which may well be capable of dismembering the whole and tearing it asunder, but never manages to rob us of the actual ground to which we cling, nor even to make us waver for only a moment with regard to our once established confidence.[21]

This ground of the work appears to be the opposite of the untranslatable, if it is indeed that which, in the work, has a definitive and immediate hold on us, which makes it speak for us, its profound *Sprachlichkeit*. From this the relative nature of a translation attached to the differences of the work may be deduced, as well as the derivative and secondary nature of criticism. Conversely, when form becomes the absolutely privileged element, as it is with the Romantics, poetic and critical translation acquire a primordial position.

Goethe's triadic scheme is put in a different light when it is confronted with other texts, those devoted to *Bildung*. There can be no doubt that the majority of the reflections Goethe devoted to translation are situated in this framework. A text written shortly before his death, in 1831, entitled *Epochen geselliger Bildung* (periods of social, or sociable, formation), distinguishes four moments of *Bildung*. The first one corresponds more or less to the "virgin" state mentioned by Herder. The three others correspond to the modes of the *Divan*:

> I. From a more or less crude mass, narrow circles of cultured people are formed; the relations are the most intimate, only the friend is trusted, only the loved one is sung to, everything has a homely and familiar aspect. These circles are closed to the outside, as they must be, since they have to secure the crude elements of their existence. They therefore tend to keep to the mother tongue, which is why this stage may rightfully be called the *idyllic*.
>
> II. These narrow circles multiply . . . the internal circulation becomes more lively, the influence of foreign languages is no longer

refused; the circles remain separated but draw closer to one another. . . . I would call this stage the *social* or the *civic*.

III. Finally the circles continue to multiply and to expand in such a way that they touch and prepare to merge. They understand that their wishes and their intentions are the same, but they are still unable to dissolve the barriers that divide them. This stage might provisionally be called the *more general*.

IV. In order to become *universal*, that goodwill and good fortune of which we may pride ourselves at present are needed. . . . A higher influence was necessary to accomplish what we live today: the unification of all cultured circles which up to now merely touched. . . . Foreign literatures are all set on an equal footing with our own, and we do not lag behind in the course of the world.[22]

If the word circle is replaced by the word nation, we have exactly the process that leads to the constitution of *Weltliteratur*. In the introduction of the journal *Propyläen*, Goethe approaches the relation of what is one's own and what is foreign from yet another angle, describing what might be called the *law of opposition*:

We do not form ourselves by merely setting in motion, lightly and comfortably, what lies within us. Every artist, like every man, is only a single being and will therefore lean towards one side. Which is why he must also absorb, as far as possible, in theory and in practice, what is opposite to his nature. The frivolous should seek out the serious and the earnest, the serious should have a light and comfortable being before his eyes, the strong should cultivate gentleness, the gentle strength, and each will develop his nature in proportion as he seems to depart from it.[23]

The relation to the foreign appears here as the encounter of that which is *opposed* to us, as the cultivation of what is antagonistic to our own nature. Such, for instance, is for Goethe the mutual relation of French and German culture at the beginning of the eighteenth century. The German *Unbändigkeit* (lack of restraint) can only help French culture to liberate itself from the straight-jacket of its classicism. But conversely, German "versatility" has everything to gain from the formal rigor of the French: Thus each culture must search in the other what it lacks as well as what is most opposed to it. The relation, then, to the foreign is characterized by the fact that one looks in it for a difference that is itself *determined*. Besides, the scene of the relation between what is one's own and what is foreign is dominated by that which, beyond their opposition, is the element of their possible coexistence: the foreign is always only an *alter ego*, and conversely, I am the foreign to a multiplicity of *alter egos*. Which entails that the relation to the foreign is above all a relation of *contemporaneity*: there can be no commerce and interaction with the dead.

Still, the contemporaneity of *alter egos* needs to be grounded in a *third term*, an almost absolute term to which all can refer, and which constitutes their ground: In the case of a culture, this ground must itself be a culture, but a culture that is the *immediate expression of Nature*. This is the *Greek culture*. For Goethe, the Greeks represent the pinnacle of humanity and *Bildung*. In the same way one must always come back to Nature, in the cycle of *Bildung* one must always come back to the Greeks. The poet states this to Eckermann on 31 January 1827:

> But, while we thus value what is foreign, we must not bind ourselves to some particular thing, and regard it as a model. We must not give this value to the Chinese, or the Serbian, or Calderón, or the *Nibelungen*; but if we really want a model, we must always return to the ancient Greeks, in whose works the beauty of human kind is always represented. All the rest we must look at only historically, appropriating to ourselves what is good, so far as it goes.[24]

The reference to Calderón or the *Nibelungen* is a barely disguised criticism to the romantic multiple overture towards foreign literatures. For Goethe, the Greeks in effect occupy the place of *Urbild* and *Vorbild* in the process of *Bildung*, a place never disputed by him. Greekness is that manifestation of the Eternally One, the originary Man, against which all cultures may be measured, whether they are Germanness, Frenchness, Italianness, or even Latinness. All the rest is "historical," either in the meaning of past (a depreciatory meaning for Goethe) or in the meaning of contemporary. Here again, we find the double level of Goethe's thought: Eternity and Contemporaneity. A double level unified in his concept of Nature.[25]

In the selective space of the translatable, the translation of the Greeks, as it is carried out by Voss and, under the direct influence of Goethe and Schiller, by Humboldt, acquires a natural precedence. Which is why Goethe looked upon the mass of romantic translations with increasing ill humor, since, as Strich rightly emphasizes, they concerned neither the Greeks nor the contemporaries:

> To be sure, German Romanticism also translated from all literatures; but what did it translate? Dante, Petrarch, Cervantes, Shakespeare, Calderón, the old Indian writers. Their contemporaries in other nations remained almost excluded from the circle of interest of German Romanticism. It knew time only as a sequence, at bottom only as a past, not as simultaneity and co-simultaneity, as a temporal community of people living together in the present.[26]

Goethe saw in it a different conception of world literature, and justifiedly so. The fact is all the more striking since, personally, he fully recognized his debt to Shakespeare and Calderón. From his point of view, the Romantics ended up in a space both infatuated with the past and—above all—dangerously syncretic. We are faced here with the opposition mentioned above between the two views of *Bildung* and the disjunctive structuring of the field of translation. Once more, Goethe's reserve is all the more notable since the *Divan* reflections propose a view of the modes of translation that is barely different from those of A. W. Schlegel and Schleiermacher. But the *Übersetzungstalent* and the romantic will to translate everything are fundamentally foreign to Goethe.

That there is an essential difference between the translation of contemporaries and the translation of authors from the past is something Goethe could teach us to appreciate better. From the past, only the works remain. From the present, we have the authors and all that is implied by it in terms of a possible living interaction. But there is more. Contemporaneity means that the translated language may also translate, that *the translator may also be translated*, that the translated language, author, and work, may *live* the fact of being-translated. In other words: If translating is considered an interaction between two languages, contemporaneity produces a double effect: The translating language is modified (which is what is always observed in the first place), but so is the translated language. Goethe must be credited for having considered the whole of the play of translating and being translated in the space of contemporaneity, for having measured its psychological, literary, national, and cultural manifestations. *Now, translation is taken up in the vast cycle of being translated*. This phenomenon is in turn reproduced on all levels of cultural trans-lation (criticism, borrowings, "influences," etc.). Thus, Goethe offers us a global view of the *mutual* relations of what is one's own and what is foreign, in which equal consideration is given to the question of what one's own is for the foreign, and thus of *its* relation to the foreign which what is our own is for it. One might even state: Before the age of *Weltliteratur*, the relation to the foreign is one of refusal, or of misunderstanding, or of disfiguring or "parodistic" annexation (the case of the Romans and of French culture until the nineteenth century), or of faithful and respecting welcome (the case of the Germans from the second part of the eighteenth century onwards). With the arrival of world literature, the relation becomes proportionally more complex as the different cultures henceforth seek to contemplate themselves in the mirror of others and to look in it for something they cannot perceive by themselves. *The captivation of oneself no longer passes merely through the captivation of the foreign, but through the captivation by the foreign of oneself.* It is Goethe's version of Hegel's mutual recognition, and the poet does by no means exclude the struggle mentioned in the *Phenomenology of Spirit*.

Goethe sought to formulate this reciprocal relation of what is one's own and what is foreign by means of various concepts which are primarily concerned with translation, but also with other intercultural or interliterary relations, like criticism: These are the concepts of *Theilnahme* (participation), *Spiegelung* (mirroring), *Verjüngung* (rejuvenation), and *Auffrischung* (regeneration). Participation indicates a certain type of relation which is both active intervention and engagement, the reverse of influence, *Influenz*, a passive relation always severely judged by Goethe, connecting it to the disease of the same name, *Influenza*. Thus he states that Carlyle shows

> a peaceful, lucid, and intimate participation with the German literary and poetical debuts; he espouses the most particular efforts of the nation, he gives value to the individual, each in his own place, and thus settles to a certain extent the conflict inevitable within the literature of any people. For to live and to act is also to choose sides and to attack. . . . And while this conflict often disturbs the horizon of an interior literature for many years, the foreigner lets the dust, smoke, and fog settle . . . and he sees those distant regions, with their light and their dark sides, light up before him, with an equanimity comparable to that with which we are used to contemplate the moon on a clear night.[27]

Thus foreign literatures become the mediators in the internal conflicts of national literatures and offer them an image of themselves they could not otherwise have. Goethe played this role, for example, in the conflicts between classics and romantics in Italy. This type of intervention in a national literature refers in turn to the notions of mirroring and regeneration, as he notes in 1827:

> Flagging national literatures are revived by the foreign.[28]

And more decisively:

> In the end every literature grows bored if it not refreshed by foreign participation. What scholar does not delight in the wonders wrought by mirroring and reflection? And what mirroring means in the moral sphere has been experienced by everyone, perhaps unconsciously; and, if one stops to consider, one will realize how much of his own formation throughout life he owes to it.[29]

Which corresponds to a principle expressed in the *Morphology*:

> The most beautiful metempsychosis is that in which we see ourselves reappear in another.[30]

Among all the "mirrorings" that may occur between two cultures, translation is certainly one of the most important, and the one which struck Goethe the most, not only because he himself had experienced

it, but because it concerns a more creative mirroring than does criticism. When a Latin translation of *Hermann and Dorothea* was brought
to Goethe, he made the following comment:

> I had not seen this poem, cherished by all, for years, and now I
> contemplated it as it were in a mirror which, as we know from experi-
> ence and more recently by entoptics, has the ability to exert a magical
> influence. Here, in a much more formed language, I saw my feelings
> and my poetry identical as well as changed; I was especially struck by
> the fact that Latin is a language that tends towards the concept and that
> transforms what, in German, hides itself in an innocent way. . . .[31]

He adds that in the Latin translation, his poem

> seemed more noble, as if it were, with regard to its form, returned to
> its origin.[32]

In the same way, Nerval's translation of *Faust* seemed to him to have
"regenerated" the German text. Regarding the English translation of
Schiller's *Wallenstein*, he states:

> Here we note something new, perhaps scarcely felt and never ex-
> pressed before: that the translator is working not for his own nation
> alone but also for the nation from whose language he takes the work.
> For it happens more often than we think, that a nation draws vigor and
> strength from a work and absorbs it fully into its own inner life, that it
> can take no further pleasure in it and obtain no further nourishment
> from it. This is particularly the case with the Germans. They are prone
> to excessive enthusiasm and, by too frequent repetitions of something
> they like, destroy some of its qualities. It is therefore good for them to
> see one of their own literary works reborn in translation.[33]

These remarks would have no more than a purely psychological
scope if they only referred to the wonder Goethe experienced when he
found his works or those of his friend Schiller again in a foreign language; these remarks would not concern the metamorphosis effected
by translation when a work unfolds in another language. But this is not
the case. In order to produce this impression of wonder, the translation
must have *effectively* placed the work in a mirror of itself that "regener-
ates" and "revives" it. It is in this sense that being translated is fundamental for a work (and for its author in the second place)—because it
places the work in an other time, a more originary time, a time in which
it seems as new as it was at its debut. In this sense, it becomes again
highly readable for those who already know it (authors or readers) in
its mother tongue. This essence of translation *for the others* certainly
remains mysterious, but it already indicates that the significance of
translation does not consist in mediating foreign works only for the
readers who do not know the language of the original. No: Translation

is an experience that concerns those translated as well as those translating; as an end product, it is ideally destined to be read by all. The effect produced on the translated work through the translation is no doubt a fundamental phenomenon, and it is Goethe's merit to have perceived it as something that refers to the mysteries of the lives of languages, works, as well as of translation as such. These mysteries are signaled by these simultaneously spatial and temporal notions of mirror reflection, regeneration, and return to the origin. Without this "participation" of the foreign, which translation is, the work "would be bored with itself," would exhaust itself in the effects it produces as a work in its linguistic space. In this sense, it *needs* to be translated, to reappear rejuvenated in the mirror of a foreign language in order to be able to offer its face of wonder to the readers of its mother tongue, i.e., its face as a work pure and simple. This metamorphosis, even metempsychosis, refers to the symbolic tenor of translation as such, of which Goethe was certainly aware, since he devoted a poem—an unpretentious one, to be sure—to it, entitled *Ein Gleichnis*, a symbol:

> Jungst pflückt' ich einen Weisenstrauß
> Trug ihn gedankenvoll nach Haus,
> Da hatten von der warmen Hand
> Die Kronen sich alle zur Erde gewandt.
> Ich setzte sie in ein frisches Glas
> Und welch ein Wunder war mir das!
> Die Köpfchen hoben sich empor,
> Die Blätterstengel im grünen Flor,
> Und allzusammen so gesund
> Als stünden sie noch auf Muttergrund.
> So war mir's als ich wundersam
> Mein Lied in fremder Sprache vernahm.[34]

The poet has picked flowers of the field and carried them home with him. Deprived of their maternal soil, they begin to wither. He then puts them in fresh water, and there they bloom again: *Thus it was when I heard, full of awe, my song in a foreign language.* The one who picks the flowers is the translator. Removed from its soil, the poem runs the risk of fading. But the translator puts it in the fresh cup of his own language, and it blossoms once again, as if it were still *on its maternal soil.* This is an awe-inspiring marvel, since neither the poem nor the flowers are still on their native soil. Even though the blossoming of flowers symbolizes what happens to the poem in translation, it is the poem in its entirety that is a symbol. Or again: Translation is a symbol. A symbol of what? Of the marvel, certainly, that occurs every day in the multiple trans-lations that make up the very fabric of the world—of the presence in our lives of the innumerable faces of metamorphosis and metempsychosis.[35]

But even as he is describing translation as a metamorphosis, even as he is inscribing it in the great cycle of vital exchanges, Goethe takes care not to assert that everything is translation. To be sure, the "mirroring" he so marvelously finds here also exists elsewhere. And first of all in the domain of human relationships—amorous, friendly, social, cultural.

Hence, it was tempting to go one step further and to formulate a theory of the generalized translation of everything into everything, of which the interlingual translation would be only a particular case. Goethe does not take this step; on the contrary, he maintains, though implicitly—and despite his unitary perception of reality—the different separated domains. The Romantics, for their part, do not have these reservations. Transforming Goethe's mirroring into a *reflection* raised to the level of an ontological principle, they edify a theory of generalized translation, of which the clearest illustration, as we shall see, is Novalis's *Encyclopedia*.

The poetological radicality of the Romantics has perennially been opposed to the allegedly "Philistine" prudence of Goethe. We would, on the contrary, like to reread the Romantics from a point of view much closer to Goethe's than to their own, and to underscore all that is negative in their speculative fever. The humanism of a Goethe will not be surpassed by symbiotically repeating the poetic absolutism of the *Athenäum*, but by radicalizing the intuitions of the man from Weimar, all of which underscore the social and historical character of translation.

5

ROMANTIC REVOLUTION AND INFINITE VERSABILITY

In his *Dialogue on Poetry*, having sketched a brief outline of the "epochs of poetry" from the Greeks through Shakespeare, Friedrich Schlegel outlines the literary situation in Germany at the end of the eighteenth century:

> Meanwhile, even here there remained a tradition whose contention was to return to the ancients and to nature, and this spark caught fire with the Germans after they had gone through all their models. Winckelmann taught that antiquity was to be viewed as a whole. . . . Goethe's universality gently reflected the poetry of almost all nations and ages. . . . Philosophy arrived in a few daring steps to the point where it could comprehend itself and the spirit of man, in whose depths it was bound to discover the primordial source of the imagination and the ideal of beauty, and thus was compelled to recognize poetry, whose essence and existence it had not even suspected. Philosophy and poetry, the two most sublime powers in man, which even in Athens in the period of their highest fruition were effective only in isolation, now intermingle in perpetual interaction in order to stimulate and develop each other. Translation of poets and imitation of their rhythms have become an art, and criticism a discipline which annihilated old errors and opened new vistas in the knowledge of antiquity. . . .
>
> Nothing further is required but that the Germans continue using these methods, that they follow the example set by Goethe, explore

the forms of art back to their sources in order to be able to revive or combine them. . . .[1]

This brief text by F. Schlegel contains so to speak *in nucleo* the entire view the Romantics of the *Athenäum* have of their age and its disruptions: The return to antiquity, the appearance of a national poetic genius of a protean stature, the self-unfolding of philosophy, the mingling of thinking and poetry, the emergence of an art of translation and of a science of criticism—these are the cultural novelties of the present. F. Schlegel here alludes not only to perfectly defined historical events, but also to those elements which are rather part of a romantic *program*: to unite philosophy and poetry, to make criticism into a science and translation into an art. It is also, and above all, of the order of a *demand*, the demand of a group of which he is the theoretical leader—a demand which we have put forward here with a false simplicity, since terms like *philosophy*, *poetry*, *art*, *science*, *criticism*, or *fantasy* have a very precise meaning in the romantic terminological cosmos, which is by no means reducible to our conceptual framework or the one that immediately precedes the Jena Romantics.

An understanding of this text, then, demands a short but close examination of the whole of the reflections of the *Athenäum* members. Only thus are we able to understand why translation is mentioned together with the great cultural realizations of the time, and what its place is among them.

The journey must begin with an examination of the *critical revolution* that emerges with Romanticism, and of which F. Schlegel and Novalis are the principal instigators. In what sense is it possible to speak of a critical revolution? Obviously, the expression refers to Kant and his "Copernican revolution," of whom the early Romantics, following Fichte, are the heirs. It also refers to the French Revolution. In both cases, a historical rupture occurs. The Kantian revolution introduces criticism into the center of philosophy, in the form of an analytic of the finite subject, which is henceforth barred from any transgression of the sensible domain, and for which any naive philosophizing is henceforth impossible. The French Revolution introduces a radical disruption of traditional social forms, also in the name of reason—which means that with Kant and the French Revolution the critical age has arrived:

> This age, in which we have the honor to live; an age that, to express it in a single word, deserves the modest but significant name of critical age, so much so that at present everything will be criticized, with the exception of the age itself, and everything will become more and more critical.[2]

This age submits everything to its "chemistry":[3] it is the age of anti-naïveté or, put in negative terms, the age of non-simplicity and of tearing apart. Romantic thinking inherits this non-simplicity, this refusal of all naïveté: It is a thinking drunk with critical pathos. At stake for it, as for all post-Kantian thinking, is the accomplishment of that which was allegedly only outlined by Kant, that is, to make his critique "more and more critical," but also to spring the bolt Kant had placed on speculation and the unfolding of the infinity of the subject. The Jena Romantics actively take part in this radicalization of Kant's thought in the wake of Fichte and Schelling.

But their place in the post-Kantian speculative field consists of *unfolding the problematic of the infinite subject in the medium of art and poetry*, and of reformulating all existing theories of art, poetry, *Bildung*, and genius, in the language of the reflection inaugurated by Fichte's *Wissenschaftslehre*, the doctrine of science. The fecundity of this project, which takes the explicit form of a project articulated in mutiple *Lehre*, surpasses by far the contemporary enterprises of the magnification of art—those of a Schelling or, later, of a Solger—because it appears in a space which is not, properly speaking, philosophical (in the academic sense) nor simply the space of poetic creation. It is well known that the works of the first Romantics are few, often unfinished, and if Novalis, for instance, had not written his *Fragments*, it is not certain that his poems and sketches for novels alone would have been sufficient to canonize him. As for F. Schlegel, his literary works (like *Lucinde*) barely go beyond the stage of experimentation. How then characterize this space? Probably by saying that it is not *the space of a work, but one of intense reflection on the absent, desired work, or the work to come*. The only finished texts left by the Romantics are their *critiques*, their *collections of fragments*, their *dialogues*, their *literary letters*, and . . . their *translations*. Translations, critiques, but also letters and fragments (considered as a literary mini-genre inherited from Chamfort, or rather as a form of finished writing, not as *Bruchstück*, piece, unfinished sketch), have in common the reference to an absent other: translation to the original, letters and dialogues to an external referent of which they treat, criticism to a literary text or the whole of literature.[4] *They are not works*, but forms of writing which entertain a profound, but also very nostalgic, relation to the work. To inhabit this relation to the already existing, absent, or imagined work, and *to think*, within this relation, *the work as such as the absolute of existence*, this is the specificity of the *Athenäum* Romanticism. But there is more: In the intimacy of this relation they have the presentiment that these forms of writing, in a certain way, also belong to the space of the work, even as they remain equally outside of it. Which could be formulated as follows: The original work needs and does not need translation; the work needs and does not need criticism; the fragments represent the whole and are not the whole; the letters and the dialogues are works and are not works. Hence the resurgence of the question: What is the literary work if it is the seat of such paradoxes? The critical revolution of the Romantics consists in a relentless questioning about this essence of the work, which was manifested to them in the fascinating intimacy of criticism and translation, of *philology* in the broad sense, as Novalis defined it in one of his fragments:

> Philology in general is the science of literature. Everything dealing with books is philological. Notes, title, epigraphs, prefaces, critiques, exegeses, commentaries, quotations, are philological. Purely philological is that which treats only of books, which relates to books and not at all to nature as original.[5]

This is also a dangerous game, since criticism and translation may appear as the absence of one's own creativity, fragmentary writing as the inability to produce finished works or systems. And in a certain way they are *also* this absence, this inability, reverberating infinitely. When Novalis writes in the margins of F. Schlegel's *Fragments*: "not a fragment," "not a genuine fragment,"[6] he is not so much measuring these by a predetermined standard as by the fact that the fragmentary writing incessantly inverts itself, or threatens to do so, into fragmented and unfinished writing in the most banal sense of the term. The bulk of Novalis's and F. Schlegel's notebooks, as they are revealed graphically by the latest German editions, bear witness to incompleteness as well as intentional fragmentation. Which entails that the riches of romantic thinking, its ability to reflect itself infinitely, to turn itself to all sides, thereby apprehending the totality, is also its absolute poverty, its profound inability (if such it has) to think at all—in the sense of the patient endurance near a theme or an object. The works written by the Romantics of the second generation (like Clemens Brentano's novels) offer an often talented caricature of this thinking without pause and without rest. It is Hegel's "bad infinite," which Hegel could easily criticize in Romanticism, even though his critique was not entirely to the point, since wealth and poverty, power and impotence, are connected absolutely here.

The critical Revolution, then, is chiefly the establishment of a certain way of thinking about the work as a medium of the infinity of the subject. This thinking borrows its arms from philosophy, but is not itself philosophy. When we speak here of work, we mean exclusively *the written or literary work*. With the exception of music, as we shall see, the Romantics have little to say about the other domains of art, no doubt because these do not entertain this paradoxical and intimate relation with criticism, translation, and different forms of fragmentary writing, which, for the Romantics, belongs to literature; no doubt also because the medium of literature is language, the most universal of all media.[7] The scattered attempts by the brothers Schlegel and Novalis to closely examine the "wonderful affinities of all the arts"[8] barely go beyond the level of generalities. In reality, their passion is exclusively the "philological," the written. Thus F. Schlegel writes in his "Letter on Philosophy:"

> But it so happens that I am an author and nothing but an author. Writing, for me, holds I do not know what secret magic: perhaps because of the twilight of eternity that hovers around it. Yes, I admit to you that I marvel about the secret power hidden in these dead traits; I wonder how the simplest expressions . . . can be so significant that it is as if they look out of clear eyes, or that they are as telling as the artless accents from the profoundest soul. . . . The silent traits [of writing] seem to me to be a more appropriate hull for these deepest, most immediate utterances of the spirit than the resounding of lips. I would almost say, in the somewhat mystical language of our H. [Novalis]: to live is to write; the sole destiny of man is to engrave the thoughts of the divinity into the tables of nature with the stylus of the creatively forming spirit.[9]

And Novalis:

> I should like to see before me, as a work of my spirit, a whole collection of books, on all of the arts and all of the sciences.[10]

> I feel like devoting my entire life to *one* novel—which alone would constitue an entire library, perhaps even the apprenticeship of a nation.[11]

This passion for the book and the written is equally nourished by the fact that these spontaneously tend to form a system, as is shown by the frequent expression of "world of books," which Novalis did not fail to point out.[12] And this latent systematicity of the written which, according to F. Schlegel, makes it possible to consider all works of literature as a single work in the process of becoming, is precisely what must be thought and developed. There is also something else: Literature is the place of a self-differentiation of which the Greeks bequeathed to us the canonical form: that of *genres*. The other arts do not provide the example of such a self-differentiation that affirms its own necessity. Moreover, the division of genres is such that it tends to reemerge every time one attempts to deny it or consider it obsolete. But historically, as we have seen above, there is another possibility, the *mixing of genres*: For the Romantics, this is what happened with the Latin and Alexandrian poets or with the moderns Shakespeare and Cervantes, and which now looks for a new figure at the dawn of the nineteenth century. Hence the following questions:

> Should poetry simply be divided up? Or should it remain one and indivisible? Or alternate between division and union?[13]

The romantic program consists in transforming what is historically only a tendency into a self-conscious intention; criticism and translation, as we shall see, are inscribed in this program.

In the first place, the issue is to produce a criticism and a theory of literature that can definitively transform, by effecting an historical rupture, the literary practice into a reflected practice assured of it absoluteness. In effect, everything happens as if the Copernican revolution in philosophy should be matched by a Copernican revolution in poetry. And one can understand why, still starting from Kant: The undertaking of the three *Critiques* does not only signify a limit to knowledge, but also a self-reflection of spirit by which spirit has access to itself, to the element of its autonomy:

> *Critique.* Always in the state of critique. The state of critique is the element of freedom.[14]

This is why F. Schlegel, in an obvious allusion to Kant and Fichte, could say that, at the end of the eighteenth century, philosophy has succeeded in understanding itself. But that is not all: The Kantian critique, ascending all the way to the transcendental imagination, discovered there "the original source of fantasy and the ideal of beauty," thus obliging philosophy "to unequivocally recognize poetry." Which means that it made possible, in its very movement, the development of a "geniology," of a "fantastics,"[15] and consequently of a Copernican revolution of poetry, by means of which poetry would gain access to its essence just as reason gained access to its essence through the transcendental method. The second revolution, to be sure, can only be the work of poetry itself, just as the revolution of philosophy is a turning carried out within philosophy itself. This entails two things. First, criticism should not be exterior to poetry; it should be a self-criticism of poetry. Second, this self-criticism cannot do without philosophy because, for the Romantics, the movement of self-reflection is nothing but *philosophizing* as such—: which is why the relation of poetry and philosophy is at once fusion and mixing. Hence F. Schlegel's two famous fragments:

> The whole history of modern poetry is a running commentary on the following brief text of philosophy: all art should become science and all science art; poetry and philosophy should be made one.[16]

The more poetry becomes science, the more it also becomes art. If poetry is to become art, if the artist is to have a thorough understanding and knowledge of his means and ends . . . the poet will have to philosophize about his art. If he is to be not merely a discoverer and an artisan, but also an expert in his field . . . then he will have to become a philologist as well.[17]

In these two texts, as in the *Dialogue on Poetry*, one witnesses a *chassé-croisé* of the notions of "art," "science," "poetry," and "philosophy," in which the Copernican revolution of poetry is at stake: the elevation of poetry to scientificity, to self-knowledge, and to artificiality, to self-formation, by way of philosophizing as reflection. Novalis expresses nothing else in his "Poeticisms:"

The way philosophies as they existed until now relate to logology, so too do poetries as they existed relate to the poetry to come. Up to now, poetries have mostly operated dynamically, the future transcendental poetry could be called organic. When it will be invented, it will be seen that all genuine poets, *without knowing it*, have created organically — but that this lack of consciousness of what they did — has had an essential influence on their works — so that largely they have been truly poetical only in detail — but on the whole ordinarily unpoetical. Logology will necessarily introduce this revolution.[18]

Appearing here is that hypervalorization of consciousness, or rather of self-knowledge, which is typical of the Jena Romantics. One of Novalis's "Logological Fragments" attempts to express the relation of poetry and philosophy:

Poetry is the hero of philosophy. Philosophy elevates poetry to the level of a principle. It teaches us the value of poetry. Philosophy is the *theory of poetry*.[19]

But it is that philosophy has become philosophizing, and this is only "a self-discussion of a superior kind—a genuine self-revelation".[20] This becoming-conscious of poetry is only the first moment—the Kantian moment—of the "logological" revolution. It must be followed by a second moment, which could be called its post-Kantian moment: the unfolding of the *infinity* of poetry. In fact, *the reflexive operation and the infinitizing operation are one and the same for the Romantics*. This is one of the consequences of the vertiginous expansion they imposed on the concept of *reflection*, transformed by them into a fundamental ontological category:

All things should be regarded as one sees the I—as one's own activity.[21]

All that can be thought thinks itself.[22]

Walter Benjamin has shown in an excellent way how this category structures the entire Romantic thinking, to the point where F. Schlegel was able write:

> The romantic spirit seems to me to be fantasizing pleasantly about itself.[23]

But this reflection is by no means a psychological movement, a way of being centered narcissistically on the self—at least not in the vulgar sense. Such a preoccupation with one's own personal "self" seems even totally foreign to the early Romantics. Reflection, here, is conceived rather as a pure specular process, as a self-reflecting, and not, as F. Schlegel depreciatingly put it, "a brooding contemplation of one's own nose."[24]

The formal structure of reflection (the movement by which I pass from "thought" to "thought of thought," then to "thought of thought of thought," etc.) provides a model of *infinitization*, to the extent that this passage is conceived as an *elevation*: It is a structure of corridors, stories, staircases, gradations, and the elevation may be considered simultaneously as an ascension, a potentiation (*Potenzierung*), and an amplification (*Erweiterung*). Thus its concrete and positive plenitude is manifested.

It is concrete because it covers the totality of reality, which appears as constituted by a multiplicity of reflective monads stimulating each other reciprocally to further reflection, as the effect of chains or series of potentiations running in all directions:

> Force is the material of matter. Soul is the force of forces. Spirit is the soul of souls. God is the spirit of spirits.[25]

It is positive because the reflective structure of reality ensures the truth of the philosophizing: all philosophizing that takes on the apparent form of philosophizing on an object is, in fact, the philosophizing of the object on itself:

> Does one *see* each body only in so far as it sees itself—and as one sees oneself? In all predicates in which we see the fossil, it sees us in turn.[26]

One of the corollaries of this theory is that we do not see objects, but doubles of ourselves:

> Thoughts are filled only with thoughts. . . . The eye sees nothing but eyes—the thinking organ nothing but thinking organs.[27]

The universe projected in this way is, in the strictest sense of the term, a specular universe, in which all exteriority, all difference, and all opposition can only be apparent and transitory.

The fact that reflection is raised to the dignity of an ontological principle frees it from all facile subjectivism, even guaranteeing its most complete objectivity. The objectivation of this category is visible when Novalis, for instance, interprets death or sickness as potentiating reflections. It is also visible in the case of two literary notions, *Witz* and *irony*, whose structure, for the Romantics, is reflexive. When Schlegel states that "the real *Witz* is conceivable only in written form,"[28] one feels his concern about interpreting this notion as a *form of the work*, not as a psychological trait of its author. One might say, paradoxically, that subjectivity as reflection is a totally objective and systematic structure—systematic because its essence is to unfold itself following the degrees of its potentiations. As Novalis writes:

> The thought of self . . . is nothing but [the operation of] systematizing as such.[29]

And F. Schlegel:

> Aren't all systems individuals just as all individuals are systems, at least in embryo and tendency?[30]

The term *organic*, which we have pointed out above in Novalis' "Poeticisms," also has the meaning of systematic: It refers to organization, rather than to organism, as with Goethe and Herder. And this is why reflection becomes capable of sustaining the theory of genius and the theory of the work.

To the extent that reflection has become an ontological category, romantic thinking becomes the running-through of reflexive chains. *Bildung* is the movement through which man takes possession of his "transcendental I," without any Kantian limitations, and practices "the expansion of his existence to infinity."[31] This running-through is defined as a potentiation. Every potentiation is an "elevation to the state of _____," and, just as well, a "lowering to the state of _____." This double determination is inevitable if reflection is to be actually infinite. That is the essence of what Novalis calls romantization:

> The world must be romanticized. In this way the originary meaning may be found again. Romanticizing is nothing but a quantitative potentiation. In this process, the lower self is identified with a better self. Just as we are such a qualitative series of powers. This process is still wholly unknown. To the extent that I give a high meaning to the common, a mysterious aspect to the habitual, an infinite appearance to the finite, the dignity of the unknown to the known, I am romanticizing it. — The operation for the higher, the unknown, the mystical, the infinite, is the reverse. . . .[32]

This double movement is also what Novalis calls elsewhere the "method of reversal."[33] Romantization, in order to be complete, must affect all strata and all series. It must be *encyclopedic*. This encyclopedism, of which, as we shall see, the romantic project of an *encyclopedia* is one illustration, consists by no means of embracing everything in a system or a "ring of sciences," as Du Bellay said in the sixteenth century;[34] but *of going through everything in an indefinite movement—* which Novalis also called (using a term to which we have already alluded) *versability*. The fragment in which this neologism appears, as a variant of versatility which seems to unite version, inversion, conversion, interversion, pouring [*versement*], etc., deals with self-limitation:

> Fichte's synthesis—genuinely chemical mix. Floating. Individuality and generality of people and—diseases. On the necessary self-limitation—infinite versability of the cultured (*gebildeten*) understanding. One can draw oneself from everything, turn and overturn everything, as one pleases.[35]

Infinite versability is the power to carry out the entire course of reflexive chains, the power of that mobility which Novalis compared to the "voluptuous" movement of a liquid in *The Disciples at Saïs*. It is also the ability to be everywhere and to be many. By this right, even though the expression appears only once in all of the *Fragments*, it may be considered as the category which, along with reflection, best represents the romantic perception of the subject, notably the productive and poetic subject, the *genius*. As such, it formulates an entire new view of *Bildung* and, as we shall see, of the work itself. More than the category of reflection, it brings us close to the speculative theory of translation, if it is true that *the theory of infinite versability is also a theory of the infinite version*.

Sturm und Drang had developed the notion of artistic genius as a tempestuous, unconscious, and natural force, engendering works as one engenders children in the ecstacy of desire. In this context Goethe, but also Shakespeare or Calderón, could be looked on as natural forces to which all theoretical reflection remained foreign. Beyond Jena Romanticism, this theory will be taken up again by nineteenth century European Romanticism. But nothing is more foreign to the *Athenäum* than the idea of a genius-artist producing in the ecstacy of a vital unconscious impulse, an ecstacy to which the artisan knowledge necessary for the composition of the final face of the work would be miraculously added. Novalis says very succinctly:

> The artist belongs to the work, not the work to the artist.[36]

For the time being it must be obvious that the "geniology" constitutes the model for the theory of the subject. And to the genius belongs, as supreme expression of subjectivity, *the power to be able to do anything and the will to will anything*: the "infinite versability." What psychoanalysis calls omnipotence will only rarely, in the history of thought, have been consecrated with such fervor as a real and positive value. Even though the reinterpretation of one thought on the basis of another is always hazardous, it may be said that romantic reflection is a supremely *narcissistic* reflection, if narcissism consists primarily in the inability to differentiate anything from oneself in a fundamental way. This refusal or this inability to differentiate oneself is not without consequences for the view of *Bildung* and of the trans-lations it implies.

The theory of genius, as omnipotent and unrealistic as it may appear to us, opens nevertheless a cultural history whose first effects are felt in the nineteenth century but which have still not finished affecting us. A great part of Nietzsche's reflection, in *The Gay Science*, for instance, is devoted to measuring the disastrous consequences of what he calls the "historical sense," that is, the cameleontic ability to creep into anything, to penetrate all spaces and all times without really inhabiting them, to ape all styles, all genres, all languages, all values—an ability which, in its monstrous development, defines the modern Western world as well as its cultural imperialism and its appropriating voracity. Nietzsche remains exemplary for us, in as much as he gathers within himself, in an obviously impossible coexistence, all cultural trends of our history. Rimbaud's trajectory presents something analogous. Actually, Romanticism rapidly withdraws in the face of the consequences of its conception of the subject, of art, and of *Bildung*, in the face of this mingling everything with everything which will effectively (but in a negative form it had certainly not expected) be realized in nineteenth-century Europe. That is the meaning of the turning towards tradition and Catholicism carried out by Novalis and F. Schlegel as of the beginning of the new century.

The infinite versability is presented in many romantic texts as a demand of *plurality*:

> On life and thought on a grand scale. — Community — *pluralism* is our innermost essence—and perhaps every man has a part of his own in what I think and do, just as I have a part in the thoughts of others.[37]

> *Doctrine of persons.* An authentically synthetic person is a person who is many persons at once—a genius. Each person is the seed of an *infinite genius.*[38]

This interior pluralism, the essence of genius, is the *analogue*, as it were, of exterior pluralism; indeed, it serves to efface any difference between interior society and exterior (actual) society: just as the individual is a society, so too society is an individual. But the genius is more than the mere plurality of persons: It is a system of persons, an organic/organized totality:

So far we have only *had* a particular *genius*—but spirit should become total *genius*.[39]

The total genius is the poetic genius, if poetry is that which "forms the *beautiful* society or the *inner totality*".[40]

This view of an organic and systematic pluralism results in the numerous theories of "sociability" outlined by the Romantics, whether it be that of love, friendship, the family, or of "syncriticism," "symphilosophy," and "sympoetry"—neologisms formed from the Greek *sun* and modeled apparently on the term *syncretism*. This term, as Novalis does in fragment 147 of his *Encyclopedia*, should be connected with *eclecticism*. The plural subjectivity is a syncretic and eclectic personality, and on the basis of this it can engage, together with its *alter egos*, in the adventures of syncriticism and sympoetry. It only pursues with others what it does with itself. The idea of syncretism contains the idea of mixing and uniting the disparate, the diverse, the separate; the idea of eclecticism contains that of touching a little bit upon everything. *To touch a little bit upon everything*—this may seem trivial; but in reality the emphasis should be placed on *everything*. And not only can the name of eclecticism be perfectly applied to the personalities of Schlegel and Novalis, it also corresponds perfectly to their theory of subjectivity, *Bildung*, and the work: The *Witz*, for instance, is completely eclectic and syncretic, and this eclecticism and this syncretism are themselves interpreted from the perspective of sociability:

> Many witty (*witzigen*) ideas are like two friendly thoughts, meeting suddenly after a long separation.[41]

Hence the long series of romantic texts celebrating the arbitrary, the *willkürlich*—a German word in which one must read caprice as well as free choice, and which constitues the ideal of cultured subjectivity:

> A truly free and cultured person ought to be able to attune himself at will to being philosophical or philological, critical or poetical, historical or rhetorical, ancient or modern; quite arbitrarily, just as one tunes an instrument, at any time and to any degree.[42]

F. Schlegel's fragment 121, published in the *Athenäum* and quoted in our introduction, synthetically resumes this theme of the arbitrary, of the plurality and the syncretic systematicity of the cultured individual. Novalis develops the same idea:

> The accomplished man must live, as it were, in many places and many people at once. . . . Then the true, grandiose present of the spirit is formed.[43]

What is particularly striking in this theory is the emphasis on the will:

Appetitus sensitivus et rationalis. — The *appetitus rationalis* is a synthetic volition. Limitation in the synthetic volition — limitation — delimitation. (I want everything *at the same time*). Elective freedom is poetic — hence, morality is fundamentally poetry. Ideal of wanting-everything, of magic will.[44]

This ideal of omnipotence, omniscience, and ubiquity serves the construction of a theory of infinite subjectivity, which frees itself by a series, itself infinite, of elevations (ironic, moral, poetic, intellectual, even corporeal) of its initial finitude. But this subjectivity would not be absolute if it was not also a *finite* subjectivity, that is to say, a subjectivity capable of self-limitation and rootedness in the limited. At this stage, romantic thinking carries out a double movement: one going in the direction of infinitization, the other in the direction of finitude. The accomplished *Bildung* is the synthesis of the two movements. Such is the theory of "transitory limits" by which Novalis seems to effect a return to Kant:

> The more the horizon (the sphere) of consciousness becomes immeasurable and manifold, the more individual greatness *disappears*, and the more the spiritual, rational greatness of man increases *visibly*—the more it reveals itself. The greater and higher the totality, the more remarkable the particular. The *capacity* for limitation grows with the lack of limits.[45]

And F. Schlegel:

> The value and the dignity of self-limitation, which is after all . . . the first and the last, the most necessary and the highest duty. Most necessary because wherever one does not restrict oneself, one is restricted by the world. . . . The highest because one can only restrict oneself at those points and places where one possesses infinite strength.[46]

In Novalis' "Dialogue I," the whole of this problematic is found in a more popularized form:

> A: For me each good book is the vehicle of a lifelong occupation—the object of an inexhaustible pleasure. Why do you restrict yourself to only a few good men of wit and intelligence? Isn't it for the same reason? Aren't we after all so limited that we are capable of wholly enjoying only a few things? And isn't it better in the end to thoroughly possess a single beautiful object than to glance past hundreds to sip everywhere, and thus to dull one's senses prematurely with many often antagonistic partial pleasures without having thereby gained anything for good?
>
> B: You speak like a religious brother. Unfortunately, you behold a pantheist in me—for whom the immeasurable world is just large enough. I restrict myself to a few men of wit and intelligence

because I must—where would I find more? So also with books. The making of books is still by far not vast enough for me. If I had the good fortune to be a father, I could not have enough children: not merely ten or twelve—at least a hundred.

A: And women, too, you greedy one?

B: No, only a *single* one, in all seriousness.

A: What a bizarre inconsistency.

B: Not more bizarre nor more inconsequent than to have only *one spirit* in me, and not a hundred. But just as my spirit must transform itself into hundreds and millions of spirits, so my wife into all the women there are. Every man is endlessly variable. Just as with the children, so with the books. I would like to have a whole collection of books before me, comprising all the arts and sciences, as the work of my spirit. And so with everything. *Wilhelm Meister's Apprenticeship* is all we have now. We should possess as many years of apprenticeship, written in the same spirit, as possible—all the years of apprenticeship of all the people who have ever lived.[47]

The most striking illustration of the principle of infinite versability at the level of projects for romantic works is constituted by Novalis's concept of an *encyclopedia* and F. Schlegel's project for a *progressive universal poetry*. We cannot deal with the study of these two concepts in depth here, but at least we want to demonstrate how the "versability" manifested in it is equivalent to the *principle of translatability of everything into everything*. In some way it is the speculative version of the *Übersetzungstalent* mentioned by A. W. Schlegel with regard to his brother. The "progressive universal poetry" wants to "mix" and to "fuse" the totality of poetic genres, forms, and expressions. The *Encyclopedia*, for its part, wants to "poeticize" all the sciences. The two projects are mutually complementary: Universal progressive poetry is encyclopedic, the *Encyclopedia* is universal and progressive.

The destiny of progressive universal poetry

is not merely to reunite all the separate genres of poetry and put poetry in touch with philosophy and rhetoric. It tries, as it should, now to mix, now to fuse, poetry and prose, genius and criticism, the poetry of art and the poetry of nature; and make poetry lively and sociable, and life and society poetical. . . . It embraces everything that is poetic, from the greatest systems of art, containing within themselves still further systems, to the sigh, the kiss that the poetizing child breathes forth in artless song.[48]

It is obvious here that versability is the operational principle of such a figure of poetry: Forms and genres spill over into one another, are converted into one another, collapse into the incessant and chaotic movement of metamorphosis which is actually the process of the abso-lutization of poetry and, for F. Schlegel, the truth of Romanticism. That this versability should be encyclopedic, for example, oriented on the Whole, is equally obvious. In F. Schlegel, for that matter, the same ambition defines the *Witz*, irony, and fragmentary writing, whose appar-ent unsystematicity is compensated by its encyclopedism. Universal pro-gressive poetry is at once "poetry of poetry," "transcendental poetry," to the extent that it "can also—more than any other form—hover at the midpoint between the presented and the presenter," and, "on the wings of poetic reflection, raise that reflection again and again to a higher power."[49] The mixing of forms, genres, and contents is presented here as the conscious radicalization of all the literary mixings that have ex-isted historically, and whose model, as we know, is the syncretism of late Latin literature. This mixing presupposes the non-heterogeneity of forms and genres (as well as the interchangeability of contents), their translatability into one another or, to formulate it even more precisely, the possibility to play infinitely with their difference and their identity.

The concept of the *Encyclopedia* will engage our attention longer, because it illustrates this principle perhaps more naively and more clearly. It is well known that Novalis conceived of an *encyclopedia* differ-ent from the idea of D'Alembert and Diderot, whose aim would be to give a "romantic-poetic view of the sciences," according to the principle that "the accomplished form of the sciences must be poetic:"[50]

> *Encyclopedistic. Universal poetics* and complete system of poetry. A science is accomplished: 1. when it is applied to everything — 2. when everything is applied to it — 3. when, considered as absolute totality, as universe — it subordinates itself, as absolute individual, to all the other sciences and arts, as relative individuals.[51]

This project of totalizing poetization of the sciences is undoubtedly born from Novalis's dream of providing a certain number of "versions" of Fichte's philosophy, somewhat as if this could be played to different tunes, or declined for the different cases. The possibility to modulate the *Wissenschaftslehre*, as the empty frame of any possible science, engenders the idea of the totalization of these modulations—the *Ency-clopedia*:

> An extremely instructive series of specific presentations of the Fich-tean and Kantian system could be conceived, e.g., a poetic presenta-tion, a chemical one, a mathematical one, a musical one, etc.[52]

The poetization of the sciences starts from the principle that all scientific categories are related and thus transferable:

All ideas are related. The family likeness is called analogy.[53]

The categories are one and indivisible.[54]

Which means that if each science is constituted by a set *x* of categories, these may be replaced, *represented*, by a set *y* of other categories, and so forth:

> *Psychology and Encyclopedistic.* Something becomes clear only through representation. One understands a matter most easily when seeing it represented. Thus the I is understood only in so far as it is represented by the non-I. The non-I is symbol of the I, and serves only for the self-understanding of the I. . . . As far as mathematics is concerned, this remark can be applied by saying that mathematics, in order to be intelligible, must be represented. A science can only be truly represented by another science.[55]

Thus one obtains a poetics of mathematics, a grammar of mathematics, a physics of mathematics, a philosophy, a history of mathematics, a mathematics of philosophy, a mathematics of nature, a mathematics of poetry, a mathematics of history, a mathematics of mathematics.[56] The same schema may be applied to all the sciences, following the schema of reversibility Novalis sometimes calls the *Umkehrungsmethode*,[57] the method of reversal: poetry of mathematics and mathematics of poetry, etc.—a schema redoubled by another, reflexive one: poetry of poetry, mathematics of mathematics. *The self-reflection of a science is the other side of its reflection in another science*, of its symbolization by another science:

> Every symbol can in turn be symbolized by what it symbolizes—countersymbol. But there is also a symbol of symbols—intersymbols. . . . Everything can be symbol of the other—symbolic function.[58]

One could speak here of generalized translatability as well as of convertibility in the monetary sense:[59] mathematics is changed into poetry like franc into dollar. But, to remain with this metaphor, this convertibility is hierarchical: Just as there are stronger and weaker currencies, so too does the movement of conversion of categories obey a law of potentiation. It goes from low to high, from empirical to abstract, from philosophical to poetic, etc., to culminate in an operation to which we shall return, called by Novalis the "elevation to the state of mystery."

Even though the scientific validity of such an undertaking may be more than doubtful, and though it tends to dislocate the categorial fields of the sciences, to create an untamed alchemy of sorts, or to apply to the objective sciences a mode of thinking that would be more appropriate to the poetic domain,[60] we want to signal above all how the

Encyclopedia clearly shows *the structural place occupied by generalized translation in romantic thinking*, even though the concept of translation appears only very rarely in it.[61] One could speak of an operative concept which is not thematized as such, but which organizes the unfolding of this thinking. In this sense, Brentano captured its truth very well when he writes in *Godwi*: "The romantic is itself a translation."[62]

We use the term *generalized translation* on purpose: all that concerns the "version" of one thing in terms of another. This notion is based on everyday language: "I have translated my thoughts as follows . . ."; "I have given my version of the facts"; "I don't manage to translate what I feel"; etc. Here, translation concerns as well the *manifestation of something*, as the *interpretation of something*, the possibility to *formulate, or reformulate, something in an other way*. Roman Jakobson would call this intratranslation. To put it in even more general terms, translation concerns everything belonging to the domain of metamorphosis, transformation, imitation, recreation, copy, echo, etc. These are actual phenomena, and it would be tempting to search their common ontological root. Romantic thinking obviously succumbed to this temptation, trying to provide a speculative basis for the universal experience of the transformability and the affinity of things. The problem of the theory of generalized translatability is always this: It tends to efface all differences. In other respects, it is true that generalized translatability corresponds to something real. And that any theory of difference encounters the reverse problem: What about the ontological site of the transformable, the convertible?

Restricted translation (between languages) could provide, as it were, the paradigm of this problem: Different languages are translatable, but they are also different, hence to a certain extent untranslatable. But other questions arise. For example: how does the translation between languages relate to what Jakobson calls the intralingual translation? That is to say, reformulation, rewording? How does translation relate to the huge domain of interpretations—a somewhat equivocal term itself? In short, at issue is *the question of the limits of the field of translation and of the translatable*.

Perhaps the point would be to articulate a multiplicity of theories of trans-lations (the theory of translation among them), refusing a theory of *the* universal trans-lation. There is a great temptation to oppose to it a theory of *difference*, whether it be psychological, linguistic, or epistemological. Such a theory is highly desirable, and it is in effect being developed today from different fields of experience. But obviously, it must question itself about the existence, if not of generalized translation, at least of its *appearance*, and even more about the *fascination* the theories of generalized translation have exerted regularly throughout history.

In their way, the Jena Romantics have lived this problematic intensely. Much more than that: It constituted the space of their thinking and their poetry. *In the first place*, they developed, with the *Encyclopedia*, the *Witz*, and the *universal progressive poetry*, a theory of generalized translatability which is the speculative and fantasizing transposition of the concrete experience of the transformable. *In the second place*, they proposed a theory of poetry which makes poetry into translation and, conversely, makes translation into a double of poetry. It is in this light that they interpreted the relation of poetry to its medium, language: All poetry would be the "translation" of natural language into language of art—a position announcing that of Mallarmé, Valéry, Proust, or Rilke. *In the third place*, they certainly surmised that restricted translation perhaps constituted the paradigm of generalized translation, but obscured this intuition by philosophically privileging generalized translation. From then on, translation was no more than one of the (interchangeable) names of the infinite versability—undoubtedly a too limited name. *In the fourth place*, they interpreted translation as the inferior double of criticism and understanding, because the latter seemed to them to bring out the essence of literary works more purely. *In the fifth place*, they passionately lived the experience of restricted translation with A. W. Schlegel, and conceived the idea of a program of total translation—thus espousing a fascination perhaps inherent to translating as such: If everything is translatable, if everything is translation, one can and must translate all the works of all the languages; the essence of translation is omnitranslation.

All these points are interconnected, even though it is important to distinguish between them. The generalized translation of the *Encyclopedia* is not the transcendental translation of poetry, but is its condition of ontological possibility. The theory of criticism is not the theory of translation; but criticism is a process of translation, and translation is a process of criticism, to the extent that both refer to the same "spiritual mimic," rooted in the principle of the convertibility of everything into everything. The *Encyclopedia* is only a fabric of intratranslations, but A. W. Schlegel's program of restricted translation has encyclopedic ambitions—through which it becomes apparent to what extent the principle of infinite versability is incessantly at work in the articulation of the different projects of the romantic Revolution. What remains now is to go through the different moments of this immense circular reflection.

6

LANGUAGE OF ART
AND LANGUAGE OF NATURE

The poet is a peculiar species of transla-
tor who translates ordinary discourse,
modified by an emotion, into the "lan-
guage of gods."

—Paul Valéry

In his *La Genèse du Romantisme allemand*, Roger Ayrault observes that
an explicit theory of language is hardly to be found in Novalis and F.
Schlegel. To be sure, the brothers Schlegel, philologists by training,
could not have not thought about language; but, in fact, it is only after
the *Athenäum* period that they contributed, with Grimm, Bopp, Humboldt, and some others, to the formation of comparative grammar and
the science of language. As for Novalis, it is true that he devotes only
little space to questions of language in his *Fragments*. What does this
mean? In the first place, it means that one would look in vain for a
philosophy like Hamann's or Herder's in the early Romantics. Rather,
such a philosophy emerges with the Schlegels well after they aban-
doned their critical, speculative, and poetological reflection.[1] It is as if
there exists a certain incompatibility between these reflections and an
objective study of language.

Still, to agree with Ayrault that neither Novalis nor F. Schlegel developed a theory of language is inaccurate, if only because their theory of
the work is a theory of poetry, which "relates directly to language."[2] On

the other hand, the Romantics did assert that language is the most universal of all the human media, though this does not mean they studied it in its own right. If the work is above all a *work of language*, language only counts as *language of the work*. Which means that the romantic theory of language is entirely dependent on the theory of the work and of poetry. It is never autonomous, never crystallized in an independent *Sprachlehre* [Doctrine of Language]. As such, it is articulated along two axes which, each in its own way, make language disappear as a reality *sui generis*: (1) Everything is language, "communication," and hence human language is a system of signs not fundamentally different from other existing systems of signs, except that it is inferior to them; (2) The "true" language, such as it appears in the work, must be conceived on the basis of mathematical and musical "languages," for example, on the basis of *pure forms* which, by virtue of their total lack of content, are "allegorical," for example, "mimes" of the structure of the world and the spirit. These forms, freed from the "tyranny" of content, are also free from the yoke of imitation.

Actual language appears in this double perspective as a *Natursprache*, a language of nature, which must be transformed into a language of art, a *Kunstsprache*:

> The common language is the language of nature—the language of books is the language of art.[3]

> Natural, mimic, imaged language.—Artificial, arbitrary, voluntary language.[4]

The language of nature is inherently purely referential, centered on a content. And the primacy of content, for the Romantics, is precisely the opposite of art.

Novalis:

> The cruder the art, the more striking the compulsion of the content.[5]

> It is crude and without spirit to communicate only because of the content — *content*, matter, should never tyrannize us.[6]

And F. Schlegel:

> As long as the artist is in the process of discovery . . . he is in a state which . . . is at the very least intolerable.[7]

This crude language must be transformed into the medium for poetry by a chain of potentiations. Here, writing as such plays an essential role:

> Elevation of the common language to the language of books. The

common language grows incessantly—*from it* the language of books is formed.[8]

The poetry of nature is the proper object of the poetry of art.[9]

The spirit is the potentiating principle—hence, *the world of writing* is potentiated nature, or technical world.[10]

Poetry implies language only as its support, its inevitable and imperfect beginning. The task of the poet is rather to produce, on the basis of the language of nature, *a pure a priori language*—a task in which mathematics, music, and even philosophy, have preceded him. In a whole series of texts, Novalis and F. Schlegel have attempted to think the totality of the arts—notably painting—as a priori creations. The foundation of this opposition of the two languages is obviously that of Nature and of Spirit, which Novalis, using a daring neologism, calls *Faktur*:

Facture is opposed to *nature*. The spirit is the artist. Facture and nature mingled—separated—united. . . . Nature engenders, spirit makes. It is much more convenient to be made than to make oneself.[11]

This nature/facture division is the fundamental affirmation of the logological revolution, and neither F. Schlegel's nor Novalis's declarations aimed at a speculative relativizing of this opposition change anything about this: That which is opposed to the *Künstlichkeit* of the artist, to everything in him that is reflection, calculation, consciousness, sobriety, lucidity, agility, and detachment, is the unconscious, obscure *Natürlichkeit*, inebriated with itself, which is characteristic of the *Sturm und Drang* genius or, more profoundly, of the popular simplicity that "flourishes" in non-reflected production, in naive "naturations" (another of Novalis's neologisms), which are to genuine poetic art what the song of birds or the murmuring of the wind in the trees is to the fugue or the sonata: mimetism, "intolerable" passion for what is expressed or represented.

The romantic criticism of content is first of all a criticism of the artist's relation to content; but it is difficult for this criticism not to be transformed into a criticism of the very notion of content, because the procedures used to open this relation (reflection, irony, etc.) tend to dissolve content or to make it into a mere support of these procedures. To affirm, as F. Schlegel does, that Goethe's irony in *Wilhelm Meister* transforms the characters of this novel into "marionettes," or "allegorical figures,"[12] is to deny any realist dimension of this work, or to consider that dimension inessential. But content is referential, it drags the work out of its own element, that of self-reference. As for imitation, its referent is the outside world, the given, the phenomenal. The task of poetry, then, is first and foremost the destruction of the natural referen-

tial structure of language (just as the romantic consciousness is a reflexive consciousness, never intentional consciousness or transcendence).
Nevertheless, the non-referential, the non-content, the non-imitative do
not mean that poetry becomes an "empty form," a pure formalization—
not any more than do music, pilosophy, or mathematics. Because self-
reference, as such, is "symbolic" or "allegorical" (contrary to the attempts of the age, the *Athenäum* tends to use both terms without
distinction). Friedrich Schlegel can state a few pages apart that "all
beauty is allegory" and that "language . . . rethought in its origin, is
identical with allegory."[13] A principle which corresponds to the non-
referential structure of reality: The self-reflection of language reflects, in
a kind of non-referential reference, the self-reflection of the real:

> All the sacred games of art are only distant imitations of the inifinite
> play of the world, this work of art which eternally gives itself its own
> law.[14]

In addition, allegory, as a principle of art, also refers to the fact that
poetic language, which is never entirely liberated from its naturalness,
can never express directly the "Almighty" [*le Très-Haut*]: by denaturaliz-
ing language through a whole series of procedures, allegorical writing
seeks to circumvent this infirmity of natural language which Novalis and
his friend never tire of proclaiming.

Novalis:

> A number of things are too delicate to be thought; many more still to
> be spoken about.[15]

> For the poet language is never too poor, but always too general.[16]

And F. Schlegel:

> Language as well behaves badly towards morality. It is never so crude
> and beggarly as when it comes to designate moral concepts.[17]

The critical Revolution, then, establishes a new relation with language which can be said to govern modern Western poetry to a great
extent—a relation in which natural language is defective with regard to
the essence and the project of poetry. From *our* perspective, this notion
of natural language should perhaps be specified. To say that language is
natural is not to deny its human, historical origin. It is to say that, for
man, language constitutes an absolute given, which constitutes him as
man, and which has its own density. This does not mean that we stand in
a passive relation to language, that we are immersed in it and dominated by its structures: We create *in* language, *with* language, we create
some language, without ever creating language *as such*. Even more than
by writing, this is shown by oral cultures, where linguistic creation is

incessant. The oral relation to language can be called "natural": It is satisfied with cultivating the potentialities of language without ever seeking to revolutionize it. The written relation, on the other hand, contains the seed of such a revolution. Novalis had this intuition when he wrote in his notebooks:

> Books are a modern genre of *historical creatures*—but a highly significant one. Perhaps they have taken the place of traditions.[18]

Literature stands in a foundational relation to history. And it is precisely because, from this point on, the relation of men to history and to themselves is mediated by the written that the latter's originary soil, "oral" natural language, no longer seems to be the vehicle of historicity. It is insufficient for the philosophical, cultural, scientific, and even poetical aims humanity has set for itself. The oral, originary naturalness of language in effect implies its non-universality, its non-rationality, its reference to and complicity with the *hic et nunc*, its infinite dispersion in languages, dialects, jargons, sociolects, idiolects, etc. Left to itself and its pure and natural, historical, and social essence, language is incessantly particularized, differentiated, tagged to the infinite dispersion of spaces and times. To be sure, one could see in this an aspect of its essential wealth. But in the perspective of modernity, it is viewed rather as that which congenitally opposes its own unfolding. In its "natural state," language is not only infinitely differentiated, but also not fixed: It is always changing, modifying, renewing itself. Writing, as is well known, introduces a brutal fixation into this moving flux, or rather, modifies the conditions of the transformation of language, as Rosenzweig forcefully stated in the text we quoted above: Henceforth, the conditions of transformation come in part from the outside. German Romanticism, whatever aversion for French classicism it may have, is inscribed in the same dimension, and draws from it the same radical consequences for poetry, by posing an abyssal (ontological, no-longer aesthetical-social) difference between the language of nature, the "common" language, and the language of poetry. And its own poetical-critical language is made in the image of this difference: It is artificial through and through.[19] This artificiality is manifested in the first place by a certain *unreadability*. The obscurity of a Heraclites, a Góngora, sometimes of a Shakespeare, or the "trobar clus" (the obscure speech of the troubadours) depends on an other register. It is either a decipherable code or a content purposely presented in an obscure way, or a more or less deliberate slippage between the language and what it aims to say. Unreadability, on the other hand, seems to be profoundly related to the non-referential. When Novalis states that the "mystery" is the "state of dignity," we are actually at the beginning of a process that will culminate in Mallarmé or

Rilke. And this infinite distancing from natural language is accompanied by a quest for a total, encyclopedic work which would be all works and which would reflect itself, a work that, in some way, could unfold in any existing language, because it is (apparently) "beyond" language. Brentano intuited this in a passage of his novel *Godwi*, to which we shall come back later, when he says about Dante and Shakespeare:

> These two poets dominate their language as well as their time. . . .
> They are like giants in their language, and their language cannot subject them, for language in general is barely sufficient for their spirit.[20]

For the moment, let us look at the two axes that structure F. Schlegel's and Novalis's reflections on language more closely.

Everything is language. This statement is found almost everywhere in the romantic texts. Everything is "sign," "symptom," "trope," "representation," "hieroglyph," "symbol," etc., calling now for an interpretation, now for a blind immersion. Nevertheless, this pure signifying of things and of the world does not communicate anything in particular; it is rather crude meaning:

> *Grammar.* Not only man speaks—the universe also *speaks*—everything speaks—infinite languages. / Doctrine of signatures.[21]

> *Grammar.* Language is Delphi.[22]

> Image—not allegory, not symbol of something foreign: symbol of itself.[23]

Such is the paradox of a communication without something that is communicated, of a universal and empty language, proposing the imminence of a future revelation or the vestiges of a past revelation to the human ear:

> All that we experience is a *communication*. Thus the world is indeed a communication—a revelation of the spirit. The time is no longer when God's spirit was intelligible. The meaning of the world has been lost. We have been left with the letter. . . .[24]

One might speak here of a universal poeticity of things, if poetry may sometimes seem to be the meaning of this language of the perpetually silent world that is perpetually in the process of speaking. This universe where everything is language, and where language is always *language of . . .* (language of flowers, of music, of colors, etc.), refers to the theory of signatures as well as to the theory of Baudelaire's correspondences, of which Tieck and the brothers Schlegel, for that matter, have given some sort of first version. But it may be said just as well that if everything is language, there is no language in the specific sense, and that human language is perpetually deficient in relation to this language of the whole. The system of linguistic signs, properly speaking, seems poverty-stricken in relation to this incessant communication of the world. Henceforth, the task of poetry is to bring human language and universal language closer together. But this does by no means come down to a naturalizing of poetry and its forms: On the contrary, to the extent that the language of things is pure mystery and pure empty significance, its task will be to create a *Kunstsprache* with the same characteristics. Novalis expressed this in a famous fragment:

> Novels, without consistence, though with associations, like dreams. Poems—merely *harmonious* and full of beautiful words, but also without any meaning or consistence—at the most isolated stanzas intelligible. . . . At most true poetry can have an overall *allegorical* meaning, and an indirect effect, like music, etc.[25]

There is a corollary to the fact that everything is language or "allegory": "Linguistic signs," writes Novalis, "are not specifically differentiated (*unterschieden*) from the other phenomena."[26] *Sign* here means both a mark making possible the designation of things, and a hieroglyph analogous to those provided to us by the world and by nature. For the Romantics, human language is the seat of a contradiction: On the one hand, as creation of the spirit, it is too abstract, too general, too distant from that which it designates. In this sense, Novalis can say that it is, for philosophy as well as for art, an "inauthentic medium of representation."[27] But on the other hand, as hieroglyph, language has an active and almost magical power:

> The designation by sounds and traits is an abstraction worthy of admiration. Three letters designate God to me; a few traits designate a million of things. . . . The doctrine of language is the dynamic of the realm of the spirit.[28]

When Novalis writes, summarily, that "the spirit can only manifest itself in a foreign and aerial form,"[29] what could be meant but language, though a poetically purified and potentiated language? Thus we read in his "Logological Fragments":

> The poet dissolves all bonds. His words are not general signs—they are sounds—magic words that make beautiful groups move around them. Just like the clothes of saints retain miraculous powers, so too have many words been sanctified by some glorious thought, and become by themselves almost a poem. For the poet, language is never too poor, always too general. He often needs recurring words, worn out by use. . . .[30]

There is a demand here that could be formulated as follows: to make an instrument of poetic expression from the most ordinary, trivial, everyday language. Rather than penetrate the signifying density of natural language, poetry must make this language more and more "aerial." *And this operation is carried out in the context of a theory of mathematical and musical "languages" that are considered to be a priori and allegorical languages.*

It should be specified that, for Novalis, music has access to its truth only through the most purified forms:

> Dance and song music are not really true music. Only subspecies of it. Sonatas — symphonies — fugues — variations —: those are authentic music.[31]

Obviously, this brutal rupture between popular and abstract music, effected by the apostle of the *Märchen* [fairy tale], sheds light on the opposition between poetry of nature and poetry of art. Above all, it makes it possible for music to become the model of poetry, without surrendering poetry to a pure and formless sentimentality.

Music can only become the background for poetry and its transformation into non-referential language because its essence is mathematical. If Novalis separates popular music so decisively from abstract music, it is because the latter is "mathematicized."

Mathematics, along with philosophy, plays a very important role in romantic thinking, according to the following principle expressed by Novalis: "Everything real created from nothing, like numbers and abstract expressions, has a marvelous affinity with things from another world . . . with a poetic, mathematical, and abstract world, as it were."[32] The romantic theory of mathematics is situated at the intersection of a purely formalist theory and a speculative doctrine of the mysticism of numbers and figures (as it can also be found in Franz von Baader). But in fact, these two theories are really one. The mystical character of mathematics lies, in effect, in its formal and a priori being. The statement from the *Monologue*, that mathematical relations and operations are a fiction as well as a reproduction of the relations of things, could just as well be made by the modern positive sciences. That this ontological and gnoseological validity is accompanied by more occult significations is a secondary point for the Romantics.

For Novalis, mathematics constitutes a model, even an object of fascination,[33] in as much as it is a product of the totally a priori, abstract, and self-centered spirit, and to the extent that the productive work of the spirit is visible in it. It is the model of an intransitive transcendental "art," whose games of signs nevertheless refer, as through an infinite distance, to the "games of the world." This non-mimetic and nonempirical *mimesis* has to guide the Copernican revolution of language and music, in order to deliver these from the "slightest suspicion of imitation."[34]

Geometry is the transcendental art of *signs*.[35]

The system of numbers is the *model* for a genuine system of linguistic signs—our letters should become numbers, our language arithmetic.[36]

Genuine mathematics is the true element of the magician. In music, it appears formally as revelation—as creative idealism.[37]

Music. Mathematics. Does music not have something of combinatory analysis, and vice versa? . . . Language is a musical instrument of ideas. The poet, the rhetorician, and the philosopher *play* and compose grammatically. A fugue is entirely logical or scientific. . . . [38]

Musical relations seem to me to be . . . the fundamental relations of nature.[39]

Texts written in praise of music are legion in Novalis (as well as in F. Schlegel). But this cult of music has nothing to do with the myth of music that had already started to flourish, in the same period, with Wackenroder; it has nothing to do (or only indirectly so) with the cult of "magic tones" that will be so fashionable with the other romantic generations. The issue here is abstract music: a compositional system of tones constituting, according to Kant's formula, a "purposiveness without purpose" or, according to the no less poignant formula of Novalis, a *monologue*. A system of perfect allegoricity, since the sounds are at once full of meaning and empty of any assignable and definite meaning. If the mathematical sign is empty, if the linguistic sign is full (too full: it says this, or that), the musical sign, for its part, is both full and empty. Hence the *poetic* importance of music, in its triple aspect of mathematical architecture, compositional structure, and infinite signification of tonal chains:

Novalis:
> Our language—it was very musical in the beginning. . . . It should once again become *song*.[40]

> *Composition of discourse*. Musical treatment of writing.[41]

> One must write as one composes.[42]

F. Schlegel:
> Many people find it strange and ridiculous when musicians speak of the thoughts in their music; and it often happens that one perceives

they have more thoughts in their music than they do about it. But whoever has a sense for the wonderful affinities of all the arts and sciences will at least not consider the matter from the dull viewpoint of so-called naturalness according to which music would be only the language of the senses, and he will consider a certain tendency of pure instrumental music toward philosophy as not impossible in itself. Doesn't pure instrumental music have to create its own text? And is not the theme in it developed, reaffirmed, varied, and contrasted in the same way as the object of meditation in a philosophical succession of ideas?[43]

Such is the task of symbolic-abstract poetry: to make the words sing philosophically in a musical and mathematical composition, where the song of the words is that which abolishes their limited meaning and gives them an infinite meaning. Such is Novalis's "poetry of the inifinite," F. Schlegel's "progressive universal poetry," when it is taken not on the level of their textual forms, but on the level of their verbal fabric. Novalis's fragment on narratives deprived of "consistence," quoted above, comes closest to defining the essence of this musicalized poetic language in an abstract sense. The Jena Romantics will undoubtedly have been the first to formulate these demands that will resurface more than a century later in Mallarmé, the Symbolists, and Valéry (in France). However, the following should be added: In the relation, henceforth anxious, that poetry will have with its model (its rival), monological music, it has an essential advantage: It may become language of language, poetry of poetry, whereas one can only speak in a derivative sense of a music of music (or a mathematics of mathematics); as soon as it is rid of all reference outside of itself, of all imitative or thematic transcendence, poetry becomes the supreme art, a *sich selbst bildendes Wesen*, a "being that forms itself."[44] That is, one might say, its supra-musical, supra-mathematical essence, its ability to be not only a priori, but transcendental in the Fichtean sense, and it is this that guarantees its profound identity with philosophy.[45]

Yet, it is strange to find that the Romantics have in no way reflected on the faculty of language to become language of language, and that Novalis's *Monologue*, the most accomplished of the Romantic *Sprachlehre*, is satisfied in this respect with the homology between language and mathematics. For the reflexive faculty of language is a property of natural language as such, indissolubly linked to its referential faculty. In the same way that self-consciousness is first and foremost intentional consciousness, language is self-reference only to the extent that it is reference, the space, even, of all the possible references where the consciousness-subject is constituted. Because they place themselves exclusively on the level of reflexive consciousness, the Romantics do not succeed in defining the level of language proper. Hence, language can only appear as the imperfect medium of a poetry destined to be the site of supreme reflection. The only theory of language the *Athenäum* is able to provide is a theory of a potentiated, romanticized, "pure" language; "pure," not in the sense that it would restore the hidden essence of the "words of the tribe" (Mallarmé), but in the sense that it has been methodically and deliberately emptied of all its natural contents and connections. To be sure, and this is an ambiguity that can be found again and again in the history of modern Western poetry, the poetic language created in this way pretends to be nothing more than the affirmation of the magical or sensory "powers" of natural language. But that is probably an illusion, and Novalis senses it when he says about poetry:

> With every finishing touch the work springs forward from the master into distant spaces—thus, with the very last touch, the master sees his so-called work separate from himself by an abyss of thought, whose expanse he himself can barely grasp.[46]

Mallarmé and Rilke formulated this law of poetic distancing with similar precision. The former writes:

> Words rise up unaided and in ecstasy; many a facet reveals its infinite rarity and is precious to our mind. For our mind is the center of this hesitancy and oscillation; it sees the words not in their usual order, but in projection (like the walls of a cave), so long as that mobility which is their principle lives on, that part of speech which is not spoken. Then quickly, before they die away, they all exchange their brilliances from afar; or they may touch, and steal a furtive glance.[47]

The latter:

> *Kein* Wort im Gedicht (ich meine hier jedes "und" oder "der", "die", "das") ist identisch mit dem gleichlautenden Gebrauchs- und Konversationswort; die reinere Gesetzmäßigkeit, das große Verhältnis, die Konstellation, die es im Vers oder in künstlerischer Prosa einnimmt, verändert es bis in den Kern seiner Natur, macht es nutzlos, unbrauchbar für den bloßen Umgang, unberührbar und bleibend. . . .[48]

The theory of poetic language, astronomically removed from the natural language, culminates in Rilke in a theory of hermeticism, in the sense that the poem closes upon itself; in Novalis and F. Schlegel, it results similarly in a theory of the "state of mystery" (*Geheimniszustand*). At the basis of this, first of all, is the idea, popular at the end of the eighteenth century, of a superior language, a Sanskrit for initiates. But the theory of the state of mystery goes further: It describes the supreme poetic operation by which language becomes both familiar and foreign, near and distant, clear and obscure, intelligible and unintelligible, communicable and incommunicable. Let us quote some of Novalis's fragments which allude to this operation from various sides:

> He who knows how to make a science—must also know how to make a non-science—he who knows how to make something intelligible, must also be able to make it unintelligible.[49]

> The art of making an object foreign, and yet known and attractive, this is the romantic poetics.[50]

> To raise to the level of mystery. The *unknown* is the *stimulus* for the faculty of knowledge. The known does not stimulate. . . . Mystification.[51]

> Mystery is the state of dignity.[52]

> The spirit strives to absorb the stimulus. The foreign attracts it. Metamorphosis of what is *foreign* into what is one's *own*; thus appropriation is the incessant activity of the spirit. Some day there will no longer be any stimulus or anything foreign—the spirit should be for itself stimulus and foreign. . . . Today the spirit is spirit by instinct—a natural spirit—it should become a rational spirit, spirit by reflection (*Besonnenheit*) and by *art*. (Nature should become art, and art a second nature).[53]

Such is also the romantic theory of the *Distant* (an echo of which might perhaps be found in Walter Benjamin, when he says in his essay on Baudelaire that beauty "is the unique appearance of something distant":)

> The unknown, the mysterious, are the *result* and the *beginning* of everything. . . . Distant philosophy sounds like music—because every call into the distance becomes vowel. . . . Thus everything at a distance becomes *poetry—poem*. Actio in distans. Distant mountains, distant people, distant events, etc., everything becomes romantic, quod idem est—hence our originarily poetic nature. Poetry of night and twilight.[54]

The place of the work is the distant, the unknown-known, the familiar foreign. In *Heinrich of Ofterdingen*, Novalis writes: "One hears foreign words and yet understands what they are intended to mean."[55] Thus we find again, but now on the purely poetic and speculative level, the relation of what is one's own and what is foreign as it constitutes German *Bildung*. In this respect, Novalis' unfinished novel may be considered as the conscious reversal (*Umkehrung*) of the relation of what is one's own and what is foreign, of the near and the distant as it structures Goethe's *Bildungsroman*, *Wilhelm Meister*. Such is the culmination of the romantic theory of the work: Raised to the state of mystery is the language where familiar words have become foreign, where everything is plunged into an unintelligible distant and yet full of meaning.

But doesn't this literary operation, which is the essence of romantization,[56] resemble the very movement of *translation*? Or rather: Doesn't translation continue, or radicalize, this movement at work in the Romantic work? Doesn't it tear the foreign work away from the finitude of its native language, of its empirical soil? Doesn't it distance it "astronomically," by inscribing it in another language, from its empirical soil? In any translation, as everyone will agree, the work is uprooted, as it were. Now, this movement of uprooting inherent in all translation, whatever its nature, is considered to be a loss, even a treason, by popular opinion. The translated text would fall short of the original because it is allegedly unable to restore the network of connivances and references that constitutes the life of the latter. Of course. But in the Romantic perspective, this network is what consecrates the finitude of the work, whose vocation is its own absoluteness. If *irony* is one of the means the Romantics imagined could elevate the work beyond its finitude, then translation must be considered as *the hyperironic procedure that completes the work of the irony immanent in the work.*[57]

In fact, this set of movements by which, in translation, the foreign becomes familiar, the familiar foreign, etc., is identical to that by which the (Romantic) work tries to deny natural language and to rid itself of any empirical connection. In this sense, the translation of a literary work is, as it were, *the translation of a translation*. And the double movement which characterizes the romantic text, which makes the near distant and the distant near, is in effect the aim of translation: In the translated text the foreign is certainly made near but, also, the near (the translator's mother tongue) is, as it were, distanced and made foreign.[58]

Now, this "metamorphosis," this "reversal," is what Novalis calls the elevation to the state of mystery. Translation, then, appears as the summit, or one of the empirical summits, of the absolutization of the work. Everything the work loses in concrete terms, it gains in transcendental reality, for example, on the level of that which constitutes it as "work."

Novalis's daring assertion that "in the final analysis, all poetry is translation"—an assertion that could have been uttered just as well by a Joë Bousquet—now becomes intelligible: If true poetry is the elevation of natural language to the state of mystery, and if translation constitutes, as it were, a doubling of this movement, then one may well state that *Dichtung* is originarily *Übersetzen*. Or: To the transcendental translation carried out by poetry (romantization) corresponds empirical translation, for example, the passage of a work from one language to another. The first "translation" works on language as language, the second on the specific language in which language in general has been worked upon by the first. Henceforth, it can be understood why the act of translating could exert such a fascination on the Romantics, though it is by no means a fascination with *the relation among existing specific languages*, but with that which, in any translation, concerns the putting to death of natural language and the flight of the work towards a stellar language which would be its pure, absolute language. Walter Benjamin's theory of translation, which would be inconceivable without his prolonged engagement with the Romantics, only expresses their intuitions more purely.

It is clear why a theory of *Kunstsprache* (just like the theory of the infinite versability of universal progressive poetry and the *Encyclopedia*) is a secret invitation to a theory of translation: In this light, *any work is translation*, whether it be an indefinite *conflation* into one another of all textual and categorial forms, or the *infinitization* of the "words of the tribe." What is customarily considered as the negativity of translation is henceforth, for the *Athenäum*, rather its *poetic positivity*. To be sure, such a speculative position goes far beyond Goethe and Herder, who remain firmly attached to an "empirical" literary and cultural perspective, and do not believe that poetry is to tear itself loose from its referential soil.[59]

This is the position which presides over the birth of what the modern epoch calls literature, as Michel Foucault forcefully showed in *The Order of Things*:

> But the word is of recent date, as is also, in our culture, the isolation of a particular language whose peculiar mode of being is "literary." This is because at the beginning of the nineteenth century, at a time when language was burying itself within its own density as an object and allowing itself to be traversed, through and through, by knowledge, it was also reconstituting itself elsewhere, in an independent form, difficult of access, folded back upon the enigma of its own origin and existing wholly in reference to the pure act of writing. Literature is the contestation of philology (of which it is nevertheless the twin figure): it leads language back from grammar to the naked power of speech, and there it encounters the untamed, imperious being of words. From the Romantic revolt against a discourse frozen in its ritual pomp, to the Mallarméan discovery of the word in its impotent power, it becomes clear what the function of literature was, in the nineteenth century, in relation to the modern mode of being of language. Against the background of this essential interaction, the rest is merely effect: literature has become progressively more differentiated from the discourse of ideas, and encloses itself within a radical intransitivity; it becomes detached from all the values that were able to keep it in general circulation during the classical age (taste, pleasure, naturalness, truth),

and creates within its own space everything that will ensure a ludic denial of them . . . ; it breaks with the whole definition of *genres* . . . and becomes merely a manifestation of a language which has no other law than that of affirming—in opposition to all other forms of discourse—its own precipitous existence; and so there is nothing for it to do but to curve back in a perpetual return upon itself, as if its discourse could have no other content than the expression of its own form; it addresses itself to itself as a writing subjectivity, or seeks to re-apprehend the essence of all literature in the movement that brought it into being.[60]

Reading this text, it is clear that the Romantic theory of the work and its language constitutes, through a whole series of literary, cultural, and historical mediations, the very soil of "modern" literature, or at least of the dominant trend in what we call the field of literature. This trend is of an intransitive order or, to use a notion newly developed by Bakhtin, *monological*. We may ask ourselves, before analyzing the Romantic texts that represent what may be called *the monologic theory of translation as the beyond of the work*, if, from now on, such a conception, such a "trend," is not what should be called into question. Shouldn't we look for that which, in modern Western literature but also *before and besides it* (in literatures peripheral to it), does not correspond to this mono-logic vocation? To rediscover this more fertile, more deeply rooted dimension which is stifled by Romantic and modern monologism, a dimension which concerns both the "lyrical" domain (which the *Athenäum*, as Lacoue-Labarthe and J.-L. Nancy have shown, does not manage to integrate) and the "novel," such as it asserts itself in the lineage unearthed by Bakhtin? To be sure, Romanticism claims such a lineage: Cervantes, Ariosto, Boccaccio, the eighteenth-century English novel, but it only retains its formal agility, not its extraordinary textual density. In *The Dialogic Imagination*, Bakhtin brutally distinguished the "mono-logism" of poetry and the "dialogism" of the novel. As such, this opposi-tion is not acceptable: If any novel is essentially dialogic, not all poetry is essentially monologic. But it is true that monologism is a temptation of poetry—that of the "stellar language," the "language of the gods"—and that the modern epoch seems to have felt this temptation more than others; starting with German Romanticism, it even theorized it. Beyond all the reformulations that must necessarily be brought to Bakhtin's thesis, it contains nevertheless the indication of a dimension—the di-alogic dimension—that may modify our experience of literature and, correlatively, of translation. Is translation only the potentiating exten-sion of the poetic monologue, or does it constitute, on the contrary, *the advent of a dialogic dimension sui generis to the work*? Such would be the question posed, in this study, by the confrontation of the theory of translation of the Romantics on the one hand, and the opposite theories of Goethe and Hölderlin on the other. A question accompanied by another: What of translation's *own place* in the monologic theory? As we shall see, this theory does not manage at all to *distinguish translation from what it is not*—criticism or poetry. In one case, translation is the business of the poets, it is *Nachdichtung*. In another, it is the business of philologers, critics, hermeneuticists. If A. W. Schlegel can still be at once a poet, translator, critic, and philologer, in the nineteenth century the division is quickly established. On the one hand there are scholarly translations, on the other literary translations, made by writers (Nerval, Baudelaire, Mallarmé, George). What is at stake in this division is that translation as such, as act, has no clearly delimited place of its own (as work of language and with language), that it is *now the aside of poetry, now the aside of philology*. And we shall see that the division in which translation as a specific act disappears is carried out by Romanticism, even as it elevated this act to speculative heights probably never before attained.

7

THE SPECULATIVE
THEORY OF TRANSLATION

While reading the texts by F. Schlegel and Novalis, particularly their fragments, one is struck by one thing: Though, as we have seen, there is a certain theory of translation immanent to their theory of literature, the passages devoted to the act of translating are few, especially when compared to those dealing with literary criticism. To be sure, neither Novalis nor F. Schlegel are translators. But is it not strange to note that their fragments devoted to the theory of the book and of writing lack all reference to translation, whereas the critical activity is incessantly mentioned? Let us consider, for instance, the following note by Novalis:

> *Encyclopedistic.* My book must contain the critical metaphysics of reviewing, of writing, of experimenting and observing, of reading, of speaking, etc.[1]

This observation extends to Novalis's unpublished notes in their entirety. One only finds the following remark, jotted down hastily along with some others:

> Every man has his own language. Language is the expression of the spirit. Individual languages. Genius of language. Ability to translate into and from other languages. Wealth and euphony of each language. The authentic expression makes the clear idea. . . . Transparent, guiding expression.[2]

In another fragment, Novalis speaks of the mutual "translation" of quality and quantity—which refers directly to the generalized convertibility of categories in his *Encyclopedia*. But it does not contain any close examination.[3]

The same could be said of the majority of F. Schlegel's texts on translation. They are short annotations, sometimes trivial, sometimes more profound, dealing above all with the problems encountered in translating ancient authors, brought to the fore by Voss.[4] Here as well, these texts could not be compared, neither qualitatively nor quantitatively, to those devoted to the notion of criticism. In effect, it seems as if the latter notion *covered* that of translation, in every sense of the term, notably that of one figure covering another exactly. For Novalis and F. Schlegel are very far from underestimating the act of translating in its literary, cultural, and historical dimension. We have seen above that the presentation of the romantic cultural field does not fail to include it. The continuation of the *Dialogue on Poetry* even mentions "[Voss's] merit as translator and as language artist, which broke new ground with an unspeakable vigor and endurance."[5] Further, F. Schlegel speaks about "German artists," and "the genius for translation that is properly theirs."[6] Obviously, one divines the imposing presence of A. W. Schlegel behind these observations. But it is in Novalis that we will find two texts that express most daringly the romantic view of translation, and the confusion, characteristic for him, between the act of translating and the act of "criticizing." The first is a fragment from *Blüthenstaub*, published in the *Athenäum* in 1798. The second is a letter of 30 November 1797, addressed to A. W. Schlegel.

Some years later, Clemens Brentano devotes a short chapter of his novel *Godwi* to romantic art and to translation, which ends with the striking assertion: "The romantic itself is a translation." An assertion that has been pointed out often in literary criticism, but never really elucidated.

At present we shall proceed to a commentary of these three texts, primarily the one by Novalis, which represents, as it were, the summary of the *Athenäum*'s view on translation. Brentano, for his part, does not belong to this group, but his text is like a distant resonance of this view, already confused and deformed, though of the utmost significance. Once these texts have been clarified, it will be our responsibility to show why, in Romantic thinking, the concept of *criticism* had to cover, displace, and to a certain extent obscure the concept of *translation*, and why, consequently, no autonomous place for the act of translating can be found in this thinking. It will be our responsibility as well to show that this covering refers to an actual problem that emerges as soon as the cultural and linguistic dimension of the work is given less attention than its absolutized poetic "nature."

Let us start, chronologically, with the oldest text, the letter to A. W. Schlegel of November 1797. At this time, the latter had just started to work on his monumental translation of Shakespeare.

> The reviewer of your Shakespeare means well. But his review is truly not poetic. And to think what could have been said about your Shakespeare, particularly in relation to the *whole*. It is among translations what "Wilhelm Meister" is among novels. Is there yet anything similar to it? Though we Germans have been translating for a long time, and however national this inclination toward translation may be—to the extent that there has been almost no German writer of note who did not also translate, truly being as imaginative here as for an original work—yet nowhere does one seem to be as uninformed as about translation. With us it can become a science and an art. Your Shakespeare is an excellent canon for the scientific observer. Apart from the Romans, we are the only nation to have felt the impulse (*Trieb*) of translation so irresistibly and to owe to it so infinitely in culture (*Bildung*). Hence the many similarities between our culture (*Kultur*) and the late Roman literary culture. This impulse is an indication of the very elevated and original character of the German people. Germanity is a cosmopolitanism mixed with the most vigorous individualism. Only for us have translations become expansions. It requires poetic morality and the sacrifice of one's personal proclivities to undertake a true translation. One translates out of a love for the beautiful and for the literature of one's home country. Translation is as much poetry (*dichten*) as the creation of one's own works—and more difficult, more rare. In the final analysis, all poetry is translation. I am convinced that the German Shakespeare today is better than the English. . . .[7]

We should comment on almost every sentence in this essential text. We shall only leave out the already clarified passages where Novalis signals the historical aspect of translation in Germany, a passage which, as we know, expresses no more than a common conviction of all German writers.

First of all, we have to note that Novalis writes this letter to A. W. Schlegel concerning a review of the latter's translation. This apparently favorable review is allegedly not "poetry." In the background of this remark is the romantic demand that any critique should also be poetry, as F. Schlegel expressed it in the *Athenäum*. Though in an indirect way, criticism is present in this text as the requirement that a review of a poetic translation should be the exposition of the essence and the truth of this translation. What essence? What truth? That remains to be seen. To Novalis, A. W. Schlegel's Shakespeare appears as a model, a work occupying among translations the rank of *Wilhelm Meister* among novels. The *Meister* is significant for the Romantics in that it appears to them to be the first modern reflexive work, the first work to present itself as work, tending towards a symbolical-allegorical dimension by means of the ironization of its content. Both F. Schlegel and Novalis devoted enthusiastic "reviews" to it, at least at the time of this letter. To say that A. W. Schlegel's translation is to translations what the *Meister* is to novels is to say that, in it, translation becomes visible *as* translation, presents itself as such, which raises it to the level of an "art" and a "science" in the sense explained in our previous chapters. It is also to say that A. W. Schlegel's Shakespeare, in a certain way, relates to its form and its content in a manner at least homologous to the manner in which the *Meister* relates to them; reflexivity, ironization, symbolization, infinite elevation to the level of *Kunstsprache*. Let us confront this passage with a sentence from the end of the letter: "I am convinced that the German Shakespeare today is better than the English." Where does such an evaluation come from? From a comparison with the original? Not in the least, even if one supposes—which is more than doubtful—that Novalis read Shakespeare in English, a reading for which he lacked sufficient linguistic and cultural knowledge. Is it a judgment of the "nationalist" type? Certainly not, since the Germanness mentioned in the letter, as for Herder, Goethe, and Schleiermacher, is above all conceived by the capacity of translating. What, then, makes it possible to say that the German Shakespeare is better than the English? A. W. Schlegel was particularly proud of having translated this Shakespeare faithfully, for example, of having rendered the passages in prose as prose and the passages in poetry as poetry.[8] Thus, in his own view, his translation was equivalent to the original, though an equivalent which, like any translation, was only an approximation. Novalis's judgment, then, seems peculiar. But it is not without motivation. The German Shakespeare is "better" *precisely because it is a translation.* To be sure, previous translations of Shakespeare are not as good as the English Shakespeare. But that is because they are prose translations, free and often made dull, which do not confront the poeticity of the Shakespearean text the way A. W. Schlegel had undertaken to do. In some sense, they are not translations that are conscious of themselves, just as the novels before the *Meister* had not fully attained the novelistic essence. As soon as the German translation of Shakespeare attempts to "mime" the original authentically, it can only go beyond it. Let us try to explain this paradox. On the "mimic" operation at work in both translation and criticism, Novalis writes in a fragment:

> The mime *voluntarily* vivifies in himself the principle of a determined individuality.
> There is symptomatic and genetic imitation. Only the latter is alive. It presupposes the most intimate union of the imagination and the understanding.

The capacity to truly awaken a foreign individuality in oneself—not merely to deceive by a superficial imitation—is still entirely unknown—and rests on a most wonderful *penetration* and spiritual mimic. The artist becomes everything he sees and wants to be.[9]

This mimic capacity penetrates the foreign individuality and reproduces it: Hence it is "genetic." In another fragment, Novalis asserts:

Naturally, we only understand the foreign by making-ourselves-foreign—transforming oneself.[10]

As we have seen, F. Schlegel, for his part, defined translation as a "philological mime" and explained the dialectics of translation in terms of creation and understanding:

In order to translate perfectly the ancient into the modern, the translator would have to have such mastery of the latter as to be able to make everything modern; but at the same time he would have to understand antiquity so well that he would be able not just to imitate it but, if necessary, re-create it.[11]

But why would this genetic and philological mime, far from merely providing a modest approximation of the original, provide a better version of it? Because it constitutes the original, through its very movement, into a *potentiation*. Its scope is not merely the original in its crude being (in this case, Shakespeare's plays in their sixteenth-century English). The original itself, in what the Romantics call its "tendency," possesses an *a priori* scope: the Idea of the Work which the work wants to be, *tends* towards (independently from the author's intentions or not), but empirically never is. In this respect, the original is only the copy—the translation, if you want—of this *a priori* figure which presides over its being and gives it its necessity.[12] Now, translation aims precisely at this Idea, this origin of the original. Through this aim, it necessarily produces a "better" text than the first, if only because the movement constituted by the passage from one language to another— the *Übersetzung*—has necessarily distanced, removed the work by force from the initial empirical layer that separated it from its own Idea: In other words, the translated work is closer to the internal scope, and further from its finite gravity. The translation, the second version of the work, brings it closer to its truth. And such is the essence of the "mimic" movement, the essence we approached when comparing the internal movement of the romantic work to the movement of translation. Criticism, as we shall see, has the same status, and F. Schlegel did not hesitate to call his review of *Wilhelm Meister* an *Übermeister*, an "Over-Meister" (just like Nietzsche says *Übermensch*, "Over-man").[13] Every *Übersetzung* is a movement in which the *Über* is a potentiating going-beyond: Thus one may say that A. W. Schlegel's Shakespeare is an

Übershakespeare. The original is inferior to its translation in the same way "Nature" is inferior to "Facture." The further one is distanced from the natural, the closer one gets to the absolute poetic core. Think of F. Schlegel's fragment on the "copies of imitations," the "examination of reviews," etc. Thus, we would have chains of works in which the latter potentiate the former:

novels prior to *Wilhelm Meister*	→	*Wilhelm Meister* (novel of the novel)	→	review of the *Meister* or *Übermeister*
Shakespeare	→	translation of Shakespeare	→	review of the translation of Shakespeare

The examination of Novalis's second text will confirm such an interpretation. But we are already in a position to better understand Novalis's assertions: that in the final analysis all poetry would be translation. This is a point we already touched upon. If poetry is essentially a going-beyond, a potentiation of "natural language," the constitution of a "stellar" language, it is in itself already translation,[14] since translation is nothing else than this movement. As restricted translation—passage from one language into another—it is certainly only one of the empirical forms of this movement. But this empirical form can undoubtedly be conceived—and Novalis, at least here, has this intuition—as the *canonical form* of the generalized translation that operates in the poetic and, moreover, also scientific work (the *Encyclopedia*). And the immanent translation that poetry is can only be conceived as a self-translation: The work translates itself, *setzt sich über*, goes beyond itself toward the ether of its own infinity. Translation, by making the original pass not only from language x into language y, but from its mother tongue (i.e., its empirical belonging) into a foreign language in general (which thus constitutes the "distant" language, the allegorical figure of the *pure language*),[15] submits it to the Grand Tour mentioned by F. Schlegel. The *Athenäum* fragment no. 297 must be reread from this perspective:

> A work of art is cultivated when it is . . . completely faithful to itself, entirely homogeneous, and nonetheless exalted above itself. Like the education of a young Englishman, the most important thing about it is the *Grand Tour*. It should have traveled through all the three or four continents of humanity, not in order to round off the edges of individuality, but to broaden its own vision and give its spirit more freedom and inner versatility; and thereby greater independence and self-sufficiency.[16]

Which amounts to saying that translation is literally *Bildung*, but a poetic and speculative *Bildung*, no longer merely literary and humanistic as it was for Goethe. Or: Translation is an *Erweiterung*, but now in an idealist sense.

In this letter, Novalis seems closer than ever to the archetypal character of translation for the poetic and literary labor. He can no more lose sight of it than the essential role of translation for the German culture escapes him. He is aware of it as much as Goethe was, if not more so. And yet, this hyperbolic reversal which makes poetry into translation, even into something more "rare" and "difficult," does not result for him in a global theory of the act of translating, because the specificity of "restricted" translation is incessantly covered over by, or identified with, potentiating translation, which is more essential in his perspective and which, under several names, characterizes the movement of the affirmation of the work on the basis of the destruction of natural language. These two forms of translation intersect *at only one point*: the fact that, in a work, the movement of destruction of the *Natursprache* obviously passes through the destruction of a particular language. One might just as well say that the act of translating consists in lighting the fire of poetic destruction from one language to another. Such are the certainly hazardous conjectures to which Novalis's thinking leads.

As can be seen, this thinking results in two extreme propositions, logical in their framework, but well capable of shocking the common sense: All poetry is translation; all translation is superior to its original. The first statement amounts to the declaration that every work is animated by a self-reflexive movement. But after all, when a Rilke declares that the words in the poem are sidereally removed from the words of the common language, he intends to express something that is valid for all poetry. It would remain to be seen if all poetry may claim such a purpose—that is to say: if all poetry is essentially monologic.

The second statement is connected to the first: If all translation is translation of translation, this movement of potentiation can only "crown" and "finish" the original. The essential is not that which, in the work, is origin, but the fact that, through its "Grand Tour," it becomes more and more "universal" and "progressive."[17] One may also say: Translation represents a superior echelon of the life of the original. A hyperbolical assertion? No doubt. But the following may be noted: It sometimes happens that translations give an impression of superiority over their original which is not merely of a literary order. We may think of Paul Celan's translation of the following verses by Jules Supervielle:[18]

Jésus, tu sais chaque feuille	[Jesus, you know each leaf
Qui verdira le forêt,	That will make the forest green,
Les racines qui recueillent	The roots that collect
Et dévorent leur secret,	And devour their secret,
la terreur de l'éphémère	the terror of the ephemeral
à l'approche de la nuit,	at the approach of the night,

et le soupir de la Terre	and the sigh of the Earth
dans le silence infini.	in the infinite silence.
Tu peux suivre les poissons	You can follow the fish
tourmentant les profondeurs,	That are tormenting the depths,
quand ils tournent et retournent	when they turn and turn again
et si s'arrêt leur coeur. . . .	And if their heart stops. . . .
Jesus, du kennst sie alle:	Jesus, you know them all:
das Blatt, das Waldgrün bringt,	the leaf that brings forest green,
die Wurzel, die ihr Tiefstes	the root that gathers
aufsammelt und vertrinkt,	and drowns its deepest,
die Angst des Taggeschöpfes,	the fear of the diurnal animal,
wenn es sich nachthin neigt,	when it inclines nightward,
das Seufzen dieser Erde	the sighing of this earth
im Raum, der sie umschweigt.	in the space silent around it.
Du kannst den Fisch begleiten,	You can accompany the fish,
dich wühlen abgrundwärts	burrow yourself toward the abyss
und mit ihm schwimmen, unten,	and swim with it, underneath,
und länger als sein Herz. . . .	and longer than its heart. . . .]

George Steiner, to whom we owe this confrontation, shows clearly how the universe Supervielle sought to capture in his somewhat dull and discursive verses is, as it were, seized and deepened in Celan's verses. One might simply say that this is a poetic recreation that can no longer be called a "translation," even if Celan believed he could call it that. Or again, that it is the opposition of two poetics. But one cannot deny oneself the impression that Celan captured *precisely* the poetic purpose of Supervielle, and that this capturing has produced a poetically superior poem. Not that Supervielle would be a lesser poet than Celan (this is not the place for such a debate), but the translation by the German poet has succeeded in "potentiating" the French poem, to place it at the level of *its own purpose*, even to purge it of the flaws that affect Supervielle's poetry in general and that concern his relation to language and poetic expression as such. If this is the case, the poem translated by Celan would be an *ÜberSupervielle*. Mallarmé's translations of Poe's poems has sometimes occasioned analogous commentaries. The rarity of these examples in the field of translation would signify, as Novalis says, that translating is something rare and difficult. It could also mean that this type of translation is only possible in a certain poetic space, defined historically by Romanticism, to which Supervielle and Celan belong as well as Poe and Mallarmé. We are very far from clearly understanding all that. But does not the fact that no translation of Shakespeare's *Sonnets* has been satisfactory (even though great poets and great translators have attempted it) indicate *a contrario* that these poems, in their poetic writing, depend on an aim that makes impossible, if not all translation, at least any "potentiating" translation? And doesn't such a potentiating translation presuppose a relation of the work to its language and to itself that is itself of the order of translation, thus calling for, making possible, and justifying the movement of its translation?

Let us start now on the second text of Novalis, from "Blüthenstaub":

> A translation is either grammatical, transforming, or mythical. Mythical translations are translations in the highest style. They present the clear, perfected state of the individual work of art. They do not give us the actual work of art, but the idea of it. There exists as yet no perfect model of such work, I believe. We encounter evident traces of it in the spirit of many critiques and descriptions of works of art. It calls for a head in which the poetic spirit and the philosophical spirit have penetrated each other in their fullness. Greek mythology is in part such a translation of a national religion. The modern Madonna is also such a myth.
>
> Grammatical translations are translations in the ordinary sense. They require a great erudition, but only discursive abilities.
>
> The transforming translations, if they are to be authentic, require the highest poetic spirit. They easily lapse into travesty, like Bürger's iambic Homer, Pope's Homer, and the French translations in their entirety. The true translator of this kind must in effect be the artist himself, able to render the idea of the whole in this or in that manner as he pleases. He must be the poet of the poet, able to let him speak simultaneously according to the poet's idea and to his own. The genius of humanity stands in a similar relation to each individual man.
>
> Not only books, everything can be translated in these three ways.[19]

This text from "Blüthenstaub" obviously alludes to A. W. Schlegel's work as a translator; but it also supposes, in a barely disguised way, F. Schlegel's work, notably his essay on *Wilhelm Meister*. The allusion to the Madonna, isolated in this context, refers to a visit by the Jena group to the museums of Dresden, where they were able to admire, among other things, Raphaël's Madonnas.[20]

Note first of all that Novalis's fragment, like Goethe's, is organized in a triadic manner: there are three types of translation. The first type (the second one in the text), "grammatical translation," seems to correspond to Goethe's prose translation, whose only aim is to render the content and the general physionomy of the original. The two other types, on the other hand, do not have an equivalent in Goethe's triad. Novalis calls the first one "mythical," the second one "transforming" (*verändernd*). Disregarding the order of the text, we will first examine the latter. There is a kind of ambiguity in the notion of *Veränderung*. According to the examples given—Bürger, Pope, the French—these are translations that merely modify the original and its forms, either by translating a versified work into prose, or one type of verse into another, etc. And this is precisely the kind of translation that is, if not condemned, at least deemed second rate by Herder, Goethe, Schleiermacher, and A. W. Schlegel. But for Novalis, the "transformation" carried out by these translations constitutes a threat only to this type, not to the essence, of translation. In truth, the "transforming" translator is the "poet of the poet"—a reflexive expression by now familiar to us, signaling the movement of potentiation mentioned above. In the same way, the genius of humanity is the man of man, the individual to the nth power. The "transforming" translator, who must possess "the highest poetic spirit," is the one who practices that "spiritual mimic" which allows for the reproduction of the "foreign individuality," as is made clear by the sentence: "He must be . . . able to let [the poet] speak simultaneously according to his own idea and the poet's idea." The "transforming" translation is, as it were, the union and the complementation of two poetic aims, producing the potentiation of the work. One may also say: If it is to represent "the highest poetic spirit" and not an arbitrary operation, the "transforming" element of this translation can only be the *poetic aim* of the translator in as much as he has become "the artist himself." Thus Celan's or Mallarmé's translation could be presented as a "transforming" translation (though faithful to the original poet's "idea" at the same time), effectively requiring "the highest poetic spirit."

But for Novalis this is not the type of translation that possesses the "highest style"—for example, the highest rank of essence. That rank is reserved for the translation called "mythical." There are few texts of Novalis that could elucidate the meaning he gives to this term. To be sure, we know that in the same period mythology constituted one of F. Schlegel's favorite themes, and that, some years later, the *Dialogue on Poetry* mentions the possibility of the creation of a new mythology that would relieve the old one, for example, Greek mythology. During his researches, Novalis states that Greek mythology is the "translation" of a "national religion." What does this mean? In one of the "Poeticisms" fragments, he writes:

> The novel, as it were, is *free history*—the mythology of history, as it were. Shouldn't a natural mythology be possible? (Mythology here in my sense, as the free poetic invention which symbolizes reality in manifold ways, etc.).[21]

In the group of fragments called "Sophie, or: of Women," he states: "Fatum is mystified history."[22]

Myth—mystery—mystique—mystification—symbol: According to the laws of the *Encyclopedia*, these terms are convertible, and refer to the same Romantic operation, the "elevation to the state of mystery."

Mythical translation is that translation which raises the original to the state of symbol, in other words, to the state of "image-of-itself," of absolute image (without referent). Let us take the two examples of Greek mythology and the Madonna, as distant as they may be from translation in the ordinary sense.

Greek mythology would be that "free history," that "free poetic invention" that transforms an historical given into a pure system of symbols: the religion of the ancient Greeks. It would produce a "text" in which the essential of this religion, for example, its ideal web, would appear. And the Madonna? Novalis speaks of the "modern Madonna," for example, the one he admired at the Dresden museum with his friends. This Madonna in effigy certainly refers to the historical Madonna of historical religion, but she is its purified figure, its image. This image, astronomically removed from the actual Virgin of Catholic dogma, is symbol of itself, shining in its own light. It is not the allegory, the sign of another thing, but it rather refers to an ideal. In Kantian terms, it is the "sensible schema" of an idea, not the representation of a real being. In this way it is celebrated in the fifteenth of Novalis's "Spiritual Songs":

> I see you in a thousand images,
> Mary, sweetly expressed,
> But none of them could paint you
> As my soul glimpses you.[23]

That this Madonna is literally "elevated to the state of mystery" is also shown by "Christendom or Europe":

> The veil is for the Virgin what the spirit is for the body; it is the indispensable organ whose folds form the letter of its sweet annunciation; the infinite play of its folds is like a cipher-music.[24]

F. Schlegel also mentions the Madonna in his *Athenäum* fragments:

> Christ has now been repeatedly deduced by a priori methods: but shouldn't the Madonna have as much right to be an original, eternal, and necessary ideal, if not of pure, then at least of male and female reason?[25]

The word *ideal* recurs in both authors. In the text from "Blüthenstaub" Novalis defines it as the "pure and accomplished" character. This character only *appears* through the mythical operation, for example, by that which we have learned to call "romantization." This operation is higher than that of the "transforming" translation, because it unites the poetic and the philosophical spirit. In mythical translation, the Idea manifests itself in the Image, becomes Image of itself. Raphaël's Madonna is not the imitation of the real Madonna, but the presentation of the pure Idea of the Madonna. Thus, here we find again, though in a different language, what Novalis expressed in his letter—with this difference that now there no longer exists a perfect model of this type of translation, not even A. W. Schlegel's Shakespeare. Not only is the latter's work not mentioned, Novalis even gives another example of mythical translation: the literary and artistic critics who aim to extract the "tendency" of the works and to grasp their necessity rather than to describe them empirically (or judge them).

The fragment from "Blüthenstaub," then, goes further than the letter to A. W. Schlegel, even as it develops the same thematic. The "transcendental" translation pushes the empirical translation more and more into the background. As such, it becomes a universal operation: "Everything can be translated in these three ways." The view Novalis gives of the middle ages in "Christendom or Europe," and of the king and queen of Prussia in "Faith and Love" are also, beyond a doubt, mythical translations of historical realities. They do not represent these realities as they are, but their "pure and perfected character."

But to the extent that translation is subjected to such a broadening, it tends to lose all specificity and to be confounded with other notions, such as the "elevation to the state of mystery," the "symbol," the "mystification," etc. In the whole of Romantic thinking, it even tends to be displaced and repressed by these concepts.[26] In fact, when we are looking for that which constitutes a theory of translation in their theory of criticism, of poetry, and of the *Encyclopedia*, we are certainly not inventing a fiction, but we, too, present the "pure and perfected character" of what this thinking eventually preferred to call by different names, and to approach from those angles in which its specificity disappears.

Nevertheless, this speculative theory determines in its way the translating practice of A. W. Schlegel and L. Tieck, even if their principles are of necessity more concrete. It does not determine them directly in their methods of translation, but it governs their deep vision of poetry and the very constitution of *their field of translations*. Indeed, the works selected by both translators correspond to those designated by romantic criticism as the models, or the sketches, of the "poetry of poetry," the "transcendental poetry," the "universal progressive" poetry, and the "poetry of the infinite." If one adds to this that these translations are all accompanied by corresponding critiques, it may be concluded that they fulfill the same function as the latter: to accumulate "materials" for the literature to come, and for the theory which is inseparable from it. As F. Schlegel writes:

> Such a theory of the novel would have to be a novel itself, which would reproduce each eternal tone of fantasy in a fantastic way. . . .
> Then creatures of the past would live in new figures, Dante's holy shadow would rise from its underworld, Laura would walk heavenly

before us, and Shakespeare would converse pleasantly with Cervantes;—there Sancho would again jest with Don Quixote.[27]

Let us now see how the connection between poetry and translation appears with another Romantic, who certainly received the impulses from the *Athenäum*, but no longer shared its speculative enthusiasm: Clemens Brentano.

Godwi, published in 1801, draws upon the novels of the time (by Goethe, Jean Paul, Tieck, etc.) in a parodic and subjective way. In the text we are about to quote, three characters are engaged in a conversation on the essence of Romanticism: Godwi himself; Maria, the poet-narrator (who speaks in the first person); and finally Haber, the "rationalist" translator of Ariosto and Tasso.[28]

It is Maria who opens this long conversation:

"Everything that stands as a mediator between our eyes and an object to be seen, bringing us closer to the distant object, but also communicating something of itself to it, is romantic."

"Then what is there between Ossian and his presentations," said Haber.

"If we knew more," I replied, "than that a harp is between them, and this harp between his great heart and his melancholy, we would know the history of the singer and of his tune."

Godwi added: "So the romantic is a perspective, or rather the color of the glass and the determination of the object by the shape of the glass."

"According to you, then, the romantic is formless," said Haber; "I rather thought it would have more form than the ancient, in such a way that its form by itself, even without content, would have a vigorous impact."

"I do not know," I continued, "what you understand by form. Frankly, the unformed has often more form than the formed can endure; and in order to bring out this surplus, we would only have to add a few curves to the Venus to make her romantic. But I call form the right limitation of something thought."

"So I could say," Godwi added, "that form itself cannot have a form, but is only the determined ceasing of a thought expanding equally toward all sides starting from one point. This something thought might be in stone, sound, color, word, or thought."

"An example suddenly comes to my mind," I replied; "you will excuse the fact that it is the so very ordinary allegory of the vanity of the world. Imagine a soap bubble, whose inner space would be its thought; its extension, then, would be the form. Yet the soap bubble has a moment in its extension when its appearance and its aspect are in perfect harmony; then its form is related to the matter, to the interior diameter in all directions, and to the light in such a way that it offers a beautiful sight. All the colors around shine in it, and the soap bubble itself is at the ultimate point of its perfection. Then it tears itself loose from the straw and floats through the air. That is what I understand by the word form, a limitation that only contains an idea, and says nothing of itself. All the rest is unform, either too much or too little."

Here Haber replied: "So Tasso's *Liberated Jerusalem* is an unform—"

"Dear Haber, I said, "you will annoy me if you do not tell me whether you do not want to understand me or do not want to annoy me."

"Do not be annoyed," he replied, "for I do neither the one nor want the other; but I am not content with your unform of the romantic, and I confront you precisely with Tasso, because I know him, and because unfortunately I feel only too strongly how clear and determined his form is. I feel it all the more because I am playing with the idea of translating him one day."

"That you feel it too strongly, is proof for me," I said; "pure form is not felt too much; and mind you do not make the reader of your translation feel it too much, for in my opinion every pure and beautiful work of art that merely presents its object is easier to translate than a romantic one that not only designates its object, but adds a coloring to this designation, for to the translator of the romantic, the form of the presentation becomes itself a work of art, which he must translate. Take for instance Tasso, precisely; what does the new rhythmical translator have to struggle with? Either he must possess Tasso's own religiousness, seriousness, and ardor, in which case we heartily implore him rather to invent himself; or if he does not possess all this, or if he is a Protestant, body and soul, then he must first translate himself into the Catholic, and thus, again, he must translate himself historically into Tasso's mentality and language; he must translate an awful lot before he comes to the actual translation, for romantic poets possess more than mere presentation, they also have themselves, and strongly so."

"But that is not the case with the pure poets," said Haber, "since they are still somewhat further removed from us."

"No," I replied; "even though they are somewhat further removed from us, and precisely because this great distance abolishes every medium between us and them that could reflect them impurely to us. The condition of your translator is mere scientificity in language and object, he should merely translate the language; in this way his translation must relate to the original like the plaster casting to the marble. We are all equally removed from them, and we shall read the same in them, since they only present, but their presentation has no color because they are form. . . ."

"The rhymes alone," I continued, "can only be rendered in our language as doggerel verse, and yet, you see, precisely these rhymes are already such a form of form. How would you produce all that? The

Italian rhyme is the tone on the basis of which the whole is played. Will your rhyme have the same tone? I do not believe you are the kind of translator who can translate from all keys and registers for another instrument, without the song . . . becoming blind, like a magnificent eagle with a paper bag over its head sitting stupidly in a corner."

Godwi laughed and said: "A question for a recipe book—how to translate an Italian eagle into German?—Answer—*Recipe* a paper bag, pull it over its head, and then the wild creature has been translated into a tamed one, it will no longer bite you; yet it is the same eagle, translated right faithfully."

"Right faithfully," I said, "for it sits among the German hens, right patiently and faithfully like a domestic animal."

"Every language," I continued, "is like a particular instrument; only those that are most similar can be translated into one another. But one music is music itself, and not a composition from the player's mood (*Gemüt*) and his type of instrument. It is created there where the instrument, the musician, and the music touch one another in equal excellence. Many translations, especially those from the Italian, will always be sounds from the concertina or the wind instruments translated for clanging and blaring instruments. . . ."

"Then you must consider Dante completely untranslatable," said Haber.

"Precisely this one less than others," I continued, "just like Shakespeare. These two poets dominate their language as well as their age. They have more passion than words and more words than tones. They bear themselves like giants in their languages, and their language cannot constrict them, since language as such is barely sufficient for their spirit, and they can well be transposed again to another smart soil. They can thrive, but a Samson must have done it. They will always be like transplanted oak trees, whose minor roots must be cut away to put them in a new furrow. But most of the other poets (*Sänger*) have very peculiar manners, which reside in the nature of their instrument; they are plays of sounds, like Shakespeare's play of words. Plays of sounds cannot be translated, though plays of words can."

"How did we get started on translations?" said Godwi.

"Because of Fiamette's romantic song," I said. "The romantic itself is a translation."

At this point the dark room lit up, a mild green luster shone from the water basin I described.

"Look, how romantic, just the way you defined it. The green glass is the medium of the sun."[29]

We have here an echo, already deformed and confused, of the romantic theory of the work: contrary to "classical" works, defined by pure form, for example, by the pure presentation of a content, "romantic" works are characterized by that "coloring" which inserts itself between our perception and the thing represented. That "coloring," in the case of a work of language, is obviously the "sonority" of the words (rhymes, alliterations, all that is commonly called the "color" of words). The romantic work musicalizes the medium of representation, and thus confuses its objectal content: At its limit, it is only the radiance, the pure resonance of the color of the medium. To romanticize is to color the form, as the green does in the water basin mentioned in the text. One recognizes here the theories of the *Athenäum*, but outside of the symbolic-abstract element specific to it, with the result that the romantic works brutally fall into the untranslatable—though with this paradox that the confusion of the form by its sonorous color is itself interpreted as a "translation." It is uncertain if Brentano himself recognized the scope of his sentence: "The romantic itself is a translation," a sentence which so exactly echos Novalis's. Or rather, this sentence is the distant echo of the deeper truth of romantic art—an echo isolated in the text. There is here a certain difficulty in connecting this statement to those dealing with poetic translation, whose emphasis is rather on the untranslatability of the Romantic work. To be sure, "for the translator of the romantic work, the form of the presentation itself becomes a work of art that he has to translate." But if this form is constituted by its sound and its color, how does one translate it? Because, for Brentano, this sonorous and colored element is precisely that which could not pass into an other language. That this is a real problem is attested to by the allusion to the Italian poets, as well as Brentano's own poetry. His two famous verses:

> O Stern und Blume, Geist und Kleid,
> Lieb, Leid und Zeit und Ewigkeit![30]

obviously do not allow a translation, at least a literal one, without losing their aura. Now, these lines are a splendid example—one of the rarest—of German Romantic poetry. Nevertheless, and this is the ambiguity of Brentano and late Romanticism, these lines are posed, as it were, on a divide: Is it a series of pure sounds whose sonorities, stimulating one another, produce an effectively untranslatable musical effect—or is it an "association" in which sound and sense mutually infinitize each other, as Novalis would have it? Both, undoubtedly, but Novalis's "association" goes well beyond the mere musicality of a poem: This musicality is *a priori* worked upon in such a way that it no longer rests simply on the fortune of natural language. It is not fortuitous, whereas Brentano's poem, in all its "magic," is like a splendid find, a magnificent throw of the dice played with signifiers and signifieds which is far from abolishing coincidence. It is rather a risky and momentaneous game with coincidence. And there the two Romanticisms are separated, there the translatable work is separated from the untranslatable work—untranslatable because it is not a *work*. In his way, Brentano notices the difference when he opposes translatable poetry (Dante and Shakespeare), whose translatability opens itself in the space that separates their "spirit" from their "language," and Italian poetry, which belongs to natural language in such a way that it no longer authorizes any translation that would not be a treason. The distinction is undoubtedly important, even though one may doubt its validity for Shakespeare and Dante, and even though one may doubt as well that it would be easier to translate plays of words than "plays of sounds."

This passage from *Godwi* is highly significant, for Brentano, so to speak, confuses the cards of Jena Romanticism in it. On the one hand he reformulates its essential intuitions: Poetry is translation; the translator must translate himself (Novalis's "spiritual mimic"); the work is defined by its musicality and its non-objectivity. Brentano's images are significant here, images in which the figure of the *void* (the transparent water basin which is the medium of the sun, the soap bubble) recurs incessantly. These almost ironic images are derived from F. Schlegel's and Novalis's best intuitions on the empty and intransitive work that can capture the distant. But the theme of musicality, though also inherited from the *Athenäum*, does even more than confuse the cards, it *inverts* them: a passage from abstract, mathematical, and composed musicality whose model is the "fugue," etc., to the musicality of the allegedly popular song, the *Lied*—in short, that sensory and sensual musicality of which the early Romanticism, at least in principle, prohibited itself any use. And immediately there appears the theme of untranslatable poetry, pure avalanche of beautiful sonorities, undoubtedly a very ancient theme, but it now takes all its force from placing poetry in the shadow of music, in that empty space between genuine poetry of art and genuine popular poetry where the essential of what we call Romanticism develops and proliferates in lyrical or novelistic almost-works, sometimes for the better, often for the worst. The same leveling of the problematic could be observed with regard to the "fantastic" and the "dream."

That the theory of the translatability of the work is suddenly inverted into the theory of its untranslatability is perhaps an inevitable dialectical turning-back by which late Romanticism seeks to affirm in its way the absolute autonomy of poetry; as in early Romanticism, this autonomy is sought beyond natural language, in the "ineffable" domain of music. And it is no coincidence that late Romantic poems have sometimes been "translated" into music in the nineteenth century, thus gaining a renown their own "musicality" could not have assured them of. To be sure, the theory of the *Athenäum* contains the seed of this reversal, just as it carries in itself *in nucleo* all the avatars of the history of modern poetry.

But at least we had to point out this strange destiny by which those who affirmed the *a priori* translatability of literature gave birth to a *poetics of untranslatability*, a far less innocent poetics than it appears to be at first sight, since in the final analysis it can only be *a regressive poetics of the incommunicable. In the absence of any positive theory of natural language*, this poetics necessarily imposes itself. The hostility the Romantics had toward a Voss, despite all their admiration for him, is understandable when one reads what he declared to Humboldt:

That which cannot be expressed in human language cannot be true.[31]

Nevertheless, one of Brentano's intuitions remains, and it would be desirable to take it up again, though transformed: the distinction between works connected to the natural language (which wrongly appear to be untranslatable) and those that attempt to establish a certain distance from it (and that would be more easily translatable). We shall come back to this in the end. The untranslatable, for its part, can only be *willed*: In the (relative) untranslatability of late romantic poetry there is a will to be closed upon itself, to incommunicability, for example, a will to escape from the domain of language, a will that goes through the idolizing of music and also through an essentially inauthentic relation to the mother tongue, sometimes bordering on folklorism. This will constitutes one of the imbalances peculiar to German Romanticism, which made it into something "sick" for Goethe.

8

TRANSLATION AS A
CRITICAL MOVEMENT

We now approach the issue mentioned throughout the previous chapter: the covering over of the concept of translation by that of criticism in F. Schlegel and Novalis. It is obvious that at least two reasons preside over this theoretical obfuscation: (1) If the center of the *Athenäum*'s poetological preoccupations was the Copernican revolution of poetry, and if this revolution necessarily passed through a critique (in the Kantian sense), literary criticism obviously tends to move into first place with them; and (2) The starting-point of Romantic reflection, at least with the Schlegel brothers, is the philological and critical activity, raised little by little to the level of a philosophical practice.[1] Novalis himself, whose formation was different, defined the "philological" as everything relating to the textual and the written. Hence two meanings of the word criticism—in one case, transcendental criticism, reflection of poetry on itself, logology; in the second, criticism of texts, i.e., literary criticism. We could speak of generalized criticism and restriced criticism, just like we did with translation. But here the two critical movements tend toward the—obviously ideal—point where they become identical, that is to say, where it seems *impossible to distinguish literature and criticism*. In effect, the literature to come carries its own criticism within it; as F. Schlegel tells us, it tries "now to mix, now to fuse together poetry and prose, genius and criticism."[2] But literary criticism, as a genre and as a discipline, carries out a reverse movement of poetization:

121

Poetry can only be criticized by poetry. A judgment about art which is not itself a work of art . . . has no civil rights in the realm of art.[3]

Novalis, after his fashion, corroborates his friend's statement:

He who is not capable of making poems will also judge them only negatively. There belongs to genuine criticism the capacity to produce oneself the products to be criticized. Only taste judges negatively.[4]

This is what the romantic texts repeat ad nauseam, and which the art of the fragment is, in part, supposed to realize: to unite reflection and poetic form. This is an entanglement that has become familiar to us in the twentieth century, but one that remains complex. For, if the immanent criticism of the work appears on one side as the condition for the possibility of its external criticism, one might as well say, as F. Schlegel does not hesitate to do, that the latter, *opening the very field of literature itself with its "fragments of the future," constitutes the condition for the possibility of the work to come.*

But it is only possible if the concept of criticism undergoes a fundamental change of meaning. To criticize a work is no longer to express a series of judgments on it on the basis of aesthetic rules or sensibility, aimed at informing or enlightening the public. It is, as Novalis said in his fragment on mythical translation, to liberate the pure Idea of the work, its "pure and perfected character," to accomplish this act of "spiritual mimic" which is the foundation of any understanding of the literary work. And it is true enough that with F. Schlegel criticism becomes "divinatory," for example, an act of comprehension. F. Schlegel expresses all this most clearly in his essays on Lessing:

. . . not so much to judge as to understand and explain. That in a work of art one must not only feel the beautiful passages, but grasp the impression of the whole. . . . And I think . . . that one understands the work completely only in the system of all the artist's works. . . . So, too, the particular in art . . . must lead to the immeasurable Whole. . . . If you want to attain the Whole . . . you may confidently assume that you will not find a natural limit anywhere . . . before having reached the center. This center is the organism of all the arts and all the sciences, the law and the history of this organism. This doctrine of formation, this physics of fantasy and art, could well be a science of its own, which I would call *encyclopedia*; but this science does not yet exist. . . . Either the source of objective laws for any positive criticism is there, or it is nowhere. If this is the case . . . true criticism cannot take notice of works which contribute nothing to the development of art and science; indeed, a true critique of that which does not stand in a relation to that organism of culture and genius, is not even possible.

. . .

If you want to try and *understand* authors or works, i.e., construct them genetically in relation to that great organism of all art and all science. . . .

The essence of higher art and form lies in the *relation to the whole*. . . . Therefore all works are One Work, all arts One Art, all poems One Poem. . . . Every poem, every work, must signify the whole, signify it actually and effectively.[5]

To *understand* a work, then, is to place it in the Whole of art and literature, to show its symbolic essence, which is to signify (*Bedeuten*) the Whole and the very Idea of art. It is to liberate the "infinite meaning" of the work. The criticism that carries out this operation can only be "positive," for example, attach itself only to those works that, in themselves, contribute to the realization of the Idea of art. Negative criticism, for its part, is of the order of the polemical. In another text on Lessing, F. Schlegel takes up the same theme:

It was not difficult to show the necessity of criticism for all literature. But the concept of criticism that was constantly given to it as foundation, was the historical concept of criticism. Only criticism as it existed until now was spoken of. But could there not be an entirely different one? . . . This is not only possible, it is also probable, for the following reason. For the Greeks, literature had already existed for a long time, it was almost at its end, when criticism began. This is not so for the Moderns, at least for us Germans. Here criticism and literature are born at the same time, yes, the former was almost born earlier; we had a knowledge . . . of foreign works, even of the most insignificant ones, before having any knowledge of ours. And still today, I do not know if we should pride ourselves more rightfully for having a criticism rather than a literature. Anyway, with the modification of this relation comes the possibility and the idea of a criticism of an entirely different kind. A criticism that would not be so much the commentary of an already existing, finished, and withered literature, as the organon of a literature still to be achieved, to be formed, even to be begun. An organon of literature, therefore a criticism that would not only explain and conserve, but that would be productive itself, at least indirectly. . . . Hence the necessity and the idea of a science of its own that seeks to determine the unity and the difference of all the higher sciences and arts.[6]

A crucial text, in which F. Schlegel defines what could be called *the Copernican revolution of criticism*: to become the condition for the possibility of the literature to come. This revolution runs parallel to the one by which poetry constitutes itself as "poetry of poetry," for example, as critical poetry. These two movements are not only parallel; they tend to collapse into one another. Thus, as we have seen, F. Schlegel states that the theory of the novel (i.e., the formal mode of realization of romantic poetry) must be a novel itself.

The critical operation is that comprehension by which, says W. Benjamin, "the limitation of the individual work of art is methodically related to the infinity of art."[7] It opens the work unto its own infinity, it is the same movement by which the work becomes "faithful to itself, entirely homogeneous, and nonetheless exalted above itself."[8] It is in this sense that F. Schlegel can add:

No literature can endure through time without a criticism.[9]

Positioned before and after the work, criticism is the agent of its potentiation. Thus F. Schlegel's essay on *Wilhelm Meister* considers itself *Übermeister* or "mythical version" of this work. "Mythical," because it relates it methodically to the Idea of which it is only the imperfect realization; because it strives to liberate this "inifinite signification" which marks its symbolical meaning. Of the realist dimension of Goethe's novel, which would connect it, for instance, to the eighteenth-century English novelistic tradition, Schlegel's criticism has no idea; and when Novalis perceives that the meaning of *Wilhelm Meister* may well be sought in that direction (that of its *content*), he hastens to condemn the work in its entirety. Likewise, F. Schlegel's essay on Lessing does not examine the real Lessing, but engages the "tendencial" Lessing, for example, what Lessing conceals in terms of "fragments of the future."

Now, this movement which surpasses the work in its immediate given by connecting it to the Whole of art, is what we have already been able to describe as the movement of mythical translation (Novalis). Then how does it happen that it appears almost always only as a critical operation? Let us first note this: The category of "comprehension" is valid for both criticism and translation:

In order to translate perfectly the ancient into the modern, the translator would have to have such mastery of the latter as to be able to make everything modern; but at the same time he would have to understand antiquity so well that he would be able not just to imitate it but, if necessary, re-create it.[10]

When F. Schlegel states, in a fragment we have already quoted, that translations are "philological mimes," he includes them in the sphere of "the philological" in general, for the same reason as "notes" and "commentaries," for example, as "critical genres." Conversely, the *Athenäum* fragment 287 equates criticism and translation:

Only then do I show that I have understood an author, when I can act in his spirit; when I can translate him and transform him without diminishing his individuality.[11]

We find once again Novalis's "spiritual mimic," valid for the translator and the critic, both of whom must study a foreign text and "reconstruct" it. To be sure, in the case of the translator, the text is both *other* and *foreign*; but this distinction carries hardly any weight for the philologer-critic confronted with ancient texts. If the aim of any reconstructive mimic of the work is to bring out its "pure and perfected character," then there should be no doubt that criticism, essentially identical to translation, is superior to it, for *it is nothing but this movement of liberation raised to pure self-consciousness: work of art surpassing the work of art, quintessence*. On the other hand, translation is and remains an interlingual activity: If it tears the work from its original empiricity, it is only to plunge it again into that of an other language. To be sure, to the extent that the work torn from its mother tongue is incarnated in another language, a fulguration, as it were, happens which allows a preview of what it would be in its pure element, far from all earthly languages, in the ethereal and diaphanous language of the Spirit—an idealist perspective for which actual language is not the right medium of the Spirit, and in which Romanticism joins Hegel. But, just as for Hegel philosophy is superior to poetry, for the *Athenäum* criticism is superior to translation. This can be formulated in yet another way: transcendental criticism and empirical criticism, restricted criticism and generalized criticism, immanent criticism and external criticism tend to be united in the finished critical text which is the bringing out of the Idea of the work as well as the auto-theory of criticism and "miniature work of art."[12] Which leads to the paradoxical consequence, as W. Benjamin put it, that "in romantic art, criticism is not only possible and necessary, but their theory inevitably contains the paradox of a higher valorization of criticism than of the work."[13] The subordinate rank of translation may be deduced from the fact that, in every concrete translation, the transcendental moment, the "translation" through which the work is raised above itself, its author, its empiricity, its own language, and even above natural language, is not carried out as purely as in criticism. Made *possible* by the work structure of the work, it is not in turn transcendentally *necessary* to it. If the critical work—pushing things, with Benjamin, to the limit of the idealist dialectic—is simultaneously possible, necessary, and ontologically superior to the original literary work, according to the law that every product to the second (or nth) power is superior to one of the first power, interlingual translation turns out to be superior to its original—*but it lacks the deep necessity of criticism*. In the potentiating realm of Romantic philology, it is only a

sub-genre, even though Novalis once called the poetical-critical operation supreme "translation," no doubt carried along by a no less momentaneous "syncriticism" with A. W. Schlegel, who was then immersed in
the grandiose, but empirical, task of translating Shakespeare.

Even though it receives the same definition as criticism, translation
does not come out on the winning side. Though displaced, relegated
ontologically to the second rank (to the point where its *literary* possibilities in the field of fragmentary writing are ignored, whereas those
of criticism are not), covered over in the sense indicated above, it has
nevertheless the same field of operation as criticism: "the works that
contribute to the development of science and art," for example, as we
know, Shakespeare, Dante, Calderón, Cervantes, etc. But even there, as
Benjamin saw very well, the Romantic program of translations is hetero-
nomous, designed *a priori* by the critical program. The inevitable de-
nouement: In the absence of any theory of this interlingual and intercultural exchange of translation that was taken up by Herder, Goethe,
and Humboldt, the act of translating is inevitably crushed by the act of
poetic creation and that of critical "reconstruction."

Nevertheless, it must be emphasized that, within this idealist perspective, the Romantics were able to show the profound relation that
connects the work as work to translation (and criticism). This relation
consists in the fact that the work, by the tension which simultaneously
unites it to and separates it from language (or at another level: to the
relation of belonging and distance that connects it to language), makes
translation possible, demands it like a need of its own, and, moreover,
makes it into an historical operation full of meaning—linguistically and
culturally as well as psychologically. This relation belongs to the work as
work, whatever may be the multiplicity of relations in which the works
may stand otherwise to their languages and language in general. The
work is that linguistic production which *calls for* translation as a destiny
of its own. Let us provisionally name this call *translatability*. It is important to distinguish this notion of translatability from common translatability or the one linguistics seeks to define. The latter is a reality.
Languages are translatable, even though the space of translatability is
loaded with the untranslatable. Linguistic untranslatability lies in the
fact that all languages are different from each other, linguistic translatability in the fact that they are all language. From which it follows that,
in this domain, translatability and untranslatability remain relative
notions.

But *literary* translatability is different, though literary translation,
obviously, also knows linguistic translatability (and untranslatability). It
consists in the fact that a work, emerging as a work, is always positioned
in a certain *distance* from its language: What constitutes it as linguistic,

cultural, and literary *novelty* is precisely the space that allows its translation into another language and, at the same time, makes this translation necessary and essential; it is indeed Schlegel's "Grand Tour." In one sense, translation is exterior to the work; it may exist without it. In another sense, translation accomplishes the work, pushes it beyond itself, but this "alienation" is already prefigured in the relation to its original language. The native strangeness of the work is joined by its strangeness (effectively increased) in the foreign language. And translation is a genuine metamorphosis for the work, an actual *Veränderung*— all the more so in proportion as the latter is more faithful, more "literal." In truth, unfaithful translation simply annuls this dialectic. The theory of what is one's own and what is foreign, of the elevation to the state of mystery (to the state of strangeness, of interpenetration of the known and the unknown), as it is put forward by Novalis, refers to this movement of metamorphosis, and it is not wrong to say that the highest translations are "mythical" and "transforming." This movement by which the work becomes "mythical" is made possible by the work itself; or, in other words, *the work is that production by which translation becomes an activity full of meaning*. Which can be seen in reverse by examining what happens (or does not happen) with other translations— those that do not deal with works, whether they be literary, critical, religious, philosophical, etc., but with texts situated either in other sectors of human exchange, or at degraded levels (without pretention to a writing of their own) of those domains. In that case, translation may be or not be technically "easy"; it only encounters texts without resistance from the linguistic point of view (certainly correct texts, but without density), or "badly written" texts, for example, texts where the ordinary relation to the language is below the relation commonly accepted; texts, in the latter case, which can only be translated by a rewriting aiming to assure the transmission of meaning barely achieved by the original. In both cases, the translation is not called for by the text; it simply emerges from the necessity of exchange and communication. *It is not really significant as an act of its own*. Meaning passes, flows, for better or for worse, from one language to an other, but all that is of the order of adaptation, not of transmutation. Translation of this type of text, whether it be literal or in a more-or-less disguised form of rewriting, does not encounter any fundamental *resistance* in them. Now, the reverse happens with a work: The incommensurable resistance it opposes to its translation—a translation it simultaneously makes possible and calls for—gives it all its meaning, no less incommensurable. And in the same movement, it buries itself in and tears itself from its language, developing the very dimension of its translatability and untranslatability. Or: *The more translatable it is, the more it is untranslatable*. Such is one of the paradoxes of the work, a parallel for which could be recognized in criticism and hermeneutics.[14]

The Romantics have been able to describe this baffling reality in their own way, because they were animated by the incessant questions: What is a work? What is the meaning of this "philological" proliferation surrounding the work, as completely finished, of texts of the second degree—notes, fragments, critiques, commentaries, quotations, translations—all these circles of texts surrounding the work, before or after it, sometimes seeming to feed on it like parasites, sometimes seeming to be its extensions, surpassing the work into vertiginously infinite spaces? What are the texts that, aiming to shed light on the work, sometimes enlighten it, sometimes obscure it, and sometimes do both at the same time? What is this pluri-literature that reading breeds around the works, and that sometimes revives them? Would there not be a work, or a genre of works, that, in its infinity and its plurality, would take up in itself, already contain within itself, in an encyclopedic way, this hyper-literature of literature? Such is the chain of questions developed to the point of obsession by Jena Romanticism. To take these up again, divorcing them from the speculative sphere that is characteristic of the Romantics, such is the desire kindled—against the imaginary fascination it exerts—by their theory of literature. In this sense, to contest the theory is also to draw its intuitions outside of the domain of Idealism, to inscribe them in those of language and culture—domains which Goethe, Herder, Humboldt, and Schleiermacher have been able to approach, though without always managing to express their multiple questions with the same philosophical clout as the Romantics. The most notable among these questions is the one we have barely touched upon here: What, in the work, makes its translation possible, necessary, and full of meaning, while at the same time making it superfluous, absurd, and impossible, even as it is made into one of the major *utopias* of the literary and linguistic activity? What is the meaning, outside of the idealist dialectic, of this movement of "potentiation" which begins with the work and is continued by criticism on the one side and translation on the other? If this potentiation is indeed a "reflection," in what relation does this Romantic "reflection" stand to Goethe's "mirroring"—a mirroring in which the work gains youth, freshness, and life? Can this distance, which calls attention to the work as work and opens the space of translation, be characterized as the Romantics characterized it—by calling it a translation itself?

9

A. W. SCHLEGEL:
THE WILL TO TRANSLATE
EVERYTHING

A. W. Schlegel is probably one of the greatest German translators who has ever lived. He had a thorough knowledge the principal modern European languages—Greek, Latin, medieval French, old German, the *langues d'oc*—as well as Sanskrit, to the Western study of which he contributed decisively. The list of his translations is impressive: Shakespeare, Dante, Petrarch, Boccaccio, Calderón, Ariosto, as well as a number of lesser known Italian, Spanish, and Portuguese poets—to which must be added the *Bhagavad Gita*.

But A. W. Schlegel is not only a great polytranslator; he is an eminent philologer, educated in the school of Heyne and Bürger, a specialist (among other things) of Sanskrit and medieval literatures, from whom more "scientific" people like Bopp, Diez, or von der Hagen have learned much.

And he is also a great critic who has written numerous articles on Shakespeare, Dante, Spanish Golden Age theater, Camoëns, Goethe, Schiller, the troubadours, India, poetry, and metrics. He gave lectures in Berlin (1801) and Vienna (1808) that played an essential role not only in Germany and Austria, but also, in part due to Mme. de Staël, throughout Europe: For the first time the intuitions of German Romanticism became accessible and effective beyond the narrow circles that gave birth to them.[1] The influence of these lectures was considerable. The entire poetic and critical gospel of the nineteenth century is derived from it.

In addition, A. W. Schlegel, together with his brother Friedrich, is the founder of the journal the *Athenäum*, whose influence on the destinies of European literature and criticism is only now beginning to be measured.[2] He also produced a poetic oeuvre, though he did not seem to attach much importance to it, knowing that his true creativity lay elsewhere.

To all this must be added that A. W. Schlegel's personality goes beyond the constellation of the Jena circle, and that his sphere of action put him in contact with the entire intellectual and literary life of the age in Germany, shown by his intense, though often stormy, relations with Schiller, Goethe, Humboldt, and Schelling. Admired, flattered, but also hated because of his pointedness and his polemical gifts,[3] he greatly surpasses his brother's celebrity at the time, though he does not have the latter's critical radicality, as well as that of Novalis, of whom he has neither the speculative gift nor the poetic talent—hence his quite unjustified reputation of mundane superficiality. Because, on the one hand, if he is not sure that he has understood (but did they understand themselves?) Novalis's and Friedrich Schlegel's project of a fragmentary writing, it is because he possesses what they lack: the ability to finish, an ability manifested primarily in his translations. Because, on the other hand, he entertains a profound relation to philosophy and poetry, though articulated in another way, more social, than his brother and Novalis. F. Schlegel felt this clearly when, in 1798, he wrote to Caroline Schlegel:

> It seems to me that modern history is only beginning, and that the world is again divided in spiritual and temporal people. You, Wilhelm, Henriette, and August, are children of the century. We, Hardenberg [Novalis], Dorothea, and myself, are the spiritual.[4]

As Marianne Thalmann indicates, A. W. Schlegel's oeuvre shows a progressive slipping: Translation is gradually put aside by criticism, and criticism is gradually supplanted by philology and comparatist studies. To be sure, A. W. Schlegel does not abandon any of these three activities, but the center of gravity of his interests is displaced, in a movement that goes *grosso modo* from the pure literary passion to the pure scholarly passion. The equivalent of this movement is found in his brother as well, showing that both belong to that modern "twin figure" formed by literature and philology, according to Michel Foucault.

But it is also clear that Schlegel the critic and philologer is rooted in Schlegel the translator. It is in the field of translation that he labors, creates, develops his entire stature; there he forms his poetic intuitions, and there, finally, he occupies a place *of his own* with regard not only to the other Romantics, but also to other intellectual personalities of the time. He is fundamentally a translator, which neither Goethe, nor Hölderlin, nor Humboldt, nor Voss, nor Schleiermacher, nor Tieck are. Behind the critic, the lecturer, the scholar, it is the man harnessed to the hard task of translating who speaks.

To be sure, this order may be reversed in turn, and it may be said as well that, behind Schlegel the translator, there is the critic and the philologer to guide his empirical choices. In the final analysis, A. W. Schlegel represents *the unity of the three figures* which, once again, sets him apart from all his contemporary translators. And this explains why he was able to propose, in a still occasional and episodic manner, a theory of translation that is above all a theory of *poetic language*.

Here, everything begins with the translation of Shakespeare, suggested by his teacher Bürger, first together with him, then on his own. The project of a *poetic* translation of Shakespeare—for, in 1796, there obviously existed numerous translations of the English playwright, most of them in prose, and best known among them the one by Wieland.[5] In an article published in the journal *Die Horen* in the same year, entitled "Something on William Shakespeare at the occasion of *Wilhelm Meister*," A. W. Schlegel, for his part, proposes right from the start to make a translation of Shakespeare that would be both faithful and poetic. The poem, he says, must be rendered

> as it is, the same way lovers do not want to be deprived of their sweethearts' freckles.[6]

Which means two things: on the one hand, a scrupulous respect for the English text, even in its "faults" and "obscurities," and the refusal to modify, embellish, and emend it, in particular there where it shocks the contemporary sensibility;[7] on the other hand, an effort to respect the metrics where the original is in verse.[8]

Demands which today may seem normal and elementary, but which did not appear so at the time, and which collided head on with the redoubtable problems that the translation of Shakespeare had always posed.

To render Shakespeare in the manifold registers of his language—rhetorical, poetic, philosophical, political, popular, etc.—is an immense task in itself. Moreover, his is a work designed for the theater, therefore having a particular orality. The poetic translation of Shakespeare must be both readable and audible, and it must be usable on a stage. The fact that Schlegel's translation is still used in German theaters today shows it has been able to solve this problem in a certain way. And A. W. Schlegel, for that matter, was perfectly aware of this.[9]

But this translation is itself based on a critical rereading of Shakespeare. Shakespeare is not a crude and formless genius (whose forms could be neglected or improved while translating, the only important thing being his "vision"), but an

> abyss of marked intention, self-consciousness, and reflection.[10]

In short, a poet who weighs his words and his works. This rereading refers to a barely older text by A. W. Schlegel, "On Poetry, Metrics, and Language" (1795), in which he puts forward an entire theory of poetry. Poetry is first and foremost a system of linguistic, metrical, and rhythmical forms manipulated by the poet with a superior know-how. In the final analysis, the poem

> consists only of verses; the verses of words; the words of syllables, the syllables of individual sounds. These latter must be examined in their harmony or dysharmony; the syllables must be counted, measured, weighed; the words must be chosen; the verses, finally, must be gracefully ordered and joined together. But that is not all. It has been remarked that the ear is pleasantly tickled when the same sound endings of words recur at determined intervals. The poet must also search for that, often exploring the domain of language from one end to the other . . . for the sake of a single ending. . . . You shall make verses in the sweat of your brow! You shall engender poems in pain![11]

This conception is found again and again in A. W. Schlegel, and it is at the heart of his practice. Thus, he states in one of his lectures:

> metre (*Silbenmaaß*) should not be just an external ornament . . . but it ranks among the essential and original prerequisites of poetry. Furthermore, since all metrical forms have a definite meaning, and their necessary character in a particular language may very well be demonstrated . . . one of the first principles of the art of translation is that, as far as the nature of a language allows, a poem should be recreated in the same meter.[12]

And in his *Lectures on Art and Literature*:

> From its birth, language is the primal matter of poetry; metrics (in the broadest sense) is the form of its reality.[13]

One might think that this is a somewhat brief and formal theory of poetry that has only very little to do with the principal intuitions of Romanticism. But that would be a mistake: The apology of form in poetry leads precisely to a theory of the *universality of poetic forms*, which is the exact *complement* of the theory of language and translation of F. Schlegel and Novalis.[14]

For A. W. Schlegel the rhythmic and metrical work of the poet ("You shall make verses in the sweat of your brow!") is necessarily of the same order of the "facture" mentioned by Novalis: It "potentiates" natural language—for which A. W. Schlegel has no more sympathy than his peers—and imposes on it the yoke of laws that result first and foremost from the poet's action. Which is exactly what he stated in his afterword to Tieck, quoted in our Introduction, and reiterated in his lectures on classical literature:

> We can . . . translate from all the most important languages into ours. Yet I do not want this to be considered an advantageous feature which just happens to be present in the composition of our language. . . . all it takes is resolve and hard work.[15]

As the *Lectures on Art and Literature* say, language itself is born from an analogous labor:

> Language is always born from the bosom of poetry. Language is not a product of nature, but a reproduction of the human spirit, which consigns to it . . . the entire mechanism of its representations. Thus, in poetry, something already formed is formed again; and its ability to take form is as unlimited as the spirit's ability to return to itself by reflections always carried to the higher power.[16]

There we have a familiar word: *reflection*. But if language is already originarily *poiesis*, poetry—in the sense of *Dichtkunst*, the art of poetry—is only its reflective doubling. Thus, A. W. Schlegel does not hesitate to take up again, transforming and in a certain way trivializing, his brother's concept of "poetry of poetry":

> It has been found strange and incomprehensible to speak of poetry of poetry; and yet, for the one who has a notion of the internal organism of spiritual existence, it is very simple for the same activity that produced something poetic to be turned on its result. Yes, it can be said without exaggeration that all poetry is actually poetry of poetry; because it already presupposes language, whose invention depends on poetic aptitude, and which is itself a poem by the whole of humanity, a poem in perpetual becoming, in perpetual metamorphosis, never finished.[17]

All this text does is to apply to language the terminology of the *Athenäum* fragment 116, devoted to "universal progressive poetry."

But the consequence of such a position is that any language, just like any man for Novalis, is "transformable without measure," and that the *forms* produced by poetic labor are transferable to another language to a certain extent. To the labor of the *production* of poetic forms corresponds that of their *reproduction* (translation). And because language is a work, "facture," and not "nature," translation is one of the aspects of the process by which language becomes more and more *work and form*: *Bildung*. Thus, the theory of the artificiality of language and its forms grounds the possibility and the necessity of poetic translation. If it is possible to translate these forms only up to a certain point, it is obvious (and A. W. Schlegel, as a "practitioner," knows it better than anyone else) *empirically* that translation incessantly runs into limits: The difficulties encountered are of the order of the translator's limitations, of his language and his culture, of the complexity of the solutions to be found in order to render this or that text, this or that metric.[18] In the worst case, they refer to the existence of that natural basis of language—mimetic, onomatopoeic—which poetry as such seeks to surpass. Which is to say (precisely in Novalis's sense): The more poetic a text is, the more it is theoretically translatable and worthy of being translated.

This theory, then, of which we offer only an outline here and which, for A. W. Schlegel, is connected without a problem to a personal awareness of the problems of translation,[19] complements the theory of *Kunstsprache*. To be sure, it does not go so far as to affirm that the translation is ontologically superior to the original, but it starts from the same bases, and provides the theory of natural language with what it lacks: a theory of the metrical forms of poetry.

The principle of the transferability of forms, which are considered the essence of poetry, does by no means entail, as Pannwitz believes, that the translator "italianizes" the German language by, for instance, using "Italian rhymes." It only transplants into its language a form which, even though it is effectively of Italian origin, tends to transcend this origin by its very nature—tends to be a kind of *poetic universal*. The translator, rather, is confronted with a multiplicity of foreign metrical forms which he aims to introduce into his mother tongue so as to expand it poetically. The formational dialectic of *Bildung* here takes on the meaning of a radical cosmopolitanism: The German language, too poor and too crude, must call upon foreign metrics to become more and more a *Kunstsprache*. It follows that any translation is and can only be a *polytranslation*. There is no privileged domain for it,[20] nor any taboo from a linguistic or literary point of view. We shall see below how Romantic polytranslation is defined. Let us simply state for the moment that it is distinct from Goethe's diversity in that it does by no means aim at a concrete cultural communication through the horizon of languages and works: it only deals with a world of absolutized and indefinitely interchangeable poetic universals, a world similar to the one of Novalis's *Encyclopedia*.

That all poetry, by virtue of its formal essence, is translatable, is a formidable discovery, an epoch-making event in the history of translation, and A. W. Schlegel is well aware of it. Novalis proudly stated in his "Blüthenstaub":

the art of writing has not yet been invented, but it is about to be.[21]

He likewise can affirm in the afterword to his translation of *Orlando furioso*, addressed to Tieck:

> Only a many-sided receptivity for foreign national poetry, which must, if possible, ripen and grow to the point of universality, makes progress in the faithful reproduction of poems possible. I believe we are on the way to invent the true art of poetic translation; this fame had been reserved for the Germans.[22]

He can even quote, alluding to the translation of *Don Quixote* that Tieck had just finished, Cervantes's famous lines on translation, stating they have now been surpassed:

> It seems to me that in translating from one language into another, provided it is not one of the queen languages, Greek and Latin, one does precisely like the one watching the tapestry of Flanders against the grain: the figures are still visible in it, but they are filled with threads that obscure them, so that they cannot be seen with the luster of the place.[23]

This is exactly what F. Schlegel expressed in his *Dialogue on Poetry* when he said that "to translate the poets and to render their rhythm is an art." This "art" is the union of the speculative theory of poetry/translation and the literary theory of the universal poetry/metric form. This union makes possible the "logological" revolution of translation, and A. W. Schlegel's letter to Tieck—from translator to translator—is its modest manifesto.

But if *all poetry is translatable*, one can now *translate everything, get started on a program of total translation*. In the same afterword, A. W. Schlegel proudly states to Tieck:

> My intention is to be able to translate everything poetically in its form and its particularity, whatever name it may have: Ancient and Modern, classical works of art and national products of nature. I cannot guarantee that I will not enter into your Spanish domain, yes, I would have occasion to learn Sanskrit and other oriental languages in a living way in order to captivate, if possible, the breath and the tone of their chants. One might call this decision heroic, if it were voluntary; but unfortunately, I cannot look upon my neighbor's poetry without coveting it with all my heart, and so I am caught in a continual poetic adultery.[24]

It is impossible not to perceive in this text the same omnipotent enthusiasm that animated Novalis in his "Dialogue" and in the fragment on "wanting everything"[25] (or, rather, that animates the entire Jena Romanticism). The *Encyclopedia* wants to poetize *all* the sciences; Romantic poetry wants to embrace *all* the genres in its "arabesques";

Schlegel's translation, for its part, wants to translate *everything*, the Ancient and the Modern, the classical and the natural, the Western and the oriental. The bookish Don Juanism of Novalis's "Dialogue" is matched by the "adultery" of the romantic translator who does not know, cannot know, any limits to his equally encyclopedic desire of translation. Rather than *polytranslation*, we should speak here of *omnitranslation*. To translate everything, that is the essential task of the true translator: It is the pure drive of infinitized translation, the pure desire to translate everything and no matter what.

But there is a difference with F. Schlegel and Novalis: Their "fragments of the future" remain mere projects, whereas A. W. Schlegel's project is realized,[26] and exactly along the programmatic axis announced in the afterword to Tieck.[27] A unique success in the history of Romanticism, even if, as we have seen, it remains connected entirely to the speculative and critical projects of the *Athenäum* by its very desire for completeness. "To translate everything" is to translate those works, past or foreign, that carry the seed of the literature to come: the works that belong to the "Roman" space of which we spoke in Chapter 3, and those that belong to the "oriental" space.[28] A. W. Schlegel does not translate contemporaries, and few Greeks. At the evening of his life, he states outright:

> I am indifferent to contemporary literature, I am only enthused by the antediluvial literature.[29]

This calls for two remarks. In the first place, to the extent that translated works seem to represent both the prefiguration and the quintessence of romantic art, the monologic principle is at work down to the choice of the texts to translate: Romantic translation only translates Romantic texts, only the "same." The experience of the foreign as foreign is foreign to them. Again the limits of *Bildung* as relation to alterity are obvious: The "own" only seeks itself on its excentric journeys, its "Grand Tours." It is only ever centrifugal in order to be more centripetal—a limit inscribed also in the theory of "wanting everything:" I am everything—everything is me—there is no radical *other*.

In the second place, it must be said that, *from the Romantic point of view*, the accusation of a selectivity infatuated with the past, formulated by Goethe, Nietzsche, and Strich, does not really apply to the project of the *Athenäum*. First of all (and it is impossible to develop this point here), Romanticism does not know any past that is not also future; for Romanticism, both the past and the future derive their equal dignity from the fact that they constitute the dimensions of the "distant" as the place of all plenitudes. In the face of this "distant," the present is the nearness that must be transformed; it is deprived of all positivity. The romantic infatuation with the past is also a futurism, and even the source of all modern futurisms.[30]

Further, the selectivity of the *Athenäum* is not arbitrary and not limiting: *Only* those works are criticized and translated that contribute "to the development of science and art," but in fact, the rest is only "negative," only "false tendency."[31] The "wanting everything" is not contradicted by the principle of selectivity: Only the works that "signify" the Whole are criticized and translated. The "false tendency" is not part of the whole.

It would be interesting to compare this desire to translate everything with the polytranslational passion that consumed modern translators like, for instance, Armand Robin. He is a multilingual translator and, moreover, highly "transforming." In his case, the polytranslational impulse is linked to a polyglot drive and to a wounded relation with the French language (his mother tongue being a Breton dialect, Fissel):

> Language, be all languages for me!
> Fifty languages, world of one voice!
>
> The heart of man, I want to learn it in Russian, Arabic, Chinese.
> For the voyage I make from you to me
> I want the visa
> Of thirty languages, thirty sciences.
>
> I am not satisfied, I do not yet know the cries of men in Japanese!
>
> I give for a Chinese word the meadows of my youth,
> The wash-house where I felt so tall.[32]

In another poem, Robin links this quest of languages to that of the true language:

> With grand gestures,
> I have for four years thrown my soul into all the languages,
> I have sought, free and mad, all the places of truth,
> Above all I have sought the dialects where man was not tamed.
> I have been on a quest for truth in all the languages.
>
> The martyrdom of my people was barred from me
>   In French.
> I have taken Croatian, Irish, Hungarian, Arabic, Chinese
>   In order to feel like a liberated man.
>
> I love foreign languages all the more
>   Pure for me, at such a distance:

In my French language (my second language) there had been all kinds
   of treason
     In it, one could say yes to infamy![33]

And in the poem "The Faith that matters":[34]

I am not Breton, French, Latvian, Chinese, English
I am all that at once.
I am the universal and general man of the entire world.[35]

But this awareness, alternatively wounded and triumphant, is reversed logically into alienation, into an infinite self-exile: the opposite
of this omnipotent cosmopolitanism that believes it can be everywhere
and be "the Word and not words":

O battle man to man against forty lives!
Replaced in my flesh by harsh foreigners,

Myself dislodged by me, replaced
By other more powerful dwellers[36]

Cases like Robin's are not infrequent in the twentieth century. To be
sure, the romantic "wanting everything" constitutes a project that goes
well beyond translation. But it may be asked if this omnipotent aim
(which, after all, is found again in literature) is not inscribed in the
dialectic of a certain type of translation, or if it does not represent one of
the profound temptations (one of the dangers) of all translation in
general. What translator, confronted with the Babel of languages, has
not thought he could "translate everything?"

It would be logical to ask now to what extent A. W. Schlegel's
translations in actuality reflect the theoretical project that underlies
them. Or: How did A. W. Schlegel *effectively* translate Shakespeare,
Dante, or Calderón? To answer these questions would require a confrontation of all his translations with the originals. Until now, such a
comparison has been barely attempted.[37] All we have is a collection of
favorable but vague judgments on Schlegel's translations and their historical importance in Germany.

In the theoretical framework of this study, it would be out of the
question to proceed to such a confrontation. Besides, the difficulties
connected to it are obvious. We shall simply try to indicate in which
general framework such a confrontation should be carried out. The
manner in which we can judge a translation of Shakespeare or Cervantes today is in part connected to the manner in which we perceive
these authors culturally. Let us say this: For us, Shakespeare (like Cervantes or Boccaccio) belongs to that constellation of European literature which, from the fifteenth to the sixteenth century, is constructed on
the basis of "popular" cultures and literatures—no less than on the

basis of the cultures and languages called "scholarly." It is impossible to appreciate these works if they are not connected to these oral roots. The same goes for a Rabelais, and also for a Luther. Thus, to translate these authors is for us to attempt to render the multiple registers of their oral language. Consequently, it is to confront the possibilities of our contemporary European languages—gone through the sieve of history and writing—with languages whose wealth, flexibility, and freedom are incomparably greater. We find again, from a different perspective, the idea of "natural genius" of the eighteenth century—with the difference that we situate this "natural genius" in the very orality of the language. The Romantic point of view is entirely different: Against the notion of "natural genius," the issue is to show in a Shakespeare the vigor of a poetic know-how that is able to realize infinitely self-conscious works. A "noble" Shakespeare, who would be a sort of Leonardo da Vinci of the theater. Here, it may be affirmed that what is important is the "Romantic" Shakespeare who mixes the noble and the base, the crude and the delicate, etc., or the Cervantes who strews his chapters with sonnets and pastoral tales, scholarly mixing satire and poetry. Given that translation had retained only the crudeness of these authors (their not very appetizing popular base), the issue—for criticism and translation—was to show that they were great poets who, when they had recourse to popular phrases, did it in play, more out of a taste for universality than a profound affinity with orality.

This means that, from the Romantic point of view, one may certainly state *theoretically* that Shakespeare, Cervantes, and Boccaccio are the *union* of the high and the low, the base and the noble. But at bottom the Romantics can no more accommodate the dimension of the low and the base than the preceding tradition: The numerous imitations of these authors in which European Romanticism indulged rather show that they constantly eclipse the "base" or subject it to a hyper-ironic treatment that annihilates it. Actually, nothing is more foreign to Romanticism than the naturalness of language, even though (and here it differs from classicism) it claims an "obscure" language charged with allegoricity (hence, sometimes, the recourse to old words, which create the impression of the "distant"). How could it then accommodate what in these authors is of the order of the obscene, the spicy, the scatological, the insult? In the critical analyses the Romantics give of them, that aspect is simply not mentioned. And in the translations? Tieck and his daughter Dorothea, finishing the translation of Shakespeare, allowed themselves to bowdlerize the crudest passages.[38] A. W. Schlegel, on the other hand, seems to have acted differently: He subtly poetized and rationalized Shakespeare (in the name of the demands of versification, for instance), but without allowing himself flagrant infidelities. Hence, as Pannwitz

says, he was unable to render the "majestic barbariousness" of Shakespeare's verses. Thus, the limit of his translation is to be found in the
Romantic view of poetry and poetic translation as well as in the general
inability of the age to accommodate that which, in foreign works, surpasses the field of its sensibility, that is, in this case, that which would
oblige *Bildung* to be something else than an educational and formative
"Grand Tour."

A. W. Schlegel's opposition to Voss, for that matter, derives from this:
The latter would have "graecicized" German too abruptly. If one over-
throws the limits of one's own language, A. W. Schlegel states in a review
of Voss's translation of the *Iliad*, one runs the risk of "no longer speaking a valid language, recognized as such, but a kind of slang (*Roth-
welsch*) one invents oneself. No necessity may be adduced to justify
such a thing."[39] Voss would have stepped over that limit between the
"foreign" and "strangeness" signaled by Humboldt.[40] That translation,
precisely, should inhabit the imprecise and undefinable borders of the
"foreign" and "strangeness" is what exceeds the perspective of classical
and Romantic *Bildung*. Likewise, F. Schlegel could harshly criticize
Luther's translation of the Bible.[41] That is because Luther does not yet
think about separating the written and the oral, the scholarly and the
popular, whereas this separation had been entirely completed by the
time of the Romantics and Goethe. The latter states in his Memoirs:

> I heard it said that one must speak the way one writes and write the
> way one speaks, whereas it seemed to me that written language and
> spoken language were, once and for all, two entirely different things,
> of which each was justified to claim its own rights.[42]

Despite Klopstock, the theory of language and translation in Germany at the end of the eighteenth century lost sight of what was primordial for Luther: to speak and to translate in the language of "the mother
in the home, the children on the street, and the common man in the
market-place." As we shall see, it was Hölderlin who was able to take up
this truth of Luther's language, not, to be sure, in this literal form, but in
the form of a poetic language enriched simultaneously by foreign languages and dialects. And thus he inaugurated a new epoch in poetry and
translation in Germany.

10

F. Schleiermacher and W. von Humboldt: Translation in the Hermeneutical-Linguistic Space

Can F. Schleiermacher and W. von Humboldt be presented together? The latter, a great representative of German classicism but in touch with all the tendencies of his time, devoted his whole life to an activity that borders on philosophy, literature, philology, but that can only be defined as a constant *concern* with language.[1] This is not a philosophy of language in the manner of Herder or Hamann nor, obviously, linguistics in the modern sense. In his texts, abstract reflection and the empirical study of language are mingled. As they are, they still exert—because of that mixture which sometimes makes them obscure—a powerful attraction today, and it is understandable that they have engaged such different minds as Chomsky or Heidegger. Perhaps it might be suggested that they represent the first modern approach to what has since been called the *symbolic* dimension.[2]

And Schleiermacher? In his youth an active member of the *Athenäum*, he devoted his entire mature life to the elaboration, in conjunction with a work as theologian and as translator (Plato), of a theory of hermeneutics. In fact, he must be considered the founder of the modern hermeneutics that claims to be a theory of the *understanding*.[3]

From Schleiermacher to Dilthey, Husserl, the "early" Heidegger, Gadamer, and Ricœur, there is a whole hermeneutical lineage, which must be distinguished from the theories of interpretation formulated by, in a certain sense, Nietzsche and Freud.[4]

The hermeneutics of understanding breaks with the limits of traditional hermeneutics (essentially that which seeks to establish rules for the interpretation of sacred texts) and intends to constitute itself as a theory of *intersubjective understanding*—let us say, of processes of "reading" that appear on the level of the communication of subject-consciousnesses. The understanding of a *text* (the exclusive object of ancient hermeneutics) is above all that of an *expressive product of a subject*. It is also the understanding of the *phenomenon of objective language* that is defined not so much by its author as by its situation in the history of the language and the culture.

Theoretically, understanding operates on all levels that may concern the inter-expressivity of subjects. But one easily guesses that its fundamental space is *language*. First of all, this is its medium of explanation. Further, understanding is generally oriented toward oral or written linguistic expressions.[5] Strictly speaking, there is also an understanding of gestures, actions, etc., but the scene where they unfold and where their meaning is brought out is necessarily language. As Gadamer says, drawing on Schleiermacher's intuitions:

> We are indebted to German Romanticism for its anticipation of the systematic meaning that the linguistic character of conversation has with regard to any act of understanding. It taught us that, in the final analysis, understanding and interpreting are one and the same. . . . *Language is rather the universal environment in which understanding itself appears.*[6]

Thus, starting from its own demands, hermeneutics encounters the dimension of language as its own dimension, and as the dimension to which man stands in a relation of both subjection and freedom:

> whenever the word (*Rede*) is not completely bound by obvious objects or external facts it merely has to express, wherever the speaker is thinking more or less independently, and therefore wants to express himself, he stands in a double relationship to language, and what he says will be understood correctly only in so far as that relationship is. On the one hand every man is in the power (*in der Gewalt*) of the language he speaks, and all his thinking is a product thereof. . . . Yet on the other hand every freely thinking, mentally self-employed man in turn shapes his own language. . . . In this sense, therefore, it is the living power of the individual which produces new forms by means of the plastic material of language. . . . Therefore each higher and free speech needs to be understood in this twofold way.[7]

The issue here is no longer language as expression or "postulate" (Novalis) of thinking, but language as the ultimate medium of any relation of man to himself, to others, and to the world: in short, that dimension of *language* and *speech* brought out by modern linguistics. Hermeneutics is indispensable because there is opacity, if not unintelligibility, in interhuman expressions. It is the bringing out of the meaning of those expressions to the extent that it is not immediately explicit.

Language as *environment*, and no longer as *instrument*, that is the novelty. For any environment is by nature, as Lacan says, "something that infinitely surpasses any intention we may put in it."

Humboldt's reflections also revolve around this nature of language:

> Thus, language is the means, if not absolute, at least sensible, by which man gives form simultaneously to himself and to the world, or rather becomes conscious of himself by projecting a world outside of himself.[8]

> Language, then, must take on the double nature of world and man if it is to convert the mutual relations of both into fruitful interaction; or, more accurately, it must abolish the specific nature of each, of the immediate reality of the object as well as the subject, in order to produce its own being anew on that basis, retaining of this double content only the ideal form.[9]

The reflections of both thinkers on the act of translation (and here we shall deal chiefly with Schleiermacher's, which are more developed) must be placed rigorously in this new framework: language as environment or as "own being." For if one were to keep to the technical or ethical principles of translation they express, one would be hard put to distinguish them from Goethe's or even A. W. Schlegel's: the same demand of "fidelity," of the exact rendering of the values of the foreign text; the same humanist discourse with its reaffirmation of the movement of *Bildung* and of the opposition to translations "after the French manner"; the same emphasis on the law of *Bildung* claiming one can only have access to oneself through the experience of the other. And it is even Schleiermacher who probably managed to formulate this law in the most precise way, mentioning "the foreign and its mediating nature."[10]

Still, the perspective is different because both are henceforth sensitive to the natural relation of man to language, to the mother tongue, to the reality of the difference of languages and, finally, to the opacity that is peculiar to the linguistic medium, an opacity which is only one of the faces of the *Verschlungenheit* mentioned by Freud and Lacan.

The result for translation is a new space, that of natural language, and that of the infinity—no less intersected—of relations anyone can have to the mother tongue and to other languages.[11] Translation is no longer instructed to surpass these (the *Athenäum*), to deride them in a sovereign manner (A. W. Schlegel), or to relativize them culturally in the space of *Weltliteratur* (Goethe). Translation must operate in the context of this dimension, which is neither private nor social, but symbolical, and in which the issue is the human in the constitution of its being.

On June 24, 1823, Schleiermacher delivered a lecture at the Berlin Royal Academy of Sciences, entitled "On the Different Methods of Translating." This lecture, later published in his *Complete Works*, was connected to the research in the domain of hermeneutics in which he was engaged at the time. It may even be said that it constitutes a chapter in this research.

Before we analyze this text, the following must be emphasized: There is no doubt that this is the only study of that period in Germany to constitute *a systematic and methodical approach of translation*.

Methodical, because, for Schleiermacher, the issue is not only to analyze, but also to deduce, on the basis of definitions, the possible methods of translation.

Systematic: Schleiermacher seeks to delimit the sphere of the act of translation in the total field of understanding, a delimitation carried out by the progressive exclusion of that which *is not* this act, and by its articulated position in this field. Once this delimitation has been effected, it becomes possible to proceed to an examination (itself systematic) of existing translations, and to create a methodology of translation applied to the different genres of *Rede*.[12] This is the path of his *Hermeneutics*.

Here, we are in the presence of a discourse on translation that claims to be rational and philosophical, and that aims to constitute a theory of translation based on a certain theory of *subjectivity*. This is also why there is constantly the question of *persons*: the translator, the interpreter, the author, the reader, etc. In this respect, we shall see that the way in which Schleiermacher defines the two types of translation that are possible for him, is characteristic: In the final analysis, they correspond to two cultural, social, and psychological types of translators. Here, translation has become an intersubjective act, the "cresting moment of life."[13]

Schleiermacher begins with a reflection on generalized translation: There is "translation" everywhere where we have to interpret a discourse, whether it be a foreigner speaking to us in a language which is not our own, a peasant calling out to us in a dialect, an unknown person speaking words we can barely understand, or whether we examine words we uttered previously, but that now seem obscure to us. . . . In all these cases we are led to an act of "translation"—and the most difficult one is not necessarily the one concerning a foreign language. In short, any communication is an act of translation/understanding to a certain degree:

> Thought and expression are essentially and internally identical—and the whole art of all understanding of speech, and therefore also of all translation is based on this conviction.[14]

But Schleiermacher is careful to immediately distinguish this *generalized translation* from *restricted translation*, that is, of translation between languages. Nevertheless, not every act of transmission between languages is necessarily translation. A second distinction must be made: between *translator* and *interpreter*. And this has to be done on the following grounds: Interpreting would be more concerned with "business matters," translation more with the domains of "science" and "art" (i.e., of philosophy and literature). This distinction is corroborated by another one: Interpreting is essentially oral, translation essentially written. These distinctions depend on mere common sense, and Schleiermacher will attempt to base them on another, more essential distinction: the distinction of *the objective and the subjective*:

> The less an author himself appears in the original, the more he acts exclusively as the grasping-organ of the object . . . the more the translation is a simple kind of interpreting.[15]

Everywhere the author appears as the mere servant of an objective content, there is interpreting—oral or written. Everywhere he tries to express himself, in the field of "science" or "art," there is translation. Further on, Schleiermacher attempts to deepen his distinction. The field of interpreting is that of the discourses in which language tends to become pure designation without density. Not only is interpreting simplified here to the extreme, it has no value in itself, being only the indifferent vehicle of a content. But in literature and philosophy, the author and his text are caught in the twofold relation to language mentioned above: There is simultaneously modification of language and expression of the subject. Philosophical wisdom, Schleiermacher says, must "be dissolved in this system of language."[16] Literary discourse is also a "living representation [of the language],"[17] even as it remains the unique expression of an individual (his speech). These two levels are at once separate and united, and the hermeneutician as well as the translator deal with it. Literature and philosophy, then, are of the domain of the "subjective," but this subjective element also means an *intimacy* with one's own language that does not exist in the case of texts connected to interpreting. Cleaving to the subjective of the subject and to the intimacy of the mother tongue, the literary or philosophical text is removed from all objectivity. This view is partially an extension of the *Athenäum*'s view, but it is also connected to this new perception of language which is being born at the time and according to which language is not so much *representation* as *expression*: Henceforth, language is supposed to be "rooted not in the things perceived, but in the active subject."[18]

Thus, the sphere of genuine translation has been "deduced":

> For, as language is an historical thing, there can be no right sense for it without a sense of its history. Languages are not invented, and thus, any arbitrary work in them and on them is foolishness; but they are gradually discovered, and scholarship and art are the powers through which this discovery is promoted and brought to fulfillment.[19]

It is the responsibility of the translator to transmit those works of science and art that make up the historical life of a language. But how can the translator render in his own language something that simultaneously falls within the scope of the intimacy of the foreign language and that of the subject expressing himself in that language? How to render the *interiority* of the other language and the foreign author? "Does not translation, considered in this way, seem a foolish enterprise?"[20]

Faced with this "foolishness," Schleiermacher mentions two practices that are supposed to resolve the difficulties of translation, even as they avoid them: *paraphrase* and *re-creation* (*Nachbildung*). In both cases, the problem is circumvented, or denied:

> But what of the genuine translator, who wants to bring those two completely separated persons, his author and his reader, truly together, and who would like to bring the latter to an understanding and enjoyment of the former as correct and complete as possible without obliging him to leave the sphere of his mother tongue, what roads are open to him?[21]

The answer to this question, which defines the general process of any translation in the most subjective way possible, is practically included in its very formulation. Suppose I would want a friend to meet someone he does not know: At the level of these two persons, either my friend will go see that someone, or the latter will visit my friend. Schleiermacher reasons in this way for translation:

> Either the translator leaves the author in peace, as much as possible, and moves the reader towards him; or he leaves the reader in peace, as much as possible, and moves the author towards him.[22]

In the first case, the translator obliges the reader to leave himself, to make an effort of decentering in order to perceive the foreign author in his being as a foreigner; in the second case, he obliges the author to shake off his strangeness in order to become familiar to the reader. What is interesting here is not so much the nature of the distinction (ethnocentric or non-ethnocentric translation) as the manner in which it is expressed: a process of an intersubjective encounter.

In this perspective, not only are there, could there be, no other methods, but all the other ways of posing the "problems" of translation are subordinated to it:

> Whatever is said about translation following the letter and translation following the meaning, faithful translation and free translation . . . must be reducible to the two [methods]. . . . the faithful translation which follows the meaning or the translation which is too literal or too free will not be the same according to one method, as it is according to the other one.[23]

This way of reordering things only has meaning because translation here has become a chapter of understanding. But that is not all: Schleiermacher devotes the remainder of his lecture to an analysis of the two methods and to a consecration of the first, examining its conditions and its meaning, then showing the fundamental absurdity of the second—for this one could be formulated as follows:

> One should translate an author in such a way as he himself would have written in German.[24]

> *In short, Schleiermacher's systematic tends to demonstrate that there is an authentic and an inauthentic translation*, just as there is an authentic understanding and communication and an inauthentic understanding and communication.

The translation that attempts to provide its reader with a text such as the foreign author would have written had he been "German," is inauthentic, because it *negates the profound relation that connects the author to his own language*. It is, Schleiermacher states, as if paternity were considered of no importance:

> Indeed, what can be the objection if a translator were to tell a reader: here, I bring you the book just as the man would have written it if he had written in German; and if the reader were to reply . . . [it is] as if you brought me the man's portrait just as he would have looked if his mother had conceived him with another father? For if the writer's particular spirit is the mother of works belonging to science and art . . . , his native language (*vaterländische Sprache*) is the father.[25]

This theory is at once the negation of other mother tongues and the negation on one's own mother tongue—it is the negation *of the very idea of a mother tongue*. The one who negates the others negates himself. And Schleiermacher shows (though without developing it) that this type of translation is connected, at least in Germany, to a cultural situation in which the national language has not yet asserted itself, in which it can neither accommodate other languages in their difference, nor pose as a "cultured" language; a situation in which the members of the linguistic community may be tempted to speak other, more "educated" languages: "As long as the mother tongue has not been formed (*gebildet*) for them, [it] remains the partial mother tongue"[26] which is "complemented" by foreign languages like Latin or French. Thus, the German cultural bilingualism will hinder, and for a long time, the literary flight of the mother tongue as well as that of translations. For bilingualism does not mean an opening to the foreign, but rather the fact of being dominated by it. As soon as the mother tongue asserts itself as language of culture, the community defined by it may think about *translating* foreign languages instead of *speaking* them. Conversely, the mother tongue cannot assert itself as language of culture as long as it has not become a language of translation, as long as those who speak it are not freely interested in what is foreign. *Inauthentic translation, then, corresponds to an inauthentic relation to the mother tongue and to other languages*. Thus, at least, things would be formulated for the German culture, because, for Schleiermacher, French translation depends either on *Nachbildung* or on the ethnocentric operation. French is like those languages that are

> the captives of too strict a bond of classical expression, outside of which all is reprehensible. Such bonded languages should expect a broadening of their sphere by having themselves spoken by foreigners who need more than their mother tongue, . . . they may incorporate foreign works by means of imitation or even by translations of the other [ethnocentric] kind.[27]

It can be seen how the theme of translation "after the French manner" is positioned here in a broader panorama, that of the type of relation a culture may entertain with the mother tongue. Which could be summarized in the following three diagrams:

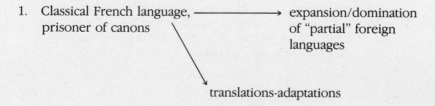

1. Classical French language, ──────→ expansion/domination
    prisoner of canons   of "partial" foreign
                                        languages

                     translations-adaptations

    ethnocentric translations

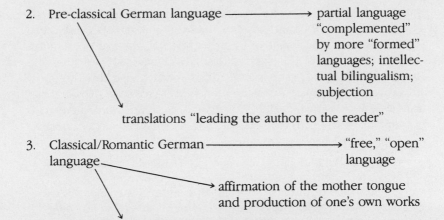

2. Pre-classical German language ————————→ partial language
    "complemented" by more "formed" languages; intellectual bilingualism; subjection

    translations "leading the author to the reader"

3. Classical/Romantic German ————————→ "free," "open" language
    language

    → affirmation of the mother tongue and production of one's own works

    non-ethnocentric translations

On this basis the nature and the historical possibility of authentic translation may be deduced. This, says Schleiermacher,

> rests on two conditions: that understanding foreign works should be a thing known and desired, and that the native language should be allowed a certain flexibility.[28]

These are the prevailing conditions at the dawn of the nineteenth century in Germany. Another condition must be added: that of the self-affirmation of the national language, even if this affirmation depends dialectically on the new relation with the foreign.

Apparently, inauthentic translation does not carry any risk for the national language and culture, except that of missing any relation with the foreign. But it only reflects or infinitely repeats the bad relation with the foreign that already exists. Authentic translation, on the other hand, obviously carries risks. The confrontation of these risks presupposes a culture that is already confident of itself and of its capacity of assimilation. Speaking of authentic translation, Schleiermacher says:

> to do this artfully and with measure, without disadvantage to one's language or oneself is probably the greatest difficulty our translator has to overcome.[29]

Because "representing what is foreign in one's mother tongue,"[30] that is what runs the risk of threatening what Schleiermacher calls in a striking way *das heimische Wohlbefinden der Sprache*, the familial (thus *heimisch* may be translated here) well-being of the language. That which Herder called its "virginity":

> This type of complaint—that such a translation must of necessity be harmful to the purity of the language and its peaceful development—has often been heard.[31]

That this "peaceful development" of the language is a myth, is shown here by Schleiermacher's entire way of thinking—because there is no isolated development of this sort, but relations of domination between languages that must be replaced by relations of freedom. The German that seeks to preserve its virginity is a language already culturally invested and dominated by the French. It is precisely where translations are made that there are fewer relations of domination. But the risk of suddenly going from one extreme to the other, and thus destabilizing the relation to the mother tongue, is a real one:

> For as true as it is . . . that a man is in a certain sense educated and a citizen of the world only through his knowledge of various languages, we must concede that just as we do not consider that type of world citizenship real which supplants love for one's country at critical moments; just so any general love which desires to equate any language . . . with the national language . . . is not a true and really civilizing love. . . . Just as a man must decide to belong to one country, just so he must adhere to one language, or he will float without any bearings above an unpleasant middle ground.[32]

This unpleasant middle ground is the risk the translator and his readers run by wanting to open themselves to the foreign, but then again, this is the price for all genuine *Bildung*. And that, for Schleiermacher, is *a certainty deriving from his consciousness as a hermeneutician as well as from his consciousness as a German intellectual*.

Let us take a slightly different example to elucidate this. It is possible to interpret the Old Testament so as to bring out its own truth, without being prejudiced *a priori* about the nature of this truth, or wanting to read, from the outset, the truth of the New Testament between the lines. Likewise, one may choose an open and dialogic relation to someone else, or prefer a relation of domination. Inauthentic translation, as Heidegger would say, is a possible *existenziell*. It is also, as Schleiermacher demonstrates very well, something culturally determined. But whatever these historical or cultural dominations may be, there is always a moment that is of the order of a *choice*, even if the choice is not necessarily a conscious one. *Bildung*, with its own limits, dangers, and positivity, is a choice: that of German classical humanism. "To present the foreign in the mother tongue," to accept that the latter be broadened, fertilized, transformed by the "foreign," to accept the "mediating nature" of the foreign, this is a choice that precedes any narrowly methodological consideration. Now, a choice is always a choice of *method*, of *met'hodos*, of a path, it is always the tracing of a field to be crossed, staked out, cultivated. And it is Schleiermacher's merit to have presented this choice as that of *authenticity*, confronting it to another possible choice, that of *inauthenticity*. Because these two concepts unite the ethical and the ontological dimension, justice and correctness.

On this ground, Schleiermacher is able to say that authentic translation must be a *massive process*:

> This method of translation must therefore be applied extensively, a transplantation of whole literatures into a language, and It makes sense and is of value only to a nation that has the definite inclination to appropriate what is foreign. Isolated works of this type are of value only as precursors.[33]

Let us say that it must be a process that is at the same time *systematic* and *plural*: translation of several languages, several literatures, multiple translation of the same work, to be sure, along the indicated path, able to complement each other reciprocally, to give rise to confrontations, discussions, etc. *Translation on a large scale is in fact the constitution of a field of translation in the linguistic and literary space*. And translation only has meaning in such a field.

Speaking about translation "on a large scale," Schleiermacher is obviously thinking of what has just happened in Germany with Voss, A. W. Schlegel, and himself, and of the historical choice German culture has made, at least since Herder:

> An inner necessity, in which a peculiar calling of our people expresses itself clearly enough, has driven us to translating on a large scale; we cannot go back, we must go on. . . . We sense that our language . . . can only thrive in all its freshness and fully develop its own power only through the most many-sided contacts with what is foreign. . . . Because of its respect for the foreign and its mediating nature, our nation may be destined to carry all the treasures of foreign science and art, together with its own, in its language, to write them into a historical whole, so to speak, which would be preserved in the center and heart of Europe. . . . This appears indeed to be the real historical aim of translation in general, as we are used to it now. To this end, however, only the method we have discussed first should be followed. . . . We should not fear great harm to our language from these endeavors. For it must be established at the onset that there is, in a language in which translation is practiced to such an extent, a proper language domain (*Sprachgebiet*) for translations, and much should be allowed of translations that should not be tolerated elsewhere. . . . We should not fail to acknowledge that much of what is beautiful and powerful in our language has in part developed through translations, or has in part been drawn from obscurity by them.[34]

There must be a particular *Sprachgebiet* for translations, a field of their own within the cultural field, for translation to be able to fulfill its mediating function. The creation of this *Sprachgebiet* is not defined as a

titanic and poetizing project, as with A. W. Schlegel, but as the realization of that *Erweiterung* of the mother tongue demanded by Herder,
Leibniz, and Lessing.

That Schleiermacher's reflection summarizes the experience in the
matter of translation of his entire epoch (with the exception of Hölderlin's), that it provides the most accomplished formulation of the law of
Bildung, that it invites us to a reflection on translation based on ethical
values, none of this can be doubted. From this point of view, Humboldt's texts, which we shall now examine briefly, do not add much; but
they have the merit of tracing very clearly the *limits* of the humanist
theory of translation, limits only Hölderlin has been able to exceed.

In 1816, Humboldt publishes his translation of Aeschylus's
Agamemnon, which he had been working on for many years, accompanied by an introduction in which he simultaneously puts forward his
view of Greek tragedy, language, and translation. This introduction distinguishes itself from contemporary texts by A. W. Schlegel by the fact
that it connects the theory of translation to a theory of language—a
theory which goes well beyond A. W. Schlegel's theory of language/
poetry, and which attempts to express what is perhaps inexpressible:
the intimacy of thinking and language:

> A word is not a mere sign for a concept, since a concept cannot come
> into being, let alone be recorded, without the help of a word; the
> indeterminate activity of the power of thinking gathers into a word,
> just as light clouds originate in a clear sky. It has now become an
> individual being with a certain character and a certain shape. . . . If
> you were to think the origin of a word in human terms (which is
> plainly impossible, merely because the act of pronouncing a word also
> presupposes the certainty of being understood, and because language
> itself can only be thought as a product of simultaneous interaction, in
> which one of the terms is not able to help the other, but in which each
> must carry out its own work and that of all the others), that origin
> would be analogous to the origin of an ideal shape in the fantasy of an
> artist. This, too, cannot be drawn from what is real, it originates from a
> pure energy of the spirit and, in the purest sense of the word, from
> nothing; from that moment on, however, it enters life and is now real
> and lasting.[35]

Let us observe that Humboldt does not seek to define this "labor" of
the spirit (and henceforth it is a "labor," not a "poetic game," despite the
comparison with the artist) in a linear way, but to grasp it in all its
mythical complexity. A little further, he writes:

> All forms of language are symbols, not the things themselves, nor
> signs agreed on, but sounds which find themselves . . . in real and, so
> to speak, mystical connections with the things and the concepts they

represent, connections which contain the objects of reality as it were dissolved in ideas. These symbols can be changed, defined, separated and united in a manner for which no limit can be imagined.[36]

Rarely has the astonishing density of the linguistic dimension been described so well, a dimension in which the producer (the spirit) is, as it were, surpassed a thousand times by his product and its infinite entanglements.

This dimension, for whose determination terms like "representation" and "expression" are insufficient, is a dimension itself dispersed in as many "local" products of the spirit: *languages*. And such is the plurality of the aims within language in general (represent? symbolize? signify? reveal? name? designate? express? link? separate? determine?), and hence of languages, that no single language, by its very idiosynchrasy, is entirely "translatable," that is, entirely "corresponding" to another:

> How . . . could a word whose meaning is not immediately given through the senses be totally identical with a word in another language?[37]

In *Hellas und Latium*, Humboldt goes even further:

> Even in the case of purely sensible objects, the terms used by different languages are far from being genuine synonyms, and by pronouncing *hippos*, equus, or horse, one does not say exactly the same thing. The same holds *a fortiori* for non-sensible objects.[38]

Here, the difference in languages acquires an abysmal depth. For what is the issue if *hippos*, equus, and horse do not *say* the same thing? Perhaps they *aim* at the same thing but do not *say* the same thing? What does *saying* mean, then?

Translation, preceded in this by literature, is what promotes the *Bildung* of language:

> Translation, and precisely the translation of poets, is . . . one of the most necessary works in a literature, in part because it opens forms of art and humanity that would otherwise have remained wholly unknown to those who do not know foreign languages . . . in part, and above all, because it leads to the broadening of the signifying and expressive capacity of one's own language.[39]

This task is first of all that of literature: Every language, says Humboldt, even the most humble of dialects, is able to express

> the highest and the deepest, the strongest and the most tender.[40]

But

> these tones slumber as in an instrument that is not played, until the nation knows how to elicit them.[41]

Which is to say that literature subtly shakes the entire edifice of linguistic symbols in order to refine them, that is, to make them capable of ever more "signifiability" and "expressivity":

> A higher, deeper, or more tender sense may be imputed on these symbols . . . and so language, without a change that is properly speaking perceptible, is heightened to a bolder sense, extended into a [medium] that represents in manifold ways.[42]

Here, translation only extends the fine-tuning of the symbolical instrument. Historically, as Humboldt knows, this refining of language by translation has played a major role in Germany.[43] And in a few decisive lines, characteristic for classical Germany, and as powerful as those of Goethe or Schleiermacher, if not more, he defines what there is of the "fidelity" of translation, trying to propose a concept of it that avoids the "French" way as well as a crude "literalness":

> If translation is to appropriate to the language and the spirit of a nation what it does not possess, or what it possesses in a different way, the first requirement is simple fidelity. This fidelity must be aimed at the true character of the original and not at its incidentals, just as every good translation originates in simple and unpretentious love of the original. . . . A necessary corollary to this conception is that a translation should have a certain colouring of strangeness over it, but the line beyond which this undeniably becomes a mistake can easily be drawn. As long as one feels the foreign, but not the strangeness, the translation has reached its highest goal; but where strangeness appears as such, probably obscures the foreign, the translator betrays that he is not up to his original. In this case the unprejudiced reader's feelings do not easily miss the dividing line.[44]

Let us reread the decisive sentence of this passage: "As long as one feels the foreign, but not the strangeness, the translation has reached its highest goal; but where strangeness appears as such, probably obscures the foreign, the translator betrays that he is not up to his original." On the one hand, what Humboldt expresses is truth itself: There is an inauthentic literalness, an insignificant strangeness that has no relation whatsoever with the genuine strangeness of the text. Likewise, there is an inauthentic relation to strangeness, which lowers it to the exotic, the incomprehensible, etc. And this is precisely what A. W. Schlegel reproached in Voss: to have created a much too "strange" pidgin of Greek and German. But the problem is to know whether the dividing line between the foreign (*das Fremde*) and strangeness (*die Fremdheit*) can be drawn "easily." If yes, how? And by whom? Humboldt replies: by the "unprejudiced" reader. But who is the unprejudiced reader? And what is an uniformed reader? Further: If the task of the translator is to broaden the signifying and expressive capacity of a language, a literature, a culture, a nation, and hence of a reader, it cannot be defined by what the latter's sensibility is able to accommodate *a priori*; it is precisely the whole purpose of translation (theoretically) to broaden this sensibility. The *Fremdheit* is not only the irrelevance of what is uselessly shocking; or, to mention a problem well known by any translator, a translation that "smacks of translation" is not necessarily bad (whereas, conversely, it might be said that a translation that does not smack at all of translation is necessarily bad). *Fremdheit* is also the strangeness of the foreign in all its force: the different, the dissimilar, that which can be given the likeness of the same only by killing it. It may be the terror of difference, but also its marvel; the foreign has always appeared in this way: demon or goddess. The dividing line between the foreign, *das Fremde*, and strangeness, *die Fremdheit* (which may be Rilke's and Freud's *Unheimlichkeit*, the "disturbing strangeness"),[45] is as difficult to draw as the one between inauthentic strangeness and authentic strangeness. Or rather, it is a line that is incessantly displaced, even as it goes on existing. And it is very precisely on this line that German classicism (but Romanticism as well) is separated from Hölderlin. In still other words, it may be said that Hölderlin was able to push back that line *beyond* what was *thinkable, conceivable* for a Humboldt or a Goethe (who nevertheless, being more liberal than an A. W. Schlegel, accepted Voss's graecizations). Which may suggest that translation is situated precisely in that obscure and dangerous region where the disproportionate strangeness of the foreign work and its language runs the risk of striking down with all its force on the translator's text and his language, thus ruining his undertaking and leaving the reader only with an *inauthentic Fremdheit*. But if a translator refuses this danger, there is the risk of falling immediately into another one: the danger of killing the dimension of the foreign. The task of the translator consists in confronting this double danger and, in a certain way, drawing the dividing line himself, without any consideration for the reader. Humboldt, demanding of translation that it make us feel the foreign, but not strangeness, *has defined the limits of all classical translation*. He has also drawn the limits of what must be the essential in the classical conception of culture and the relation to languages: to promote the balance of the movement of *Bildung*, but without exposing this movement to the disproportion of the "violent motion" of the foreign. Which may mean, in the final analysis: to refuse the strangeness of the foreign as profoundly as the ethnocentrism of French classicism.[46]

11

HÖLDERLIN:
THE NATIONAL AND THE FOREIGN

Hölderlin's translations, as well as their relation to the whole of his poetic work and his thinking, have been closely studied.[1] Given the exceeding rarity of this kind of study, we must see in them the sure sign of their profound singularity. We have neither the intention nor the pretension to proceed to a confrontation of Hölderlin's translations with their originals. We shall simply attempt to show what constitutes the singularity, the historicity, as well as the surprising modernity of these translations—which is possible only by examining, even summarily, their own space, a space which is that of poetry, of thought, and even of Hölderlin's existence. We also want to show that the Swabian poet's translations, even as they belong entirely to their age and even have precursors (particularly Voss), announce a problematic of translation which is already our own. In their time, most notably by Schiller, these translations have been considered "the work of a madman," even though personalities like Brentano and Bettina von Arnim were able to greet them with enthusiasm. But only in the twentieth century, starting with N. von Hellingrath, have they been recognized as epoch-making in the history of not only German, but Western translation. Thus they have risen to the rare level of historic translations. For instance, the impact of the translation of *Antigone* may be measured by the fact that it served as the libretto for Carl Orff's opera *Antigona*, and that it was performed numerous times in an adaptation by Brecht, most notably by one of the most important companies of the second half of the twentieth century, the *Living Theater*.

As W. Benjamin pointed out, Hölderlin's translations, at the very least those of Sophocles, are the last works the poet produced before falling into schizophrenia. If we believe W. Benjamin, there would be a connection between the radicality of these translations and Hölderlin's break-down:

> Hölderlin's translations are prototypes of their kind. . . . For this very reason Hölderlin's translations in particular are subject to the enormous danger inherent in all translations: the gates of language thus expanded and modified may slam shut and enclose the translator with silence; . . . in them meaning plunges from abyss to abyss until it threatens to become lost in the bottomless depths of language.[2]

Perhaps psychoanalysis will enable us to measure the relation between schizofrenia, the relation to languages, and translation in a better way.[3]

Hölderlin's translations are part and parcel of his poetic trajectory, of his conception of language, poetry, and that which he himself calls the "experience [*épreuve*] of the foreign"—to such an extent that the customary categories of poetry and translation can only be applied with difficulty in his case. Hölderlin is a very great poet; he is also a very great translator, a very great "thinker" and also (if we may say so) a very great schizophrenic.[4] Though he took a decisive part in the construction of German Idealism with his friends Schelling and Hegel, he follows his own path, which will move him further and further away from this field and lead him to a reformulation of *Bildung* that, in fact, will literally burst its framework.

Hölderlin the translator barely elaborated on the principles of his translations. We find some brief observations in the "Remarks on Oedipus" and the "Remarks on Antigone," and in some letters of the same period. But, as we shall see, they carry weight. The difficult speculative texts devoted to poetry do not deal directly with the questions of translation either. Before examining the complex problematic of the "own" and the "foreign" that dominates the "Remarks" and the letters to Böhlendorff, Wilmans, and Seckendorf, we would want to mention a twofold particularity of Hölderlin's *poetic language* that will allow a better access to the space of his translations.

It has often been said that there is nothing more transparent, clearer—even in its obscurity—nothing more "chaste" and "pure" than Hölderlin's poetry. Nothing less sensual, less carnal. And yet, this poetry is by no means abstract, ethereal, or even symbolic in the sense of the Romantics. Likewise, his general thematic could not be clearer, more precise, and more delimited in its several polarities: the Limited and the Unlimited, the High and the Low, the Greek and the Hesperic, the Homeland and the Foreign, Heaven and Earth, etc., all polarities that are generally seized in an almost "geographical" manner, even if this is a poetic, mythical, and even historical geography. The great German and European streams, the Alps, native Swabia, German cities, Greece and its high places, the Orient and the South: A map could be drawn of Hölderlin's places. Now, the language of the poet seems to agree profoundly with this geographical thematic in that, even in its stripped form, *it tends to incorporate "Greek" and "native" linguistic elements simultaneously*; in this case, a German that has managed to integrate Hölderlin's maternal dialect, Swabian, but also a linguistic treasury going back, starting from Klopstock, Voss, and Herder, to Luther and old German. In a modest but highly illuminating book, Rolf Zuberbühler has patiently explored what he calls "Hölderlin's renovation of the language out of its etymological origins."

This renovation, which is totally conscious for Hölderlin, consists in drawing on the linguistic base of the German language, using the words while giving them back their, if not "originary," at least their ancient meaning in the poem. Thus, for instance, when Hölderlin uses the word *Fürst*, prince, he gives it back the meaning of *Vorderster* (the one before the first) or *Erster* (the first).[5] The adverb *gern* (gladly)—an essential one for him—points back to its root, *gehren, begehren* (to desire).[6] *Ort* (place) is often used in his poems in the ancient meaning, still found in Luther, of *Ende* (end).[7] *Hold* (favorable, gracious, propitious) is connected to the German dialectal *helden*, which means to incline, and *Halde* (slope).[8] *Meinen* [to mean, to believe, to think] goes back to the old German *minnen* [to love].[9] Zuberbühler gives many examples of such an "etymological" approach by Hölderlin. To be sure, this type of approach is not unusual at the end of the eighteenth century, notably in Klopstock and Herder. But for Hölderlin, this recourse, not so much to the etymology as to the *more speaking* significations German words were able to have in what could be called their dialectal epoch (middle ages, Luther), becomes an original and complex law of poetic creation. That this is a conscious recourse is brought out by a line from the poet's youth:

> Sprechen will ich, wie dein Luther spricht.[10]

Hölderlin borrows numerous words from Luther's Bible (*Blik, Arbeit, Beruf, Zukunft, Geist*), and some of his verses are directly inspired by it. Thus,

> Doch uns ist gegeben,
> Auf keiner Stätte zu ruhn[11]

rhythmically reproduces Luther's translation of Phil. I: 29,

Denn euch ist gegeben um Christus willen zu tun. . . .[12]

Here the recourse to the old Lutheran speech, a frequent one at the time,[13] is situated in a poetic movement that goes well beyond Klopstock's and Herder's quest for nationalist origins. This movement aims at recovering the *Sprachlichkeit*, the speaking force of the common language which derives from its multi-dialectal roots. To locate Hölderlin's manifold borrowings from Luther, Klopstock, Pietism, etc., is to indicate the same momentum that drives him to the integration into his poetic language of elements of his maternal dialect, Swabian.[14] On this level, Hölderlin's proximity to the founding father of the German language, the translator Luther, is obvious. But we have a name for this movement: *it is the return to natural language, the* Natursprache *and its powers*. With this difference that the natural language is also the native language. In fact, the Swabian poet teaches us that *the natural language is always also the native language*. But that is not all. It would be stupid to consider Hölderlin a "localist" poet, like Hebel. He does not write in a dialect, but in the *Hoch- und Schrift-Sprache*.[15] Moreover, his poetry integrates—no less decisively—a host of lexical, metrical, and rhythmical elements of a foreign language: Greek. Here again, Zuberbühler's study provides numerous examples: The expression, or rather the neologism, *unstädtisch* renders the Greek ἄπολις, the expression *des Tages Engel* renders the Greek ἄγγελος, etc. It may be said, then, that Hölderlin's poetic language is constituted in the double movement of a return to the meanings of the natural and native language, and of an appropriation of the *Sprachlichkeit* of a foreign language, Greek, which is itself essentially dialectal. By its radicality, this movement has no equivalent in the poetry of the time which, with Romanticism, seeks to edify a *Kunstsprache* or, with Goethe, a poetry that is solidly confined to the domain of the classical *Schriftsprache*.

Now, the unique character of Hölderlin's poetry may be defined by two expressions Heidegger used concerning the poem "Remembrance" (*Andenken*): "The experience [*épreuve*] of the foreign and the practicing of what is one's own."[16] This is a *double law* Hölderlin formulated in a letter to Böhlendorff, dated 4 December 1804:

We learn nothing with more difficulty than to freely use the national. And, I believe that it is precisely the clarity of the presentation that is so natural to us as is for the Greeks the fire from heaven. For exactly that reason they will have to be surpassed in beautiful passion . . . rather than in that Homeric presence of mind and talent for presentation.

It sounds paradoxical. Yet I argue once again . . . : [that] in the progress of education the truly national will become the ever less attractive. Hence the Greeks are less master of the sacred pathos, because to them it was inborn, whereas they excel in their talent for presentation, beginning with Homer, because this exceptional man was sufficiently sensitive to conquer the Western *Junonian sobriety* for his Apollonian empire and thus to veritably appropriate what is foreign.

With us it is the reverse. Hence it is also so dangerous to deduce the rules of art for oneself exclusively from Greek excellence. I have labored long over this and know by now that, with the exception of what must be the highest for the Greeks and for us—namely, the living relationship and destiny—we must not share anything identical with them.

Yet what is familiar must be learned as well as what is foreign. This is why the Greeks are so indispensable for us. It is only that we will not follow them in our own, national [spirit], as I said, the *free* use of *what is one's own* is the most difficult.[17]

This famous letter refers to one of the turning-points of Hölderlin's poetry: At the outset, the poet certainly has an immense fascination for the Greek world, frequently taking on an aspect of nostalgia. But gradually, Hölderlin goes from the image of a Greece that would be the place of natural perfection, which was after all very common since Winckelmann, to a Greece in which "what is one's own," the original element, would be what he seeks to bring out with expressions like the *fire from heaven*, the *sacred pathos*, or the *aorgic*. That is, a Greece closer to Nietzsche's view or, more generally, to the modern view: the violent world of myth. Through all these characteristics, Greece appears as that which, in its origin and its trajectory, is foreign to us, even *the foreign* as such. And this is exactly as we have indicated, F. Schlegel's intuition. If the Greek trajectory goes from the "sacred pathos" to the "Junonian sobriety," the trajectory of the modern Western world consists rather in conquering the "pathos," which is foreign to it, given that what is its "own" is precisely this very "Junonian sobriety." If the Greeks had not conquered this "sobriety," they would have been engulfed, as it were, by the "fire from heaven" (Empedocles' temptation); but without this same fire from heaven, the West runs the risk of falling into a mortal prosaic element, into what Hölderlin calls the "lack of destiny," the *Schiksaallose*.[18] Thus, the two trajectories are literally opposed, which means that Greece cannot be a model:

And thus the Greek modes of representation and poetic forms are also more subordinated to the patriotic ones.[19]

On 12 March 1804, Hölderlin writes to Seckendorff:

The fable, the poetic face of history, and the architectonic of the heaven, keep me busy primarily at the moment, in particular the national, to the extent that it differs from the Greek.[20]

But this does not at all mean that the poet would be abandoning the Greeks in order to devote himself henceforth to the "high and pure exaltation of the songs of the fatherland."[21] If this were the case, there would be a Greek phase in Hölderlin, followed by a national phase. But this is not the case. There is much rather a *simultaneous* double movement—the same one we indicated on the level of Hölderlin's language—which connects the "experience [*épreuve*] of the foreign" (of the fire from heaven, the sacred pathos, the aorgic, the South, Greece, the Orient) and the "practicing of what is one's own" (homeland, the native, the national).

In his commentary on "Remembrance," Heidegger writes:

The love of not being at home for the sake of coming home to what is one's own, is the essential law of the destiny by which the poet is destined to the foundation of the history of the "fatherland."[22]

This formulation does not accurately define Hölderlin's law, and Heidegger is no doubt aware of it when he writes in a note appended to his commentary:

To what extent the law of historicity composed in these lines may be derived from the principle of unconditioned subjectivity of the German absolute metaphysics of Schelling and Hegel, according to whose teaching the being-with-itself of the spirit presupposes first the return to itself, which in turn presupposes the being-outside-itself, to what extent this reference to metaphysics, even if it uncovers "historically correct" relations, does not obscure rather than illumine the poetic law, all this we can only propose to thinking here.[23]

In effect, the movement of leaving and returning to itself of Spirit, as it is defined by Schelling and Hegel, but also by F. Schlegel, as we have seen, is also the *speculative reformulation* of the law of classical *Bildung*: What is one's own gains access to itself only by *experience*, namely the experience of the foreign. This experience may be the *Reise*, the romantic journey of Heinrich von Ofterdingen, at the end of which what is one's own and what is foreign discover their poetic identity, or the *Apprenticeship Years* of Wilhelm Meister, during which Wilhelm slowly discovers the virtues of self-limitation, far from the attacks of the "demonic."

Hölderlin's thinking does not depend on either of these two laws; its complexity bursts the simplicity of the schema of *Bildung*: It is neither the apprenticeship of the infinite, nor of the finite. In fact, it brings forth something more profound and more risky. On the one hand, the movement toward what is one's own and the movement toward the foreign do not succeed each other in a linear fashion, in the sense that the second would be like the mere condition of the first. Rather, the poem "The Journey" (*Die Wanderung*) sings the experience [*épreuve*] of the foreign and the attachment to what is one's own simultaneously:

> Most happy Swabia, my mother
> Whom like the more shining, your sister
> Lombarda over there
> A hundred rivulets thread.
> . . . .
> . . . ; for close to the hearth of
> The house you dwell, . . .
>
> . . . Therefore
> Innate in you is loyalty. For whatever dwells
> Close to the origin is loathe to leave the place.
> And so your children, the towns by the distantly glimmering lake,
> By Neckar's meadows, and by the Rhine,
> All them affirm that
> No dwelling-place could be better.
>
> But I am bound for the Caucasus!

Nevertheless, somewhat further, having celebrated "Homer's country," Hölderlin states:

> Yet not to stay I am minded
> Ungracious and intractable is
> The taciturn whom I fled from, my mother.[24]

In the first version of "The Only One" (*Der Einzige*), he still remembers that love of the foreign which continually tends to supplant the love of what is one's own:

> What is it that
> To the ancient, the happy shores
> Binds me, so that I love them
> Still more than my own homeland?[25]

Conversely, other poems celebrated the homeland as what belongs most to the poet:

> . . . Mine
> To speak of my country. Let no one
> Begrudge me that.[26]

But, enigmatically, the homeland seems the most difficult, at least in its "free" use:

At one time I questioned the Muse, and she
Replied to me,
In the end you will find it.
No mortal can grasp it. . . .
But, like the laurel, forbidden fruit
Your country is, above all.[27]

"Mnemosyne," more than any of Hölderlin's poems, has expressed the danger that lies in the love of the foreign, a danger that can only be averted by the love of the "homeland:"

A sign are we, without meaning
Without pain we are and have nearly
Lost our language in foreign lands
. . .

   But what we love? We see sunshine
On the floor and motes of dust
And the shadow of our native woods.[28]

The end of the poem returns to the foreign country, though it is presented as a country of the dead:

By the figtree
My Achilles died
And Ajax lies
By the grottoes of the sea
By streams, with Skamandros as neighbor.

What is opened here, simultaneously, is a dimension in which each of the poles, what is one's own and what is foreign, taken in its immediation, is equally *dangerous*: The foreign, the fire from heaven, could annihilate the one who comes too close, but what is one's own, the homeland, *also* hides the danger of an engulfment. In both cases, there is the threat of falling into the purely Indifferentiated, of a mortal fusion with Immediacy. This is precisely the danger mentioned by the third version of "The Only One:"

. . . Namely always the world rejoices
Away from this earth, leaving it
Bare; where the human cannot retain it.[29]

This entire problematic is summarized, as it were, in one of the latter versions of "Bread and Wine":

. . . The spirit namely is at home
Not in the beginning, not at the source. The homeland sears him,
The spirit loves the colony, and brave forgetting.
Our flowers and the shadows of our forests rejoice

The smothered one. The animator would almost be burned.[30]

With an unsurpassable rigor the double law of the "spirit" finds expression here: On the one hand, "the homeland devours him"; on the other, "the shadows of our forests" save him. The movement by which the "spirit" escapes the mortal (devouring) immediacy of the homeland is also the movement that threatens to consume it by the searing light of the foreign. Henceforth, as the experience [*épreuve*] of the foreign protects from the bad homeland, so does the apprenticeship of the homeland protect from the fire from heaven—from the foreign. The two movements are inseparable: The task of poetry consists in *mastering* the imbalances inherent to the experience of what is one's own and the experience of the foreign. This task is stated in "Patmos" with the utmost clarity:

> We have served Mother Earth
> And lately have served the sunlight,
> Unwittingly, but what the Father
> Who reigns over all loves most
> Is that the solid letter
> Be given scrupulous care, and the existing
> Be well interpreted. This German song observes.[31]

Likewise, in "The Vatican":

> To preserve God pure and with discrimination
> Is the task entrusted to us,
> Lest, because much depends
> On this, through a penitence, through a mistake
> In the sign
> God's day of judgment set in.[32]

To institute a balance, a measure in this dimension, to carry out a task of *differentiation*—or rather, poetry, *song*, establishes "what remains" ("Remembrance"), that is, that differentiated dimension in which the experience of the foreign and the experience of what is one's own arrive at being dominated. Poetry is able to play this foundational role because it is language, *letter* and *sign*, because it maintains itself, as Hölderlin says,

> under the more real Zeus, who . . . not only *stays* between this earth
> and the ferocious world of the dead, but who also *forces* the the
> eternally anti-human course of nature, on its way to the other world,
> more decidedly down onto earth.[33]

Poetry, as the putting into work of the dialogue (*Gespräch*) constituted by the language in the song (*Gesang*), is the place of this fight by which the reign of the Differentiated is instituted. As the place of this

struggle, of the establishment of Difference, language is "the most per-
ilous of goods,"[34] because it can *itself* be the prey of the indistinction it
is charged to avert. Hölderlin was well aware of this, as he was able to
say in "The Vatican":

> Turkish, and the owl, well versed in writings,
> Speaks like hoarse women in a city destroyed. But
> They catch the meaning. Yet often like a fire
> Confusion of tongues breaks out.[35]

This general problematic of Hölderlin's poetry, put forward very
summarily here, *has its rigorous counterpart in the movement of his
language*. The latter must go through the experience [*épreuve*] of the
foreign language (Greek) as well as the apprenticeship of the native
language (German and its dialectal roots). It might be said that the
language should simultaneously be "swabianized" and "graecicized" in
order to become more properly its own, in order to become song of
the Native Earth, the institution of a "Nation."

In the space of the mother tongue, the dialect is that which, at least
potentially, best expresses the essence of what is one's own and of the
"native." The mother tongue or national language is the "daughter" of
its dialects; but, because it dominates them by dint of being the common language, it is also their "mother." The relation of language to *its*
dialects is a mutual and differentiated relation; the dialects are dialects
of *that* language—they have no meaning, no being as dialect outside of
that space.

But conversely, common language needs dialects, lest it be infinitely
impoverished and fall into "fatelessness." Dialects, and more generally
the dialectal creativity, constitute so many *sources* of the language because, on the one hand, every language has a dialectal origin and, on the
other, because the dialects, connected to but different from it, feed the
great "stream" of the national language like as many rivers. In their
Sprachlichkeit, their own "speaking," dialects are the closest possible to
the terrestrial being of man, his "native" being. But, on the other hand,
they can only develop this "speaking" in the common language. For Hölderlin, then, the return to Swabian and the German dialectal past is, even
partially and, as it were, modestly,[36] (as it was, later, for G. M. Hopkins) to
carry out the "free" apprenticeship of what is one's own—that which
properly belongs to the very language he makes sing in his poems.

But to "graecicize" German is to subject it to the experience
[*épreuve*] of the foreign, of the most foreign language there is, because
it carries within itself what is most foreign to "us," the "fire from heav-
en," though it has been able to become the language of "Junonian
sobriety" and of rational "logos."

If Hölderlin had merely "dialectized" or "graecicized" his poetic language, its balancing double dimension and its differentiating power would disappear: a localist (or pseudo-localist) poetry would be the result, or a pidgin of Greek and German. After all, such cases are not uncommon in literature. But poetry, as the dimension of the Differentiated, the Articulated, the Measured, can only have the common language as its element: that is, the language that has been delimited simultaneously in relation to the dialects it "caps" without stifling them, and in relation to other languages. In a certain way, the double delimitation of which Bakhtin speaks, and which we mentioned above in connection with Luther, is repeated here. Through the "dialogue" with the Greek and the "return" to the dialectal element of the German, poetry gives the common language access to its own dimension—the equilibrium between the foreign language and the dialect that forms its origin.[37]

In this context, Hölderlin's translations from the Greek poets obey a total necessity at all levels. *They signal the furthest point of the graecization of German at work in his poetry*.

But it may also be said, conversely, that the most "native" German is used to render the speaking force of the Greek. Thus, already on the simple level of words, we witness again the same double movement. The line:

Was ist's, du scheinst ein rotes Wort zu färben

translates verse 20 of *Antigone* with such literality as to confine it to the absurd:

Τί δ'ἔστι; δηλοις γάρ τι καλχαίνουσ' ἔπος.

Indeed, καλχαινα originally means to have the color purple, to have a dark complexion. Hence the sliding of its meaning toward: being somber, tormented, etc. There where Mazon, for instance, translates (in agreement with the dictionary, which, for that matter, refers to verse 20 of *Antigone* for the derived meaning of this verb):

What's the matter; something is bothering you, clearly.[38]

Hölderlin prefers to reinstate the first meaning of the Greek word:

What is it? You seem to paint a purple word.[39]

Here, then, to translate literally is to translate the first meaning.

But on the other hand, numerous Greek words are rendered by terms going back to the *Mittelhochdeutsch*, or to Luther's German. Ποδῶν ἀρετᾶ is translated by *mit . . . der Füße Tugend* (with the "virtue" of the feet) instead of *mit der Kraft der Füße* (with the force of the feet) which would be more obvious. Here, *Tugend* is taken in its etymological sense, going back to the verb *taugen*, to be valid, to have value. Πόνος, normally translated as *Mühsal* (difficulty) is rendered as *Arbeit*, work, labor, in the old sense. Δεσποινα *Herrin*, mistress, is rendered by *Frau*, woman, in the meaning this word has in *Mittelhochdeutsch*.[40] Zuberbühler provides an impressive list of such examples, and shows that this is a deliberate choice on the part of the poet. Thus the German of the middle ages and of Luther's Bible is used to translate Pindar and Sophocles, not because of an arbitrary taste for the "ancient," but because Hölderlin wants to find again the speaking force of the German words.

A double movement, then, in which German must literally speak literal Greek, must be forced, as it were, violated, transformed, and perhaps fertilized by the foreign language. This literalness can also be found on the syntactic and the lexical level, and this is what gives Hölderlin's translations their sovereign and violent archaism. Nevertheless, we must insist that this literalness would be difficultly understood if one did not see that in order to translate what he interprets as the literalness of the original text—to have a purple color, instead of being tormented—Hölderlin went back to the etymological sources of German, to that which is literalness and origin in this language. From then on, translation becomes the encounter—shock and fusion—of two archaisms, and it is this, and not a vague literalness, that gives this operation all its meaning, and that obviously connects it to the rest of Hölderlin's undertaking. Except that in this case one of the poles of this undertaking—the brutal transfer of Greek into German—seems to have priority over the other: as if Hölderlin, at the very moment when he developed his problematic of differentiation, of the "native return," went forward in a dangerous way into that zone where the delimitation of languages borders on the confusion of languages.

Nevertheless, this movement is complicated and approaches its mastery by this: On several occasions, the *original text*, in its language and its content, is violated, and violated in a very precise way—namely in terms of a fundamental tendency that the text itself, according to Hölderlin, would have repressed:

> I hope to give of Greek art, which is foreign to us because of its adaptation to the Greek nature and flaws which it has always been able to accommodate, a more lively presentation than usual by bringing out more the oriental element it has denied, and by correcting its artistic flaw where it is encountered.[41]

Translation is instructed to reveal the originary element of the original text. Jean Beaufret writes in this respect:

To orientalize the translation of Sophocles, then, is to make Greek tragedy more ardent than it can appear to the modern reader who, contrary to the Greeks, excells culturally in *excentric enthusiasm*.[42]

Still, things are not all that simple, because Hölderlin writes to his publisher a few months later:

I believe I have written entirely against the excentric enthusiasm, and thus to have achieved Greek simplicity.[43]

And Beaufret adds quite correctly to his commentary:

To orientalize translation, then, is to remove Greek tragedy from its surroundings only by conserving its unequaled sobriety as well.

Thus, Hölderlin's "corrections" have a double meaning, and in this complex perspective all the "distances of translation" have to be studied, because if it is *like a traitor*, it is no less *in a holy way* that the modern poet comports himself in relation to the Greek original.[44]

A double movement, then, of "orientalization" of the translation, but also of captivation of the "simplicity," that is, the "sobriety" by which the original work is what it is. As Beaufret says:

A balance of two excesses, of the *Unförmliches* and the *Allzuförmliches*, of the aorgic disproportion and the excessive respect of forms.[45]

In this perspective, to translate καλχαίνουσ ἔπος as *ein rotes Wort zu färben*, is in effect, even if it is only in a detail, to bring out what Antigone's words contain in terms of, to use the striking expression from Hölderlin's "Remarks," *tödtendfactische*, of "deadly factical."[46] And to this purpose, exactly like in German, it is to return to a certain originary *literalness* of the text. Literal translation goes toward this literalness and even, in a sort of hyperbolical movement, restores it where the original text tends to veil it or to "deny" it. In fact, the original is not an inert given, but the site of a struggle, at all of its levels. Hölderlin described this struggle as that of "pathos" and "sobriety," or of the *Unförmliches* and the *Allzuförmliches*. Translation re-produces this struggle, even reactivates it, but as it were *in reverse*: If Sophocles goes from the fire from heaven to the Junonian sobriety (Greek trajectory), the modern translator goes from that sobriety to the fire from heaven (Western trajectory). But this movement remains itself measured, in that it also tries to "achieve the Greek simplicity." If Sophocles denies the fire from heaven, the oriental which is his own, he only does so up to a certain point; for his part, the translator denies sobriety only up to a certain point.

Could it be said that Hölderlin, starting from a certain "interpretation" of the Greeks, has arbitrarily modified Sophocles, as seems to be

the case in the passage in *Antigone* devoted to Danaë, where he renders
the line:

> She held and kept the seed of the golden rain which was Zeus [47]

as:

> She counted to the father of time
> The strokes of the hours, the golden ones

and thus produced a simultaneously fascinating and deviating mix
of objective literalness and subjective recreation? To be sure, any translation of a work starts from a reading of it, and Hölderlin's translations
are determined by his view of poetry and the Greeks. But perhaps the
concept of *interpretation* is insufficient. Every interpretation is the reconstruction of meaning carried out by a subject. What is this reconstruction based on? On the subject's field of vision, on his "perspective."
Perspectivism is a reality. But when we read a work, not *everything* is
interpretation. Beneath or beyond this, there is the pure apprehension
of the work Goethe alluded to in *Dichtung und Wahrheit* when he
extensively mentioned its "ground." It can be said of this "ground" that
it irradiates, and that in turn it illumines the subject's perspective. In this
sense, Hölderlin's view of the Greeks is not an interpretation. And this is
so true because, since Hölderlin, all those who approached the Greek
world approached the *same* reality (whatever their formulations may
have been).[48]

But that is not all. Where does this experience that precedes all
interpretation and protects it against all subjective arbitrariness come
from? The answer here must be: from that reading which *translation*
itself is. If that is not the case, one should maintain that Hölderlin
scaffolded a theory of Greek art, of tragedy, etc., which he then applied
to his translations. But in fact, his view of the Greeks and of tragedy
emerges from his experience as a poet on the one hand, and *from his
experience as translator* on the other. Only the translator (and not the
mere reader, even if he is a critic) can perceive what in a text is of the
order of the "denied," because only translation makes *appear* the struggle that took place in the original and that led to the balance *it is*. Valéry
intuited this very well:

> The labor of translation, carried out with a concern for a certain
> approximation of the form, in a way makes us seek to put our steps in
> what remains of the steps of the author's; and not to shape a text on
> the basis of another; but to go back to the virtual period of the latter's
> formation.[49]

Hölderlin's corrections, modifications, etc., proceed from this profound relation, *possible only in translation*, to the work and the virtual

period of its formation; which is why they are neither arbitrary nor belong to the domain of interpretation: At most, it can be said that there may be other translations that, starting from the same profound relation, may arrive at different results. In this sense, Hölderlin touched an *essential* possibility, even a necessity, of the act of translation, and he formulated them with great rigor. Because it "goes back to the virtual period of its formation," a translation stands in a relation to a work which is not only *sui generis*, but deeper, more "responsible" than other relations: It has the power to reveal that which, in the work, is origin (conversely, it has the power to obscure this possibility itself), which indicates that it has with the work a certain relation of *violence*. Where there is revelation of something hidden there is violence. And the violence of translation refers also to the no less violent immediacy presiding over the mutual delimitation of languages and their crossbreeding. That there is cross-breeding here, and not peaceful acclimation, that the images of sex and struggle prevail over those of gardening and culture (Herder, Goethe), is precisely what Hölderlin shows in a passage devoted to the essence of the tragic:

> The presentation of the tragic rests primarily on the tremendous—how the god and man mate and how natural force and man's innermost boundlessly unite in wrath—conceiving of itself, [rests] on the boundless union purifying itself through boundless separation. . . . Everything is speech against speech, one cancelling the other.[50]

Here, translation appears as one of the places where the measured and the disproportionate, fusion and differentiation confront one another—as a place of danger (the "confusion of languages"), but also of fruitfulness. That poetry is also such a place means that translation is a *poetic act*: not, as with the Romantics, that poetry is an act of translation, even if it is "transcendental," but that translation belongs to the differentiating space of the poetic, a space which is that of the confusion of languages as well as that of their delimitation. Hölderlin's translations are historic, because they are the first in Germany since Luther to inhabit the place where cultures and languages are delimited. That these translations, *a priori*, seem to be placed under a sign opposed to Luther—*Verdeutschung* on the one hand, *Griechischung* on the other—should not lead us astray if, on the one hand, a secret *Verdeutschung* is carried out in Hölderlin and if, on the other hand, the kind of *Verdeutschung* in Luther stands in a relation of correspondence to the very language of the Bible which passes through orality and which is closer than the relation of the Latin translation. What we, with Rosenzweig, have called historic translation can only be "historic" *because that type*

*of cross-breeding/differentiating relation with the foreign language
and the foreign work happens in it.*

Because of this type of historicity, Hölderlin's translations appear to
us simultaneously as *rooted in a tradition, anchored in an origin*
(Luther) and *constituting the space of modern Western translation.* In
fact, they bear witness to a choice that is inherent in the act of translation
in all times. Either this act yields to the cultural injunctions that have
been aimed at the appropriation and the reduction of the foreign since
the beginning of Western translation (from Saint Jerome to Nietzsche)
or, by virtue of its privileged position of a *between*, it contests these
injunctions, thus becoming a culturally creative act; this contestation,
raised to the level of a consciousness, as this can be seen with someone
like Pannwitz, is the essence of *modern* translation. To be sure, this
modernity has nothing to do with that of the *Athenäum*, that of monologic poetry/translation.[51] Its nature may be measured even better if we
briefly examine certain twentieth-century translations that, very obviously, are situated in Hölderlin's lineage.

Let us take the example of Klossowski's *Enéide*.[52] From the very first
lines, the reader, first of all dumbfounded by the syntactic disruptions
imposed on the French language by Klossowski trying to render Virgil's
Latin literally, goes through a strange experience: To be sure, this is
certainly a latinized French, as R. Pannwitz wished, but the strange
thing is that this latinization produces, in the strongest sense of this
word, a series of *manifestations*. In the first place, Virgil's epic *appears*
in the way it could emerge at the moment of its "formation"—which
might help us to measure the scope of Goethe's remarks on the "rejuvenation" of a work through its translation. Whereas less literal translations bar us from any access to the truth and the immediacy of the
epic's speaking:

> Virgil's epic poem is in effect a theater in which the words *mime* the
> gestures. . . . The words adopt a certain attitude, not the body; the
> words are woven, not the clothes; the words sparkle, not the ar-
> mour. . . . This is why we wanted, above all else, to restrict ourselves
> to the texture of the original.[53]

But there is more: in a sort of mutual mirroring (Goethe's
Spiegelung once again!), the two languages *appear*, in the struggle in
which they are engaged, as it were at *their own borders*: the Latin in the
French (first face of the translation) and the French invested by the Latin
(second face), showing us, paradoxically as it were, a *pure* Latin and a
pure French. What is notable for the reader who accepts entrusting
himself to the movement of Klossowski's translation is the metamorphosis of the French, which makes it appear, not as a sub-cross-

breeding of French and Latin, but rather as a new language, or rather, rejuvenated and renovated, raised to a level of hitherto hidden powers. Thus, there is indeed a *coupling of languages*, but even as they mix, the languages also manifest their pure *difference*. French on one side, Latin on the other, and yet the two are united in that space of cross-breeding which translation is, and perhaps exclusively.

For it is clear that when this mixing happens elsewhere, the risk is great that it would be caught in interlingual power relations.[54] These are relations that tend to annul the difference of languages, and often to stifle the specificity of the dominated language, which is deemed "inferior," whereas the meaning of translation is rather a profound egalitarianism. This was clearly felt by Goethe, but realized by Hölderlin, who accepted to the full extent the risks it carried: the loss of the language (of the own language, of language as such) in the "foreign land."

Nevertheless, the nature of "literal" (using this word for lack of another, more subtle term) translation is such that it can in no case be transformed into a model or a methodological recipe. Just like it exceeds all "interpretation," it exceeds all methodology. Let us say that this translation first manifests itself at certain determined historical and cultural moments, as Rosenzweig rightly said. It emerges from a profound need of the language, the culture, and the literature, and it is this need, perceptible historically, that guards against the arbitrariness of an attempt at individual experimentation (of which many examples are known in the history of translation, as Steiner showed in *After Babel*). Hölderlin's translations, ahead of their epoch, were nevertheless historically motivated. And in our day, this is the case for translations like Klossowski's. All evidence points to the fact that they correspond to a *crisis* of our culture, in the first place the shaking-up of its ethnocentrism. It is the crisis of an ideological, cultural, literary, and poetic position which has attained its final consequences. This does not mean that all translation should become "literal," because this type of translation only makes sense for a certain type of works, whose relation to their languages is such that it requires this differential coupling of literal translation. The case could not be clearer in the case of the *Enéide*, and Klossowski explained it perfectly well. The same goes for the (re)translation of the Bible, the Greeks, the works from the East and the Far East, and a certain number of Western works. But, for instance, a literal, or anglicizing, translation of Henry James would not make sense. To be sure, James should not be "gallicized," but his work demands a different type of approach.[55]

We are still far from overseeing this entire problematic, and the danger of constituting typologies somewhat hastily, by wanting to escape the infinite empiricism of the majority of the translators (translation would be a matter of "intuition," different from work to work, not allowing for any theorization, etc.), is great. What remains is that Hölderlin was the first, by the radicality of his undertaking, to expose us to the necessity of a global and thorough reflection on the act of translation in the baffling multiplicity of its registers.[56]

CONCLUSION

I. The Archeology of Translation

Every conclusion is a rereading attempting to retrace the path opened, staked out, and articulated by the introduction, but whose course has partially turned out to be different than was initially envisioned. The present study attempted to analyze the German Romantics' theory of translation by, on the one hand, situating it within their theories and programs as a whole and, on the other hand, confronting it with other, contemporary reflections: those of Herder, Goethe, Schleiermacher, and Humboldt, which are theories of *Bildung*, and that of Hölderlin, which extends beyond the framework of the former, and beyond its entire epoch. We also attempted to show how the tradition of translation in Germany, which starts with Luther, defined itself in opposition to a culture—that of French classicism—in whose unfolding translation did not play a decisive role.

Next, it appeared that all the theories of translation developed in the Romantic and classical period in Germany constitute the foundation for the principal currents of modern Western translation, be it *poetic* translation—as it is manifested in a Nerval, a Baudelaire, a Mallarmé, an S. George, or a Benjamin, whose origins are obviously to be found in German Romanticism—or the great re-translations carried out in Germany in the twentieth century, which can claim Humboldt or Schleiermacher as their precursors. Hölderlin's translations, for their part, inaugurated a new epoch in the history of Western translation that is still in its initial stages.

In that sense, our study may appear to be an *archaeology of European translation*, centered on its key phase at the dawn of the nineteenth century. An archaeology which belongs to that reflection of translation on itself—at once historical, theoretical, and cultural—which is henceforth inseparable from the practice of translation. That translation should become a "science" and an "art," as the Jena Romantics demanded of criticism, that is in effect its *modern* destiny. But for translation, this means first of all: to appear, to manifest itself. For two centuries, literature has had its manifestos. Translation, on the other hand, has always inhabited the non-manifest: "Effacement be the splendor of my being," as the poet-translator Philippe Jacottet once said.[1] Indeed, since time immemorial translation has been a practice obscured and repressed by those who carried it out as well as by those who benefited from it. In this respect, classical and Romantic Germany is an exception that is well worth meditating upon. But whatever the immediate intensity of its relation to translation has been, it is no less undeniable that it has only been able to offer *fragments* of a genuine theory of translation. That Goethe, Hölderlin, the Romantics, and Humboldt, from different angles, provide us with invaluable "materials" for such a theory has been keenly felt in the twentieth century by such thinkers as W. Benjamin, W. Schadewaldt, and F. Rosenzweig. But those "materials," dealing primarily with the poetic and cultural dimension of translation, must be rethought in the light of our twentieth-century experience, and replaced into a domain of our own.

Indeed, the twentieth century has seen the manifestation of the problematic of translation (together with that of language and languages) from different perspectives.

Above all, we must mention the question of the *re-translation* of works fundamental to our Western culture: primarily the Bible, but also Greek poetry and philosophy, Latin poetry, and the great texts that presided over the birth of modern literature (Dante, Schakespeare, Rabelais, Cervantes, etc.). To be sure, any translation is bound to age, and it is the destiny of all translations of the "classics" of universal literature to be retranslated sooner or later. But retranslation in the twentieth century has a more specific historical and cultural meaning: to *reopen the access* to works whose unsettling and questioning power ended up being threatened at once by their "glory" (too much clarity obscures, too great radiance exhausts) and by translations belonging to a phase of Western conscience that is no longer ours. Thus, as we have seen, our view of the Greeks, the Old Testament, or even Shakespeare, is fundamentally different from the classicist, humanist, or Romantic views. This will to reopen the access to great texts of our historical tradition extends to the field of translation, hermeneutics, and philosophy at the same time. This is obvious in the case of the Bible: Think of Buber, Rosenzweig, or Meschonnic. But it suffices to think of the great rereadings of Greek philosophy attempted by Heidegger, to see that here as well the task of thinking has *become* a task of translation. In the same way the hermeneutic of the sacred texts is unthinkable without a retranslation of them, the rereading of the Greeks cannot be conceived by Heidegger and his disciples without a translation from the Greeks toward ourselves and from ourselves toward the Greeks, a translation that claims to be (in Heidegger's vocabulary) "listening to the Greek words." And it is evident that this operation of translation, henceforth immanent to philosophy, has had enormous cultural reverberations (in Germany, but also elsewhere). What should be emphasized here is *how, in the twentieth century, translation becomes a concern of thinking itself in its attempt to reread the Western religious and philosophical tradition.* It is in this light that the act of translation is finally being recognized in its historical essence. In "The Principle of Reason," speaking about the great translations of the history of philosophy, Heidegger writes:

> By this we mean those translations that, in a period when their time has come, transpose (*übertragen*) a work of thinking or poetry. . . . In such cases, the translation is not only interpretation (*Auslegung*) but also tradition (*Überlieferung*). As tradition, it belongs to the innermost movement of history.[2]

But this concern with translation, in our century, does not only deal with philosophy and religious thinking. It can also be found in the field of the "humanities" or, more precisely, in psychoanalysis, ethnology, and linguistics.

The relations of psychoanalysis to translation are highly complex, and we do not pretend to measure their entire magnitude. It is well known that Freud arrived in France through translations that tended to distort the essential aspect of his conceptual and terminological inventiveness. It was necessary for Lacan, with the same patience of a Heidegger reading the Greek texts, to interrogate Freud's writing in an attempt of rereading/translation in order to open for us Freud's *Grundwörter* (basic words) on the one hand (*Trieb, Anlehnung , Verneinung, Verwerfung*, etc.), and the infinite complexity of the weave of his language and his images on the other. We see here how (re)translation also becomes one of the major concerns of a reflection, and a path that reopens the authentic access of a thinking. But psychoanalysis undoubtedly stands in an even more profound relation to translation, to the extent that it questions man's relation to language, languages, and the so called "mother" tongue in a way fundamentally different from that of the tradition—a questioning accompanied by a reflection on the work and on writing, destined to gradually upset our view of them and, undoubtedly, to contribute to a turning-point in literature. The few, and still sparse, remarks on translation found in Lacan, O. Mannoni, Abraham, and Torok could perhaps, when they are further developed, also change a certain awareness of the act of translation and the processes at work in it—certainly on the level of the translator himself (in his *drive* for translation, the translator is that individual who represents an entire community in its relation to another community and its works), but also on the level of what we have called the *translatability* of the work. Renan said:

> A work not translated is only half published.[3]

What is—at bottom—this *lack* translation intends to supplant? What hidden face of the work, what reverse side of the text should appear through it? If we want to go beyond the Romantic notion of "potentiation," to deepen Goethe's perception of the rejuvenating "mirroring," perhaps we need a theory of the work and of translation that calls upon psychoanalytic thinking.

In its own way, ethnology also encounters the problem of languages, cultures, and translation. If it were only because it, too, as a discourse on the *foreign* (and on what is supposed to be *the most foreign*: the "savage"), constitutes a kind of translation, exposed to the same alternatives as Schleiermacher's translator: to lead the reader to the foreign, or to lead the foreign to the reader. Obviously, a modern translator concerned about struggling against ethnocentrism can learn much from the reflections of a Clastres or a Jaulin, for instance. It is no less obvious that the ethnological writing should at times (and essentially) become a translation: think of Clastres's *Le Grand Parler*[4] or of the Peruvian writer-ethnologist J.-M. Arguedas's translations of Quecha poetry.

For its part, linguistics (and it is appropriate to add to this the research of Anglo-Saxon analytic philosophy, itself oriented to linguistic questions) also encounters translation as an immanent reality. Think of Jakobson's famous text, "Linguistic Aspects of Translation:"

> Equivalence in difference is the cardinal problem of language and the pivotal concern of linguistics. Like any receiver of verbal messages, the linguist acts as their interpreter. No linguistic specimen may be interpreted by the science of languauge without a translation of its signs into other signs of the same system or into signs of another system. Any comparison of two languages implies an examination of their mutual translatability; the widespread practice of interlingual communication, particularly translating activities, must be kept under constant scrutiny by linguistic science.[5]

It is remarkable that in this text, Jakobson should simultaneously define the *object* of linguistics (language and its process of "equivalence in difference") and the *practice* of this science in terms of translation. To be sure, this is another case of generalized translation:

> For us, both as linguists and as ordinary word-users, the meaning of any linguistic sign is its translation into some further, alternative sign, especially by a sign "in which it is more fully developed," as Peirce insistently stated. . . . We distinguish three ways of interpreting a verbal sign: it may be translated into other signs of the same language, into another language, or into another, non-verbal system of symbols.[6]

This generalized translation, within which Jakobson, in an effort to dominate the unmasterable concept of translation, situates "reformulation," "translation properly speaking, " and "transmutation," is itself connected to what we have called, with regard to the Romantics, the reflexive structure of language:

> An ability to speak a given language implies an ability to talk *about* this language.[7]

Again, as for Novalis (but in a rewording that has no longer anything speculative), we see *reflexivity* and *translatability* connected.

Without a doubt, linguistics is not only a discipline that claims to be "scientific" and whose knowledge would be as foreign to our experience as that of mathematical physics. It is a certain perception of language and man's relation to language, even if it is not, like translation, an *experience*. In that sense, it must be asserted that translation can never constitute a mere branch of linguistics, philology, criticism (as the Romantics believed), or hermeneutics: Whether it be of philosophy, religion, literature, poetry, etc., translation constitutes a dimension *sui generis*. A dimension which produces a certain *knowledge*. But this experience (and the knowledge it provides) may in return be illumined and partially transformed by other experiences, other practices, a different knowledge. And it is obvious that linguistics, in the twentieth century, can enrich the translating consciousness; and vice versa, for that matter. Jakobson's linguistics interrogates poets; it might also interrogate translators. And this is, in effect, the reciprocal game proposed by Haroldo de Campos in Brasil.[8]

Ezra Pound's translations, and his reflection on poetry, criticism, and translation, are of a fundamental importance here, and it would be interesting to confront the theory of *criticism by translation* with the Romantic theories of translation by criticism. Pound's reflections, like those of Meschonnic, *Po&sie*, and *Change*, attempt to define what may be, in the twentieth century, a theory and a practice of *poetic translation*.

We did not intend here to present a panorama (necessarily sketchy and partial) of the contemporary efforts in the theory of translation, but above all to emphasize this: The field of translation, which has become practically decentralized and structured on the international level,[9] is slowly, very slowly, beginning to become less obscure and to assert itself as a field of its own, as the several domains in which the "problems" of translation are posed are gradually beginning to question themselves (often for the first time) on translation and its different registers. For translation is not a mere mediation: It is a process in which our entire relation to the Other is played out. Now this consciousness, already present in Romantic and classical Germany, is reemerging with a force that is all the greater in proportion as all the certainties of our intellectual tradition and even our "modernity" are shaken up. That much needs to be retranslated; that we must go through the experience [*épreuve*] of translation, incessantly; that in this experience [*épreuve*] we must struggle relentlessly against our fundamental reductionism, but also remain open to that which, in all translation, remains mysterious and unmasterable, properly speaking in-visible (we do not know the nature of the face of the foreign work that will appear in our language, regardless of our efforts to make the voice of that work speak in our language at all cost); that we must expect much from this undertaking of "eccentric" translation, perhaps an enriching of our language, perhaps even an inflection of our literary creativity; that we have to question the act of translation in all its registers, and to open it to other contemporary interrogations,[10] reflect on its nature, but also on its history as well as on its obscuring—this seems to us to characterize the present age of translation.

When we read what the German classical and Romantic age managed to write on the act of translating and its meaning (cultural, linguistic, speculative, etc.), we find not only a number of theories that, in some form or other, still determine our present, for better or for worse. We also find a consciousness, and above all an inhabiting of language that is essentially *less threatened than ours*.

Let us take, for instance, the case of the expansion of our language that we expect from non-ethnocentric translation. Clearly, the Germany of Goethe and Schleiermacher expected the same gains from its translation enterprises, even though their perspective seems too limited to us *today*. But in the meantime, something happened that has been denounced by numerous authors of our century, and that has to do with the destruction of the *Sprachlichkeit* (the speaking power of the great modern languages) to the benefit of a system-language of communication becoming more and more emptied of its own density and significance. One may think here of the impoverishment of oral creativity, the death of dialects, the receding of literature in an increasingly closed space in which it is no longer capable to "figure" the world. The degradation of language (natural language) is certainly a commonplace. *Our* common place. At the end of *After Babel*, Steiner mentions the dangers threatening planetary English. In fact, these dangers concern all languages, and all the dimensions of our existence. Henceforth, they place the task of translating in a new, or at least infinitely more crude light: The issue is to defend language and the relations among languages against the increasing homogenization of communication systems— because they endanger the entire realm of belonging and difference. Annihilation of dialects and local speech; trivialization of national languages; leveling of the differences among them for the benefit of a model of non-language for which English served as guinea pig (and as victim), a model by virtue of which automatic translation would become thinkable; cancerous proliferation of specialized languages at the bosom of the common language[11]—this is a process that thoroughly attacks language and the *natural* relation of human beings to language. To reopen the paths of the tradition; to open a relation, finally accurate (not dominating or narcissistic), to other cultures, and notably those of what has now become the "Third World"; to mobilize the resources of our language to bring it up to the level of those several openings—all of this, obviously, is to struggle against that destructive phenomenon, even if there are other ways to avert it. And that is, perhaps, what is essential to the modern translating consciousness: a maximal demand of "knowledge" at the service of a certain realimentation of the speaking force of language, to *inhabit and defend Babel* with a certain lucidity at the time when the Tower-of-Manifold-Languages (i.e., that of Differences) is threatened by the expansion of an uprooting jargon which is not even Esperanto, that naive humanist dream that now reveals its nightmarish face.

The history of Western translation has not yet been written. The modern translating consciousness is unthinkable without a knowledge of its history: its origins, its epochs, its wanderings. May the present work constitute at least the beginning of the writing of one of the most captivating chapters of that history.

II. *Translation as a New Object of Knowledge*

Translation as a new object of knowledge: This means two things. First of all, as experience and as operation, it is the carrier of a knowledge *sui generis* on languages, literatures, cultures, movements of exchange and contact, etc. The issue is to manifest and articulate his knowledge *sui generis*, to confront it with other modes of knowledge and experience concerning these domains. In this sense, translation must be considered rather as *subject* of knowledge, as origin and source of knowledge.

In the second place, this knowledge, in order to become a "knowledge" in the strict sense, should take on a definite, quasi-institutional and established form, suited to further its development in a field of research and teachability. This has sometimes been called traductology (other, less fortunate names have also been suggested).[12] But that does not mean, at least not in the first place, that translation should become the object of a specific "discipline" concerning a separate "region" or "domain," precisely because it is not anything separate itself. In fact, traductology, as a form or field of knowledge, could primarily be compared to Michel Foucault's "archaeology," Jacques Derrida's "grammatology," or the "poetology" developed in Germany by Beda Allemann. Rather than being "regional" disciplines, these types of reflection bear upon dimensions already intersected by other, established disciplines, but intersected in such a way that the immanent wealth of their content can no longer fully appear.

Translation constitutes such a dimension. Carrying its own knowledge, it can only become the subject of this knowledge if it opens itself to a traductology in the sense outlined here.

The issue, then, will be to found—or to radicalize already existing and often decisive attempts at foundation—a space of reflection, and thus of research. As we indicated at the beginning of this study, this space will cover the field of translation within other fields of interlinguistic, interliterary, and intercultural communication, as well as the history of translation and the theory of literary translation—"literature" encompassing literature in the strict sense as well as philosophy, the humanities, and religious texts. The knowledge which will take this space as its theme will be autonomous: In itself, it will neither depend on applied linguistics, nor comparative literature, nor poetics, nor the study of foreign languages and literatures, etc., even though all these established disciplines, in their own way, claim the field of translation. Yet, to the extent that this field, by its very nature, intersects a multiplicity of domains, and chiefly those of the disciplines mentioned above, there will necessarily be some interaction between these and traductology. No reflection on translation can do without the contributions of linguistics and literary theory. Traductology is interdisciplinary *par excellence*, precisely because it is situated *between* several disciplines, often far apart.

Its starting point rests on a few fundamental hypotheses. The first one is this: Even as it is a particular case of interlingual, intercultural, and interliterary communication, translation is also the *model* for any process of this kind. Goethe has taught us this. This does not mean that all the problems that may be posed by this communication appear decoded and, as it were, in a condensed form in the operation of translation, and that it would then be possible to understand and analyze the other modes of intercommunication from the perspective of translation. It may be said that translation occupies an analogous place to that of language within other sign systems. As Benveniste said, in one sense language is only a sign system among others; but in another, it is the system of systems, the one that makes possible the interpretation of all others. This fact will be confirmed by the relation of mutual envelopment between the generalized theory of translation and the restricted theory. From Novalis to George Steiner and Michel Serres, we have witnessed the edification of theories in which any type of "change" (of "trans-lation") is interpreted as a translation, not only in the aesthetic domain, but also in that of the sciences and, finally, in human experience in general. A trace of this peculiar extension of the concept of translation is also found in Roman Jakobson's classic text on translation. This generalized theory of translation or, as Michel Serres says, of "duction,"[13] has recently been criticized by Henri Meschonnic. The extension of this concept would result in depriving it of all content, whereas, on the contrary, much would be gained in the development of a restricted theory of translation. Still, it remains a fact that the concept of translation continues to overflow any limited definition it can be given. This semantic—and epistemological—overflowing seems inevitable and, for that matter, it corresponds to the common perception that translation is always much more than translation. It will be better, then, to articulate a restricted and a generalized theory of translation, without dissolving (as is the case for the German Romantics) the former in the latter. Which amounts to saying that the restricted theory should function as the archetype of any theory of "changes" or of "trans-lations." The position of this archetype is characterized by a paradox: *its uniqueness*. The relation that links a translation to its original is unique in its kind. No other relation—from one text to another, from one language to another, from one culture to another—is comparable to it. And it is precisely this uniqueness that makes for the *significant density* of translation; to interpret the other exchanges in terms of translation is to want (rightly or wrongly) to give them the same significant density.

Traductology's second hypothesis is that translation, be it literature or philosophy or even humanities, plays a role that is not merely one of transmission: On the contrary, this role is tendentially *constitutive* of all literature, all philosophy, and all human science. Giordano Bruno expressed this with all the lyricism belonging to his epoch:

From translation comes all science.

The hyperbolical character of this sentence should not mask the truth of its content. We will briefly explicate here in what respect translation plays this constitutive role and in what respect—and this is a decisive corollary—it remained obscured and denied as a constitutive moment, so as to appear only as a simple operation of mediation (of meaning). If translation had not been obscured as the constitutive (and hence historical) factor of literature and knowledge, something like "traductology" would long since have been in existence, with the same right as "criticism."

But, as we have seen, when translation is being interfered with, we approach a repressed domain, filled with resistances.

In the area of literature, modern poetics, and even comparative literature[14] have shown that the relation of works (first writing) and translations (second writing) is characterized by a reciprocal engendering. Far from being only the mere "derivation" of an original supposed to be absolute, as the Law still defines it, the translation is *a priori* present in any original: Any work, as far as one can go back, is already to several degrees a fabric of translations or a creation that has something to do with the translating operation, inasmuch as it posits itself as "translatable," which means simultaneously "worthy of being translated," "capable of translation," and "having to be translated" in order to reach its plenitude as work. The possibility and the injunction of translation do not define a text after the fact: They constitute the work *as work* and, in fact, must lead to a new definition of its structure. This may easily be verified by analyzing Latin literature or medieval works.[15]

This is not without consequences for disciplines like poetics, comparative literature, or the study of foreign languages and literatures. The analysis of transtextualities, undertaken methodically by poetics, implies, in addition to research concerning hypertextuality, intertextuality, paratextuality, and metatextuality, a reflection on that specific transtextuality constituted by translation, following the lead J. L. Borges intuitively indicated:

No problem is as concordant with literature and with the modest mystery of literature as is the problem posed by a translation.[16]

Novalis and A. W. Schlegel, but also Baudelaire, Proust, and Valéry, intuited this "concordant" relation between "literature" and translation. They even went so far as to assert that the writer's operation and the translator's are identical.[17] Nevertheless, it is necessary to mark the limits of this identification that is so typically Romantic: These limits are defined by the irreducibility of the relation between original and translation. No translation has meaning other than as translation of an original. For its part, literature does not know any relation of this kind, even if it has a nostalgia for it.[18]

Similarly, comparative literature presupposes "traductology" as a partially integratable complement. The comparative study of different literatures is obviously based on their interaction. Now, interaction has translations as the condition for its possibility. No "influence" without translation, even if (we encounter again the reciprocal envelopment) the converse can be stated as well.

In the philosophical domain, translation also plays an essential role. Historically, from the Greeks to the Romans, from the Middle Ages to the Renaissance and beyond, philosophy developed through a series of translations that have been much more than a mere "transfer of content." As Heidegger has shown concerning the translation of Aristotelian concepts or of "the principle of reason," the principal *Grundwörter* (fundamental words) that articulate philosophical discourse have been translated every time by a process in which interpretation and neology, borrowing and reformulation, coexisted or alternated. And every translation of a *Grundwort* has entailed a new perception of past or present philosophies: think of Hegel's *Aufhebung* that became *relève* in Jacques Derrida. The history of philosophical translation "errors" constitutes one of the most captivating chapters of this process—because these "errors" are never insignificant.[19] In the twentieth century, translation has entered the philosophical horizon as an explicit and crucial *question* with thinkers as different as Wittgenstein, Karl Popper, Quine, Heidegger, Gadamer and, most recently, Michel Serres and, above all Jacques Derrida.

In the modern human sciences the same "circle" is found, the same essential interweaving between translation and the constitution of a discipline. As we have seen, psychoanalysis first encountered translation as one of the problems of its own renovation. But this led it to question itself more and more about the essence of translation and—this is important for us—to rediscover the place the concept of translation held as an operational concept *within Freud's own thinking*. This is shown by a letter from Freud to Fließ shortly before the appearance of *Die Traumdeutung*:

> I explain the particularity of psychoneuroses to myself by the fact that *translation*, for certain materials, *has not been carried out*, which has certain consequences. . . . *The failing of translation* is called *repression* in clinical terms. The motive of the latter is always a *disconnecting of displeasure* that would happen by *translation*, as if displeasure would provoke a disturbance of thinking that would not allow the *labor of translation*.[20]

Orientalism also presupposes the problematic of translation. On the one hand, research itself is accompanied by translation, whether it is of works, of quotations, or of *Grundwörter*. On the other hand, the very essence of its project, as Massignon indicated, supposes a certain "decentering" that is itself an essential moment of the operation of translation: to translate oneself toward. . . .

> In order to understand the other, one should not annex it, but become its host. . . . To understand something other is not to *annex* the thing, but to transfer oneself by a decentering to the very center of the other.[21]

Edward Saïd, in *Orientalism*—a very controversial work, for that matter—has shown that, historically, Orientalism found itself badly armed to confront the problematic of its necessary decentering, inasmuch as a certain ideological surcharge, in the nineteenth century, led it to "ethnocentric" translations. This "failing of translation," to take up Freud's term, signals an organic "absence" of this discipline, with which it is gradually parting. But it also signals the point where a traductology could collaborate with it. In fact, one of the axes of traductology is to elaborate a theory of *non-ethnocentric translation* with a generalized field of application. This theory is both *descriptive* and *normative*.

It is descriptive in that it analyzes the systems of deformation that weigh upon any operation of translation and is able to propose a counter-system on the basis of that analysis.[22] It is normative in that the alternatives it defines concerning the direction of translation are mandatory. These alternatives go far beyond the traditional divisions of translation theory into "supporters of the letter" and "supporters of the spirit." Thus, starting from this framework, every domain can elaborate its own methodology of translation. For instance, traductology is not supposed to settle the problems of the translation of Chinese poetry for, if it descended to that level, its task would obviously be empirically infinite. But there is a level where the problems are the same for the sinologist, the specialist of Serbian literature, or of Greek tragedy. This level concerns the problematic of translation itself and the systems of constraints that French (and any great "national" language) poses for translation. This level is that of *pure translating competence*. And it is the one lacking in most specialists of a given domain, which taints their attempts at translation with epistemological naïveté. This is the case because, even as they recognize that the problematic of translation is essential for them (it concerns, in part, the becoming of their discipline), they end up degrading this problematic to the level of a simple technical procedure. At this stage, we are once again confronted with the obscured, denied status of translation, and the violent resistances it arouses.

These resistances constitute an essential chapter of traductology. Originally, they seem to be of a religious and cultural order. At a first level, they are ordered around *untranslatability as a value*. What is essential in a text is not translatable or, supposing it is, should not be translated. In the case of the Bible, the Jewish translation represents this extreme position. Just as the "Law" should not be "translated" from the oral to the written, the sacred text should not be translated into other languages, lest it lose its "sacred" character. This double refusal indicates in reverse the essential connection between the written and translation, in order to be able to question both of them better. The rejection of translation traverses the whole history of the West, with the dogma, never made explicit and continually refuted practically, of the untranslatability of poetry, without mentioning the famous "prejudicial objection" against translation in general.[23] A very recent example will show the deaf persistence of this rejection. In an article devoted to the necessity of the diffusion of the French language and literature, Bernard Catry mentions the possibility of stimulating, on the official level, "the translation into foreign languages of French works." This, the author believes, might lead foreign readers to subsequently read those same works in the original language, and thus to learn French. And he adds in passing:

To be sure, Sartre in English is no longer Sartre.[24]

The "to be sure" that opens this short sentence indicates that Catry considers translation a makeshift and a total treason. It contains a devalorization that is never made explicit. Obviously, it is an entire culture (in this case, French culture) defending itself against the "exile" of its "sacred monsters."

One easily understands from this that translation is considered suspect and, in the end, culturally negative. At the other end of the spectrum, it is rather its significant density that is denied, by the opposite axiom of *universal translatability*. Essential to translation would be the transmission of "meaning," that is, the universal content of any text. As soon as this is postulated, translation acquires the shallowness of a humble mediation of meaning. In his *Aesthetics*, Hegel stated that poetry could be translated from one language into another (and even into prose) without any loss, because spiritual content prevails in it. But when one states, more modestly, that "not words, but ideas are translated,"[25] one only repeats, at a non-speculative level, what Hegel said. Every time translation rebels against the narrowing of this operation and pretends to be a transmission of *forms*, of *signifiers*, resistances proliferate. These resistances are well known by every translator: The issue would be to provide a translation that "does not smack of translation," to propose a text "the way the author would have written it if he were French," or, more trivially, to produce a translation in "clear and elegant French." The result is that translation appears either as the modest transmission of meaning, or as the suspect activity of injecting the language with "strangeness."[26] In both cases, translation is denied and obscured.

One of the fundamental tasks of traductology is to fight this obscuring, which is manifest additionally in the prejudicial objection against the *reflection of translation*. This reflection collides with a series of oppositions: the conflict between theorist and non-theorist translators, of translators and theorists of translation. In the first case, a majority of translators proclaim that translation is a purely intuitive activity, which can never really be conceptualized. In the second case, there is an opposition between theorists without practice and "practitioners" without theory. The result is a tenacious putting-into-question of the possibility of a traductology that would cover both the theoretical and the practical field and that would be developed on the basis of the *experience* of translation—more specifically, on the basis of *its very nature as experience*. Abstract theorists and empirical practitioners concur in the assertion that the experience of translation is not, should not and could not be theorizable. Now, this presupposition is a negation of the meaning of the act of translation: By definition, this act is a *second and reflexive* activity. Reflexivity is essential to it, and with it systematicity. In fact, the coherence of a translation is measured by the degree of its systematicity. And systematicity is unthinkable without reflexivity. This reflexivity goes from the interpretive reading of texts to the reasoned elaboration of an entire system of "choices" of translation. Of course, it is accompanied by a necessary intuitiveness. But this reciprocal play of reflexivity and intuitiveness, as we have seen, makes translation much more similar to a "science" than to an "art." In the same way that, in the case of a science, an entire system of deformation must be overcome before it can constitute a rigorous categorial horizon, translation likewise, must confront a field of linguistic, literary, and cultural deformation in order to be able to realize its pure aim. That this end is rarely attained only confirms the necessity of a traductology that would accomplish a "Copernican revolution" of translation.

To finish, let us clarify the position of traductology in relation to the *linguistic* approach to translation. We start from the presupposition that the two approaches are both distinct and complementary. In his *Problèmes théoriques de la traduction*, Georges Mounin poses the problem of the untranslatables: Morphologically, syntactically, lexically, etc., languages tend to make all translation impossible, except at a level of approximation where the "losses" are higher than the "gains." Thus,

Mounin says, the translation of the approximately fifty words for bread in the region of Aix-en-Provence would pose "insoluble problems" if "a French novel of some merit would have the world of baking in this region as its setting."[27] Examples of this kind may be multiplied infinitely and, of course, on other levels than that of the "semantic fields" of the author. This observation is indisputable, even if Mounin attempts to minimize its scope in the last part of his book. Linguistically speaking, we are facing a *band of untranslatability*. But if one puts oneself on the level of the *translation of a text*, the problem changes completely. To be sure, every text is written in a language; and in fact, the multiplicity of terms mentioned, whether it appears in an oral or a written sequence, remains in itself "untranslatable" in the sense that the other language will not have the corresponding terms. But at the level of a work, the problem is not to know whether or not there are equivalents for these terms. *Because the level of translatability is different*. Faced with a multiplicity of terms without equivalence in his own language, the translator will be confronted with different choices: gallicization (in *Captain Grant's Children* Jules Verne translates *pampas* as "the pampasian plains"), borrowing (*pampa* in contemporary French), or semi-gallicization (*porteño*, inhabitant of Buenos Aires, becomes *portègne*). The alleged untranslatability is dissolved in total translatability by simply having recourse to modes of relation that exist naturally and historically between languages, but adapted in this case to the demands of the translation of a *text*: borrowing and neologism for the lexical domain. It is the structure itself of the text that will dictate what must be "translated" or "not translated" (in the usual sense), *the non-translation of a term counting as an eminent mode of translation*. Other modalities complement this recourse to types of interlingual exchanges. For instance, a term or a structure *x* will be canceled at a point *X* in the text, possibly to be replaced by a term or a structure *y* at point *Y*: this is the procedure of *compensation*, recommended already by Du Bellay. Or the positing of a term or a structure *x* situated at point *X* in the text at another point *Y* of that text where the target language can accommodate it better: This is the procedure of *displacement*. Or again, *homologous replacement*: An element *x*, literally untranslatable, is replaced by an element *y* that is homologous to it in the text. These are not, as one tends to believe, makeshift procedures, but modalities that define the meaning itself of all literary translation, *inasmuch as it encounters what is linguistically (and sometimes culturally) untranslatable and dissolves it in actual literary translatability without, of course, slipping into paraphrase or an opaque literalness*. These modalities are based to a large extent on what Efim Etkind called the "potential language."[28] For any language, a rigorous correspondence with another language may be postulated, but on a *virtual* level. To develop these potentialities (which vary from language to language) is the task of translation *which thereby proceeds toward the discovery of the "kinship" of languages*. This task could not be simply artistic; it supposes an extensive knowledge of the entire diachronic and synchronic space of the target language. Thus, the translation of Spanish diminutives requires a thorough study of French diminutives (their history, the mode of their formation and integration, etc.), without which one would believe oneself faced with "untranslatables." The abstract theorist of translation and the intuitive practitioner encounter the same limitation, which comes from the fact that they have no awareness of the "heterological" wealth of the target language.

The modalities mentioned above are usually no longer classified in the category of translation—for instance by Jakobson or Max Bense—but in that of "creative transposition," the definition of which for that matter, remains indeterminate. But in fact this "transposition" is the very essence of translation, and the former can only be opposed to the latter on the basis of a petty and imaginary (the perfect correspondence, the *adequatio*), even speculative concept of translation. On the contrary, translation must be defined on the basis of its actual operation, which does not at all mean that all modalities are equivalent, and that there would not exist modalities that amount to non-translations or bad translations. As we have seen, these phenomena of non-translations and bad translations must be taken into account by traductology for, as George Steiner said, without exaggerating too much:

> It must be admitted that since Babel ninety percent of translations have been wrong and that it will remain that way.[29]

These remarks are aimed at making clear that the linguistic and the traductological approach are different and, at the same time, complementary, since translation can only realize its pure aim on the basis of linguistic knowledge, if at least it wants to go beyond an empiricity that destines 90 percent of its products to being "wrong." In other words, the "Copernican revolution" of the sciences of language must make possible the "Copernican revolution" of translation, without at all being the only foundation, and without translation ever becoming a branch of "applied linguistics." Traductology will only be constituted in collaboration with linguistics and poetics; it has much to learn from socio- and ethnolinguistics, as well as from psychoanalysis and philosophy.

From that point on, *science of translation* would have a double meaning: a science taking the knowledge of translation as its object, and the "scientificization" of the practice of translation. In this respect, it must be noted that France has remained far behind other countries in this domain, like Germany, the Anglo-Saxon countries, the Soviet Union, and the Eastern countries. This theoretical delay has as its corollary a delay on the practical level, both quantitative and qualitative. The opening of a domain of traductological reflection, then, will fill the void whose grave consequences are appearing little by little, and which contibute to a chronical crisis in France of both translation and culture.

The Manifestation of Translation

1. Cf. Pierre Leyris, "Pourquoi retraduire Shakespeare," foreword to Shakespeare's *Oeuvres* (Paris: Club du Livre, 1962–64).

2. *The Poet's Tongues: Multilingualism in Literature*, New York: Cambridge University Press, 1970.

3. This position may be compared to that of non-French writers writing in French. This concerns primarily the literatures of francophone countries, but also works written in French by writers who do not belong to francophone areas at all, like Beckett. We shall categorize these products under the heading of "foreign French." They have been written in French by "foreigners," and bear the marks of that strangeness in their language and in their thematics. Though it sometimes resembles the French of the people of France, their language is separated from it by a more or less sensible abyss, like the one separating our French from the French passages in *War and Peace* and *The Magic Mountain*. This foreign French has a close relation with the French of translation. In the one case, there are foreigners writing in French and thus imprinting our language with the seal of their strangeness; in the other, there are foreign works rewritten in French, inhabiting our language and thereby also marking our language with their strangeness. Beckett is the most striking example of the proximity of these two kinds of French, since he has written some of his works in French and himself translated others from English. In a good deal of these cases, these works belong to a bilingual or multilingual space, in which French occupies a peculiar place: that of a minority language, either dominated or dominant, and confronted in any case with other languages in often antagonistic relations. This situation is very different from the one in France, since our country, despite the existence of regional languages, tends toward a monolingual existence. It engenders works marked by a double sign: As foreign works using French, a "peripheral" French, they

tend to be of the vernacular type, adapting popular expressivity. As works written in French, they tend—in order to manifest a belonging and an opposition to dominant neighbor languages—to use a "purer" French than the French of France. Both tendencies may be found in the same work, as in the case of an Edouard Glissant or a Simone Schwartz-Bart. In all of these cases, the foreign French text seems "other" than the French text written in France. These two antagonistic tendencies make it similar to the writing of the translator who, confronted with an "other" foreign text, is tempted at the same time to defend his own language (overgallicization) as well as to open it to the foreign element. The structural parallelism is striking, and it is no surprise that the aim of the translator—to enrich his language—is also the aim of a good deal of writers. The Mauritian poet Edouard Maunick states: "I would like to inseminate the French language" ("Ecrire, mais dans quelle langue?" [Write, but in which language?] *Le Monde*, 11 March 1983).

Introduction

1. In Winfried Sdun, *Probleme und Theorien des Übersetzens* (Munich: Hueber, 1967), p. 50.

2. Quoted in Fritz Strich, *Goethe und die Weltliteratur* (Bern: Francke, 1957), pp. 18, 47.

3. August Wilhelm Schlegel, Afterword to Tieck, in *Athenäum* II, 2, p. 280–81.

4. Novalis, *Briefe und Dokumente*, vol. 4 of *Werke Briefe Dokumente*, ed. Ewald Wasmuth (Heidelberg: Schneider, 1954), p. 367. [Letter to A. W. Schlegel, 30 November 1797].

5. Friedrich Schleiermacher, "On the Different Methods of Translating," in André Lefevere, *Translating Literature: The German Tradition from Luther Rosenzweig* (Assen/Amsterdam: Van Gorcum, 1977), p. 88.

6. Wilhelm von Humboldt, "Einleitung zu 'Agamemnon'," in Lefevere, p. 42.

7. In Sdun, p. 29.

8. Novalis, p. 368.

9. Letter of 11 February 1792, quoted in Sdun, p. 117.

10. Johann Georg Hamann, *Sämtliche Werke* II, ed. Josef Nadler (Wien: Herder, 1950), p. 199. (An excellent French translation of this text, by J.-F. Courtine, can be found in *Poësie*, no. 3 (1980): 3–51).

11. For the analysis of this expression, see Chapter 5, p. 78.

12. Rudolph Pannwitz, *Die Krisis der europäischen Kultur* (Nürnberg: Carl, 1947), p. 192.

13. Walter Benjamin, *Der Begriff der Kunstkritik in der deutschen Romantik*, in *Gesammelte Schriften* I, 1 (Frankfurt am Main: Suhrkamp, 1974), p. 76

14. Armel Guerne, "Hic et nunc," in *Le Romantisme allemand*, ed. Albert Béguin (Paris: Cahiers du Sud, 1949), p. 357. Guerne develops this point of view elsewhere: "How often does Novalis, in his Fragments, dream of a language more euphonic than his own! . . . This is . . . what enables us to grasp why there is such a tendency in Novalis to gallicize his German, right down to his vocabulary, and to move about in it spiritually in Latin. . . . It cannot be denied that Novalis's work, internally had its raison d'être in French . . . a kind of initial need, the satisfaction of which gives him, or "gives him back," something, despite everything that gets lost in the process of . . . the re-thinking . . . and the translation" (*La Délirante*, no. 4–5 [1972], p. 185–6). Which explains, though without justifying its great arbitrariness, Guerne's own "gallicizing" translation of Novalis.

15. Novalis, *Fragmente I*, vol. 2 of *Werke Briefe Dokumente*, ed. Ewald Wasmuth (Heidelberg: Schneider, 1957) no. 1694, p. 449.

16. Ibid., no. 38, p. 18.

17. *Friedrich Schlegel's* Lucinde *and the Fragments*, tr. Peter Firchow (Minneapolis: University of Minnesota Press, 1971), p. 177 (*Athenäum Fragment* no. 121). Cf. the text by F. Schlegel quoted by Beda Allemann in *Ironie und Dichtung* (Pfullingen: Neske, 1969): "The good critic and characterizer should observe in a faithful, conscientious, and versatile way, like the physicist, measure exactly like the mathematician, classify carefully like the botanist, dissect like the anatomist, feel like the musician, imitate like the actor, embrace practically like a lover, survey like a philosopher, study cyclically like a sculptor, be strict like a judge, religious like an antiquarian, comprehend the moment like the politician, etc." (p. 58) In short, to turn himself into everything, to be versed in everything, to turn everything into everything—this is the romantic "talent of the translator."

18. Novalis, "Monologue," tr. Alexander Gelley, in *German Romantic Criticism*, ed. A. Leslie Wilson (New York: Continuum, 1982), p. 82–83.

19. August Wilhelm Schlegel, Afterword to Tieck, *Athenäum* II, 2, pp. 282–83.

20. Novalis, *Fragmente II*, vol. 3 of *Werke Briefe Dokumente*, ed. Ewald Wasmuth (Heidelberg: Schneider, 1957), no. 1922, p. 53.

21. Pannwitz, p. 193.

22. For a discussion of the "monologic" and the "intransitive," see Tzvetan Todorov, *Theories of the Symbol* and Mikhaïl Bakhtin, *The Dialogic Imagination*.

23. Antoine Berman, "Lettres à Fouad El-Etr sur le Romantisme allemand," in *La Délirante*, no. 3 (1968), pp. 85–117.

24. Nor is it in Romanticism. We are only concerned here with the incessantly mystified Jena Romanticism.

25. See Antoine Berman, "L'Amérique latine dans sa littérature," *Cultures* 6 (1979) and "La traduction des oeuvres latino-américaines," *Lendemains* 8 (1982).

26. See our Conclusion.

27. Which clearly shows the extent to which the theme of translation remains culturally and ideologically obscured. Cf. Andreas Huyssen, *Die frühromantische Konzeption von Übersetzung und Aneignung. Studien zur frühromantischen Utopie einer deutschen Weltliteratur* (Zürich/Freiburg-i.-Br.: Atlantis, 1969).

28. Walter Benjamin, *Der Begriff*, p.76.

29. "The Task of the Translator," tr. Harry Zohn, in *Illuminations* (New York: Harcourt, Brace and World, 1968), p. 76.

30. After these lines had been written, a remarkable exhibition was organized by the Deutsche Schillergesellschaft in Marbach (Federal Republic of Germany) in 1982, entitled *Weltliteratur—Die Lust am Übersetzen im Jahrhundert Goethes* ("World Literature—the Pleasure of Translation in Goethe's Century"). The catalogue of this exhibition (700 pages) contains, in addition to an abundant iconography, almost all of the available documents on the practice of translation in the period we are examining here. Henceforth this basic work will be indispensable for any work on translation in classical and Romantic Germany.

Luther: Translation as Foundation

1. Johann Wolfgang von Goethe, "Noten und Abhandlungen zur besseren Verständnis des West-östlichen Divan," in Lefevere, *Translating Literature*, p. 35.

2. Johann Wolfgang von Goethe, *The Autobiography of Johann Wolfgang Goethe* [*Dichtung und Wahrheit*], tr. John Oxenford, (Chicago: Chicago University Press, 1974) vol.2, pp.112–13.

3. Martin Luther, "On Translating: An Open Letter," tr. Charles M. Jacobs, revised by E. Theodore Bachmann, in *Luther's Works*, vol. 35, *Word and Sacrament I*, ed. E. Theodore Bachmann (Philadelphia: Muhlenberg Press, 1960), p. 181.

4. Ibid., pp. 188–89.

5. Ibid., p. 189.

6. Ibid., p. 189–90.

7. Mikhaïl Bakhtin, *Rabelais and his World*, tr. H. Iswolsky (Cambridge, MA: MIT Press, 1968), p. 465. [The French translation, from which Berman quotes, renders "This line drawn between the languages" as "la *délimitation* des langages" (the delimitation of languages) hence Berman's use of *delimitation* in the next line.—TR.]

8. Ibid., p. 468 and pp. 469–70.

9. Ibid., p. 470.

10. "The creation of written German took place in connection with the translation of the Bible by Luther." (Hermann Broch)

11. Novalis to F. Schlegel, 7 November 1798: "There is in your letter one of the most striking examples of our interior synorganization and synevolution. You mention your Bible-project, and in my studies of science in general . . . I, too, have arrived at the Bible—the Bible as the *ideal* of *all* books. Once developed, the theory of the Bible will provide the theory of writing or of the formation of words in general—which is at the same time the doctrine of the symbolic and indirect construction of the creative spirit. . . . All my activity . . . must be nothing else than a critique of the Bible-project—an essay on a universal method of biblification." (Novalis, *Briefe und Dokumente*, p. 404)

12. Franz Rosenzweig, "Die Schrift und Luther," in Hans Joachim Störig, *Das Problem des Übersetzens* (Darmstadt:Wissenschaftliche Buchgesellschaft, 1969), pp. 199–203.

13. Ibid., p. 215.

14. Luther, "On Translating," p. 194.

15. Martin Luther, "Defense of the Translation of the Psalms," tr. E. Theodore Bachmann, in *Luther's Works*, vol. 35, p. 216. (Also in Störig, pp. 196–97.) Regarding his own translation of the Psalms, Moses Men-

delsohn writes in 1783: "I have taken such little delight in innovation that, with regard to language, I have even remained closer to Dr. Luther than to later translators. Wherever the former has *translated correctly*, it seems to me he has also *germanized* felicitously; I have not even feared the Hebrew phrases he once introduced into the language, even though they might not be authentic German" (quoted in *Weltliteratur*, p. 127).

16. Ibid., p. 222 (also in Störig, p. 196).

17. Saint Jerome, "Letter to Pammachius," in Störig, p. 3.

18. See Chapter 10.

19. We shall see in our chapter on Hölderlin how the latter is very deeply connected to Luther, in his work as a poet as well as in his work as a translator. Herder, Klopstock, and A. W. Schlegel also refer to Luther's Bible, but only Hölderlin managed, in a certain way, to take up the work on the German language that Luther accomplished *as a translator*. The relation to the German language of someone like Nietzsche—as a *polemical* thinker—is likewise hardly conceivable without a long association with Luther. The relation of this thinker to foreign languages—primarily French and Italian—also shows that, like Hölderlin, he seeks the truth of his own language in a certain "experience" [*épreuve*] of foreign languages. But the other pole, the rootedness in what Hölderlin calls the "native" and Luther the language of "the woman in the home" or of "the common man in the marketplace," is missing in Nietzsche.

20. Walter Benjamin, "Conversation with André Gide," in *Mythe et Violence*, p. 281 ["Gesprach mit André Gide", *Gesammelte Schriften* IV, 1, p. 506].

21. A position still worth consideration: The contemporary flight of the "history of mentalities," i.e., of the material, social, and cultural base of our society and more specifically of its *oral* past, at the very moment when those foundations, together with orality, seem to be radically breaking down, leads to the question: What is going on here? Is it nostalgia? A search for origins? The solemn burial of values considered fascinating, but obsolete? What position do the historians of the oral past take with regard to our present and the possible defense of popular cultures? The same question would be asked concerning ethnology. We have here an extremely important process which is by no means foreign to the peculiar interests of an historical and cultural theory of translation. German and French Romanticism have also faced, in their own way, this set of questions. Nietzsche saw a vital danger in the "chameleontic faculty" constituted by the "historical sense": He at-

tempted to reverse the situation by making it into a movement of appropriation. This union of appropriation and domination, of identification and reduction, etc., has been characteristic of the European cultural reality up to this day. Now it is being called into question from several points of view.

22. *Athenäum* Fragment no. 229, tr. Firchow, p.194.

Herder: Fidelity and Expansion

1. Rosenzweig, p. 194.

2. August Wilhelm Schlegel, *Geschichte der klassischen Literatur* (Stuttgart: Kohlhammer, 1964), p. 17. Quoted in Lefevere, *Translating Literature*, p. 52.

3. Collardeau has given a remarkable summary of the French problematic at the end of the eighteenth century: "If there is any merit in translating, it is perhaps only to perfect the original, if possible, to embellish it, to appropriate it, to give it a national air and, in some way, to naturalize this foreign plant." (Quoted in Van der Meerschen, "Traduction française, problèmes de fidélité et de qualité," in "Traduzione-tradizione," special issue of *Lectures* 4–5 [1980], p. 18).

4. Wolfgang Schadewaldt, "Das Problem des Übersetzens," in Störig, pp. 225–26.

5. In Sdun, p. 21.

6. Ibid., p. 22.

7. The *Literaturbriefe*, whose full title is *Briefe, die neueste Literatur betreffend* [Letters concerning the newest literature], no doubt constitute the first of the German literary periodicals. Lessing was its chief animator, together with Thomas Abbt and Moses Mendelsohn.

8. A space which, for him, refers to Luther: "It is Luther who awakened and liberated that sleeping giant, the German language" (*Fragmente*, quoted in Rolf Zuberbühler, *Hölderlins Erneuerung der Sprache aus ihren etymologischen Ursprüngen* [Berlin: Erich Schmidt, 1969], p. 23).

9. In Sdun, p. 26.

10. In J. Murat, *Klopstock* (Paris: Les Belles Lettres, 1959), p. 282.

11. In Sdun, p. 26.

12. Ibid., pp. 25–26.

13. Ibid., p. 26.

14. Ibid., pp. 26–27.

15. Jean Paul, *Vorschule der Aesthetik* (Munich: Hanser, 1963), p. 304.

Bildung and the Demand of Translation

1. *Bild* (image), *Einbildungskraft* (imagination), *Ausbildung* (development), *Bildsamkeit* (flexibility, "formability"), etc.

2. Martin Heidegger, "Andenken," in *Erläuterungen zu Hölderlins Dichtung* (Frankfurt am Main: Klostermann, 1981), p. 90n.

3. Novalis, "Aufzeichnungen zu den Lehrlingen zu Sais" in *Die Dichtungen*, vol. 1 of *Werke Briefe Dokumente*, ed. Ewald Wasmuth (Heidelberg: Schneider, 1953), p. 211.

4. F. Schlegel, "Critical" fragment no. 78, tr. Firchow, p. 152.

5. Novalis, *Fragmente I*, no. 1393, pp. 369–70.

6. Novalis, *Fragmente II*, no. 1837, p. 18.

7. Friedrich Schlegel, "Über die Philosophie (an Dorothea)," *Athenäum* II, 1, p. 27. (*Kritische Friedrich Schlegel Ausgabe*, vol. 8: *Studien zur Philosophie und Theologie*, ed. Ernst Behler and Ursula Struc-Oppenberg [Munich: Ferdinand Schöningh, 1975], p. 55.)

8. Novalis, *Fragmente I*, no. 1409, p. 373.

9. Novalis, *Fragmente II*, no. 2383, p. 162.

10. Novalis, *Fragmente I*, nos. 988, 992, p. 271.

11. Friedrich Nietzsche, *Beyond Good and Evil*, tr. Walter Kaufmann (New York: Random House, 1966), p. 160.

12. Friedrich Nietzsche, *The Gay Science*, tr. Walter Kaufmann (New York: Vintage Books, 1976), pp. 136–38 (no. 83).

13. Saint Jerome, p. 9.

14. F. Schlegel, *Dialogue on Poetry and Literary Aphorisms*, tr. Ernst Behler and Roman Struc (University Park, PA: Pennsylvania State University Press, 1965), p. 64.

15. Ibid., p. 83.

16. F. Schlegel, "Über die Philosophie," p. 84.

17. [Here, and throughout, "trans-lation" is used to render the French *translation*, which has the more general meaning of transposition (Latin *translatio*), as distinct from translation (French *traduction*) in the strict sense of interlingual transposition.—TR.]

18. Friedrich Schleiermacher, "On the Methods of Translating," in Lefevere, p. 88. See also Chapter 6.

19. "Never have the ancients been read . . . as much as now, the understanding admirers of Shakespeare are no longer rare, the Italian poets have their friends, the Spanish poets are read as zealously as is possible in Germany, the translation of Calderón promises the best of influences, it may be expected that the songs of the Provençals, the romances of the North, and the blossoms of the Indian imagination will not remain foreign to us much longer. . . . Under these propitious conditions it is perhaps time to remind ourselves again of the older German poetry." (L. Tieck, quoted in *Weltliteratur*, p. 486).

20. Cf. Alexander von Humboldt, *L'Amérique espagnole en 1800 vue par un savant allemand* (Paris: Calmann-Lévy, 1965).

21. Friedrich Schlegel, *Dialogue on Poetry*, tr. Behler and Struc, p. 77.

22. Novalis, *Fragmente I*, no. 1712, p. 458.

23. *Athenäum* fragment no. 297, tr. Firchow, p. 204.

24. As the romantic voyage could sometimes be, called by Tieck "the voyage into the blue."

25. August Wilhelm Schlegel, *Die Kunstlehre* (Stuttgart: Kohlhammer, 1963), p. 230.

26. F. Schlegel, *Ideas*, no. 102, tr. Firchow, p. 250.

27. F. Schlegel, *Athenäum* fragment no. 147, tr. Firchow, p. 180.

28. Goethe, "Noten und Abhandlungen," in Lefevere, p. 36.

29. F. Schlegel, *Dialogue on Poetry*, tr. Behler and Struc, pp. 78–79.

30. Humboldt, "Einleitung zu 'Agamemnon'," in Lefevere, p. 42.

31. "We do not want to possess Greek culture, it must possess us." (Herder, "Letters for the Advancement of humanity," quoted in *Weltliteratur*, p. 318). Cf. Hammer in the Preface to his 1812 translation of Hafitz: "[the translator] wanted not so much to translate the Persian poet to the German reader than to translate the German reader to the Persian poet." (quoted in *Weltliteratur*, p. 398)

32. F. Schlegel, "Critical" fragment no. 46, tr. Firchow, p. 149.

33. *Athenäum* fragment no. 277, tr. Firehow, p. 201.

34. Nietzsche, *Twilight of the Idols*, in *The Portable Nietzsche*, ed. and tr. Walter Kaufmann (New York: Viking Penguin, 1982), p. 557.

35. *Athenäum* fragment no. 239, tr. Firchow, p. 195–96.

36. F. Schlegel, "Über die Philosophie," p. 62.

37. [The French word for *novel* (*roman*) and the adjective derived from it (*romanesque*) makes its place in this filiation from ancient Rome to German Romanticism more obvious than it appears in English. Berman also plays upon this etymological connection between Roman culture and the novel in the next paragraph (*Roman/roman*), an effect with is unfortunately lost in the translation.—TR.]

38. Novalis, "Blüthenstaub," in *Schriften* II, ed. Richard Samuel (Stuttgart: Kohlhammer, 1965), p. 437.

39. Novalis, *Fragmente II*, no. 1921, p. 53.

40. Friedrich Hölderlin, letter of 4 December 1801 (in *Essays and Letters on Theory*, tr. Thomas Pfau [Albany, NY: State University of New York Press, 1988], p. 150.

41. [See note 37 above—TR.]

42. Klopstock expressed this brutally: "Do not talk to me about translating something from the French, or another foreign language; however beautiful it may be, you no longer have the right to it. The only translation I shall still allow of a German is a translation from the Greek." (Letter to Gleim, 7 September 1769, in *Ausgewählte Werke*, ed. K. A. Schleiden [Munich: Hanser, 1962], p. 1164).

Goethe: Translation and World Literature

1. Quoted in F. Strich, p. 54.

2. Ibid., p. 26.

3. Johann Wolfgang von Goethe, "Nature," in *Scientific Studies*, ed. and tr. Douglas Hiller (New York: Suhrkamp, 1988), p. 3.

4. Qouted in Strich, p. 24.

5. Ibid., p. 56.

6. Ibid., p. 26.

7. Ibid., p. 17.

8. Goethe, *Conversations with Eckermann*, tr. John Oxenford (San Francisco: North Point Press, 1984), p. 133 (31 January 1827).

9. Ibid., pp. 23–24.

10. Ibid., p. 24.

11. Ibid., p. 25, our emphasis.

12. Ibid., pp. 20–21.

13. Ibid., p. 18.

14. Ibid., p. 30.

15. Goethe, *Conversations with Eckermann*, p. 62.

16. Goethe's position concerning nationalism is expressed as early as 1801 in the journal *Propyläen*: "Perhaps people will soon be convinced that there is no such thing as patriotic art or patriotic science. Like all good things, both belong to the whole world and can only be furthered by a general, free exchange among all contemporaries, constantly bearing in mind what has remained and is known to us from the past" (quoted in Strich, p. 49). In fact, nationalism puts Goethe's entire view of cultural interactions into question, which is not to say that he champions a hollow and abstract cosmopolitanism: "The issue is not that nations should think alike, but that they should become aware of each other, understand each other, and even if they cannot mutually love each other, they should at least learn to tolerate each other" (ibid., p. 26). "One must get to know everyone's particularities, in order to leave them to everyone, and precisely to be able to enter into relation with them: for the properties of a nation are like its language or its currency, they facilitate intercourse, and even make it possible in the first place" (ibid., p. 26).

17. "Noten und Abhandlungen," p. 35–36. The scheme Goethe proposes here is triadic, conform to the concept of *Bildung*. In the text devoted to Wieland, it is dual (as it is in Schleiermacher, who really only develops it more systematically): "There are two maxims in translation: one requires that the author of a foreign nation be brought across to us in such a way that we can look on him ours; the other requires that we should adapt ourselves to the foreign. . . . The advantages of both are sufficiently known to educated people through perfect examples ("Zu brüderlichem Andenken Wielands," in Lefevere, p. 39).

18. Quoted in Strich, p. 19.

19. Goethe, "Über Literatur und Leben," in *Gedenkausgabe*, Bd.9, p. 633.

20. Goethe, *The Autobiography of J. W. von Goethe*, tr. John Oxenford, vol. 2, (Chicago: Chicago University Press), p. 112.

21. Ibid., p. 131.

22. Quoted in Strich, p. 65.

23. Ibid., p. 55.

24. Goethe, *Conversations with Eckermann*, p. 133.

25. "All is eternally present in her. . . . The present is eternity for her" (Goethe, "Nature," p. 5).

26. Strich, p. 24–25. This remark, though correct in itself, is far from exhausting the problem. The Romantics have a different perception of the present than Goethe. But they cannot be characterized as infatuated with the past—they are rather futurists. Cf. our chapter on A. W. Schlegel.

27. Quoted in Strich, p. 37–38.

28. Ibid., p. 34.

29. Ibid., p. 34.

30. Ibid., p. 33.

31. Ibid., p. 36.

32. Ibid., p. 36.

33. Ibid., p. 36.

34. Ibid., p. 35. Approximating translation: "I recently picked a bunch of flowers of the field, brought them home pensively; the warmth of my hand made the crowns bend down; I put them in a glass of fresh water, and what a marvel it was! The little heads raised themselves again, stems and leaves became green, and it all seemed as healthy as if the flowers were still in their maternal soil. It was this way for me when I, full of awe, heard my song in a foreign language." [For a poetic translation, by Vernon Watkins, see *Selected Poems*, ed. Christopher Middleton (Boston: Suhrkamp/Insel, 1983), pp. 254–55.—TR.]

35. Hofmannsthal develops the same idea: "Languages belong to the most beautiful things on this world. . . . They are like marvelous musical instruments. . . . And yet, it is impossible to make them vibrate completely. Yes, when we have become deaf to the beauty of our own language, the first foreign language to come on the scene has an indescribable magic for us; we only have to transfer our faded thoughts into

it to watch them come alive like flowers put in fresh water." (*Die pro-saischen Schriften gesammelt*, Bd.2 [Berlin: Fischer, 1907], p. 105).

Romantic Revolution and Infinite Versability

1. F. Schlegel, *Dialogue on Poetry*, tr. Behler and Struc, p. 73–74.

2. Friedrich Schlegel, *Kritische Schriften* (Munich: Hanser, 1964), p. 532.

3. Ibid., p. 83.

4. Furthermore, F. Schlegel considers letters and dialogues to be fragments: "A dialogue is a chain or garland of fragments. An exchange of letters is a dialogue on a larger scale, and Memorabilia constitute a system of fragments" (*Athenäum* fragment no. 77; Firchow, p. 170). Translation, for its part, is placed in the framework of notes and and commentaries: "Notes are philological epigrams; translations are phi-lological mimes; many commentaries, where the text is only the point of departure or the non-I, are philological idylls" ("Critical" fragment no. 75; Firchow, p. 152).

5. Novalis, *Fragmente I*, no. 1256, p. 339.

6. Novalis, *Schriften* II, p. 623.

7. F. Schlegel, *Kritische Schriften*, p. 419.

8. *Athenäum* fragment no. 444, tr. Firchow, p. 239.

9. "Über die Philosophie," p. 3.

10. Novalis, "Dialogue I," tr. Alexander Gelley, in *German Roman-tic Criticism*, p. 80.

11. Novalis, *Briefe und Dokumente*, p. 459.

12. Novalis, *Fragmente II*, no. 1839, p. 19.

13. *Athenäum* fragment no. 434, tr. Firchow, p. 237.

14. Novalis, *Fragmente I*, no. 26, p. 15.

15. Ibid., no. 1466, p. 391.

16. "Critical" fragment no. 15, tr. Firchow, p. 157.

17. *Athenäum* fragment no. 55, tr. Firchow, p. 199.

18. Novalis, *Fragmente II*, no. 1902, p. 44.

19. Ibid., no. 1925 p. 55.

20. Ibid., no. 1968, p. 70.

21. Novalis, *Fragmente I*, no. 1152, p. 307.

22. Novalis, *Fragmente II*, no. 2263, p. 132.

23. *Athenäum* fragment no. 418, tr. Firchow, p. 231.

24. *Athenäum* fragment no. 121, tr. Firchow, pp. 176–77.

25. Novalis, *Fragmente II*, no. 2281, p. 139.

26. Ibid., no. 2263, p. 132.

27. Ibid., no. 2128, p. 104.

28. *Athenäum* fragment no. 394, tr. Firchow, p. 227.

29. Novalis, *Fragmente I*, no. 1054, p. 292.

30. *Athenäum* fragment no. 242, tr. Firchow, p. 196.

31. Novalis, *Fragmente II*, no. 1913, p. 49.

32. Ibid., no. 1921, p. 53.

33. Novalis, *Fragmente I*, nos. 61, 236, 1710.

34. Du Bellay, *Défense et illustration de la langue française* (Paris: Gallimard, 1967), p. 221.

35. Novalis, *Fragmente II*, no. 2369, pp. 159–60.

36. Ibid., no. 2431, p. 172.

37. Novalis, *Fragmente I*, no. 1733, p. 467.

38. Ibid., no. 1695, p. 449.

39. Novalis, *Fragmente II*, no. 2307, p. 143.

40. Ibid., no. 1820, p. 13.

41. *Athenäum* fragment no. 37, tr. Firchow, p. 166.

42. "Critical" fragment no. 55, tr. Firchow, p. 149.

43. Novalis, *Fragmente II*, no. 2173, p. 114.

44. Novalis, *Fragmente I*, no. 1711, p. 457. Hence the concept of "magical idealism."

45. Ibid., no. 291, p. 94.

46. "Critical" fragment no. 37, tr. Firchow, p. 147.

47. Novalis, "Dialogue I," tr. Alexander Gelley, in *German Romantic Criticism*, p. 80–81. Cf. also *Fragmente I*, no. 68: "Ars *litteraria*.

Everything a scholar does, says, speaks, suffers, hears, etc. must be an artistic, technical, scientific product or some such operation. He speaks in epigrams, acts in a play, he is a dialogist, he represents conferences and sciences—he tells anecdotes, stories, fairytales, novels, he feels poetically; when he draws, he draws as an artist, as a musician; his life is a novel—thus he sees and hears everything—thus he reads. In short, the genuine scholar is the completely cultured (*gebildete*) man—who gives everything he touches and everything he does a scientific, ideal, and syncritical form" (p. 29).

48. *Athenäum* fragment no. 116, tr. Firchow, p. 175.

49. Ibid.

50. Novalis, *Fragmente I*, no. 40, p. 18.

51. Ibid., no. 1335, p. 358.

52. Ibid., no. 239, p. 79.

53. Novalis, *Fragmente II*, no. 1952, p. 64. "Family likeness" is in French in the text ("air de famille").

54. Novalis, *Fragmente I*, no. 120, p. 40. "One and indivisible" is in French in the text ("unes et indivisibles").

55. Ibid., no. 1694, pp. 448–49.

56. Ibid., no. 308, p. 99.

57. Ibid., no. 61, p. 27.

58. Novalis, *Fragmente II*, no. 2084, p. 93. Novalis goes on: "On the confusion of the symbol with the symbolized—or their identification—on the belief in a true, complete representation—and the relation of image and original—on the appearance and the substance . . . all superstition and all error, in all times and all peoples and all individuals, rest." The interchangeability of symbols and categories excludes their absolutization. One of the consequences of this position is that there is no natural truth of language—hence the romantic criticism of the *Natursprache*. See the next chapter.

59. The metaphor of money is also found in "The Paintings," a dialogue by A. W. Schlegel published in the *Athenäum* (II, 1:44–49), in which the copy of an ancient work is presented as a process of translation: "Ah, if my drawing were a translation! But it is barely a destitute abstract. . . . If I want to translate (*übertragen*) everything that I perceive at the edges, the result would be . . . petty; and with every part that I melt together into larger masses something of the original mean-

ing is lost. . . . I watch insistently and repeatedly; I collect the impressions . . . but then I must translate them into words internally. . . . Society and mutual social contact are the essential. . . . It is with spiritual wealth as with money. What is the good of having a lot and keeping it locked away? For true comfort what matters most is that it circulates multiply and rapidly." (Quoted in *Weltliteratur*, p. 502). This text shows how the Jena Romantics interpret everything from the viewpoint of translation, and how translation in turn is referred back to a larger "circulation," of which money, as for Goethe, is the symbol. The romantic "sympilosophy" is a translation.

60. "The tree may become a blossoming flame, man a speaking flame—an animal a walking flame" (Novalis, *Fragmente I*, no. 967, p. 267). "Animal nature of the flame" (*Fragmente I*, no. 994, p. 272). Bachelard would speak here of metaphors of the material imagination.

61. "The philosopher translates the actual world into the world of thought and vice versa" (Novalis, *Fragmente II*, no. 1956, p. 65)

62. Clemens Brentano, *Werke II*, p. 262. See Chapter 7.

Language of Art and Language of Nature

1. It is only in 1808 that F. Schlegel publishes his *Essay on the language and the philosophy of the Indians*.

2. Novalis, *Fragmente I*, no.1394, p. 370.

3. Ibid., no. 1272, p. 343.

4. Ibid., no. 1277, p. 345.

5. Novalis, *Fragmente II*, no. 1865, p. 30.

6. Ibid., no. 2032, p. 83.

7. "Critical" fragment no. 37, tr. Firchow, p. 147.

8. Novalis, *Fragmente I*, no. 1271, p. 343.

9. Ibid., no. 1411, p. 373.

10. Ibid., no. 395, p. 123.

11. Ibid., no. 163, p. 55. The last sentence is in French in the original: "Il est beaucoup plus commode d'être fait que de se faire soi-même."

12. F. Schlegel, *Kritische Schriften*, p. 471.

13. *Dialogue on Poetry*, tr. Behler and Struc, pp. 89, 115.

14. F. Schlegel, *Kritische Schriften*, p. 471.

15. Novalis, "Blüthenstaub," p. 440.

16. Novalis, *Fragmente II*, no. 1916, p. 50.

17. *Athenäum* fragment no. 428, tr. Firchow, p. 234. It is perhaps in this context that Guerne's remark on the relative gallicization of Novalis's language may be better understood, a phenomenon which is after all evident in the choice of the pseudonym "Novalis" by a man whose real name is Hardenberg: in Latin, *novalis* means a plot of land newly cleared for cultivation (*novalia* in English). The native German would be the *Natursprache*, French the *Kunstsprache*, as French and, above all, as *other* language. The recourse to "Romance" expressions would serve to raise the natural language to the level of an artificial language, to enhance the distance with the former. This is the reverse of Luther's movement, which seeks both a popular language and good German. Novalis noted this particularity of Luther's language, though seeming to confuse it with the romantic mingling of the noble and the base: "Mix of the crude, the common, the proverbial, with the noble, the high, the poetic. *Dr. Luther's language*" (*Fragmente I*, no. 1402, p. 372). An abyss separates Luther's position from Novalis's, i.e., the position of the idealist dialectic of the constitution of a transcendental, poetical-philosophical language. The same process of de-Germanization could be seen at the stylistic level in F. Schlegel: the literary form of the *Witz*—of the fragment—remains the French "mot d'esprit," the "trait" (Chamfort).

18. Novalis, *Fragmente I*, no. 1360, p. 363.

19. Friedrich Schlegel has expressed this taste for the artificial and its connection with reflexivity very well: "It is sublime taste always to like things better when they have been raised to the second power. For example, copies of imitations, evaluations of reviews, commentaries on notes. . . . " (*Athenäum* fragment no. 110, Firchow, p. 174). Apart from the striking modernity of the text, the relation to translation—called elsewhere "philological mimes" ("Critical" fragment no. 75, tr. Firchow, p. 152)—is obvious. Here artificiality consists of removing oneself ever further from whatever original.

20. Clemens Brentano, *Werke* II (Munich: Hanser, 1963), p. 262.

21. Novalis, *Fragmente I*, no. 479, p. 149.

22. Ibid., no. 1296, p. 348.

23. Novalis, *Fragmente II*, no. 1957, p. 65.

24. Ibid., no. 2228. p. 126.

25. Novalis, *Fragmente I*, no. 1473, p. 392.

26. Ibid., no. 1285, p. 347.

27. Ibid., no. 1275, p. 344.

28. *Blüthenstaub*, p. 412.

29. Ibid.

30. Novalis, *Fragmente II*, no. 1916, p. 50.

31. Novalis, *Fragmente I*, no. 1327, pp. 254–55.

32. Quoted in Eva Fiesel, *Die Sprachphilosophie der deutschen Romantik* (Hildesheim/New York: Olms, 1973), p. 33.

33. Cf. the astonishing "Mathematical Fragments" in *Fragmente I*, no. 401, pp. 124–26.

34. Novalis, *Fragmente II*, no. 1855, p. 24.

35. Novalis, *Fragmente I*, no. 343, p. 111.

36. Ibid., no. 328, p. 109. Cf. also nos. 387 and 291.

37. Ibid., no. 401, p. 126.

38. Ibid., no. 1320, p. 353.

39. Ibid., no. 1326, p. 354.

40. Ibid., no. 1313, pp. 350–51.

41. Ibid., no. 1383, p. 368.

42. Ibid., no. 1400, p. 371.

43. *Athenäum* fraagment no. 444, tr. Firchow, p. 239.

44. Novalis, *Fragmente I*, no. 1398, p. 371.

45. No other literary romantic text measures up to this musicalizing reflexivity advocated by the *Athenäum*. One will have to wait until the twentieth century to see such texts emerge. *A la recherche du temps perdu* by Proust and *Virgil's Death* by Broch are the most striking illustrations of the literary fecundity of Novalis's and Schlegel's principles. As regards Proust, Anne Henry's works—notably *Marcel Proust: théories pour une esthéthique* (Paris: Klinksieck, 1981)—have shown the influence of Schelling, the philosopher closest to the *Athenäum* group, on this author and his literary project, through a whole series of mediations. Reflexivity is inherent in Proust's writing and inscribed in the very

title of the work (*recherche*). The remark by Proust, according to which the task of the author is identical to that of the translator, and another one asserting that every work, as work, seems to be written in a foreign language, testify to his belonging to the "literary space" opened by the *Athenäum*. "With him, we enter into a new aesthetic that no longer has its roots in the lived, but in the solidity of the theoretical" (R. Jaccard, "Proust théoricien," *Le Monde*, 5 August 1982). This aesthetic is not new: It is the aesthetic of reflexivity developed by F. Schlegel.

46. Novalis, *Fragmente II*, no. 2431, pp. 171–72.

47. "Mystery in Literature," in *Mallarmé: Selected Prose, Poetry, Essays, and Letters*, tr. Bradford Cook (Baltimore: Johns Hopkins University Press, 1956), p. 33.

48. "No word in the poem (I mean here every 'and' or 'the,' 'a' or 'it') is *identical* to the corresponding word in conversation and everyday use; the purer lawfulness, the larger relation, the constellation it occupies in verse or artistic prose, changes it to the core of its nature, makes it useless, unusable for mere intercourse, untouchable and durable." Quoted in George Steiner, *After Babel* (New York: Oxford University Press, 1975), p. 241.

49. Novalis, *Fragmente I*, no. 1043, p. 288.

50. Ibid., no. 1434, p. 381.

51. Ibid., no. 1687, p. 446.

52. Ibid., no. 1752, p. 472.

53. Novalis, *Fragmente II*, no. 2386, p. 163.

54. Novalis, *Fragmente I*, no. 133, p. 43. Cf. also nos. 91 (p. 33) and the famous fragment no. 1847: "Poetry dissolves the foreign existence into its own" (Novalis, *Fragmente II*, p. 22).

55. *Heinrich von Ofterdingen*, tr. Palmer Hilty (New York: Ungar, 1964), p. 32.

56. "Romanticism.   Absolutization—Universalization—*classification* of the individual moment, of the individual situation, etc., is the actual essence of *romanticizing*" (Novalis, *Fragmente I*, no. 1440, p. 383).

57. As Benjamin observed, when he said of translation, "Thus translation, ironically, transplants the original into a more definitive linguistic realm, since it can no longer be displaced by a secondary rendering. . . . It is no mere coincidence that the word "ironic" here brings the Romantics to mind" ("The Task of the Translator" in *Illuminations*, p. 75-76).

58. In *La Part du feu*, Blanchot admirably expressed this movement: "Let us admit that one of the objects of literature is to create a language and a work where the dead word would be really dead. . . . It appears that this new language should be to the common language what a text to be translated is to the language that translates it: a set of words or events which we no doubt marvelously understand and grasp, but which in their very familiarity make us feel our ignorance, as if we discovered that the easiest words and the most natural things may suddenly become unknown to us. That the literary work wants to keep its distances, that it seeks to remove itself from any interval that always makes the best translation . . . into a foreign work, this explains (in part) the symbolist taste for rare terms, the search of exoticism. . . . *Traduit du silence* [Translated from the silence], this title by Joë Bousquet is like the wish of an entire literature that would want to remain translation in the pure state, a lightened translation of something to be translated, an effort to retain of language the only distance that language seeks to keep in regard to itself and that, at the limit, must result in its disappearance" (p. 181). We are very close to Romanticism here—as the reference to Bousquet confirms. Or rather, Blanchot's reflection seems totally caught in the space of literature opened by the *Athenäum*.

59. Quite the contrary: Goethe's theory of "occasional poetry," asserted many times in his conversations with Eckermann, is radically opposed to that of romantic poetry. For him, the occasion is that by which poetry is rooted in contemporaneity and naturalness.

60. Michel Foucault, *The Order of Things*, (New York: Random House, 1970), p. 300.

The Speculative Theory of Translation

1. Novalis, *Fragmente I*, no. 10, p. 11.

2. Ibid., no. 1280, p. 346.

3. Ibid., no. 489, p. 153.

4. "Critical" fragment nos. 73, 76, 119; *Athenäum* nos. 229, 392, 393, 402.

5. F. Schlegel, *Dialogue on Poetry*, p. 79.

6. Ibid., p. 87.

7. Novalis, *Briefe und Dokumente*, pp. 367–68.

8. See Chapter 9.

9. Novalis, *Fragmente II*, no. 1890, p. 41. That the act of translating effectively rests on such a penetration of the foreign individuality and on a "genetic mimic" is attested to by the experience of any literary translator: The translator's relation to the text he is translating (to its author and its language) is such that he enters into the zone of the work where it is, though finished, still being generated. The translator penetrates, so to speak, into the intimacy of the author with his language, there where his deprived language seeks to invest and metamorphosize the common, public language. And it is on the basis of the penetration of this relation that the translator may hope to "mime" the foreign work in his language. The *critical* act, on the contrary, rests on an approach, not a penetration. In this sense, it is not an *experience*, and the translator is closer to the actor or the writer than to the critic. Or rather his mode of identification is different. The Romantics tend to confuse these relations under the generic term "mimic." The field of this "mimic" is infinite and without delimitations: Once again we find the theory of infinite versability, a theory that may be able to account for the critical activity, but certainly not for the translating, or *a fortiori* the poetic activity. The theory of self-limitation here is nothing but an insufficient parapet.

10. Novalis, *Fragmente I*, no. 236, p. 77.

11. *Athenäum* fragment no. 393, tr. Firchow, p. 226. See also no. 401: "In order to understand someone who only partially understands himself, one must first understand him completely and better than he himself does, but then only partially and precisely as much as he does himself" (tr. Firchow, pp. 227–28). Obviously, all these axioms are valid for both criticism and translation. Schleiermacher will draw a lesson from F. Schlegel's reflection, by edifying a systematic theory of hermeneutics, i.e., of interpretation and understanding, and by developing his theory of translation against this background. See Chapter 10.

12. Novalis, *Fragmente II*, no. 2411: "Each work of art has within itself an a priori ideal, a necessity in itself to be there. Only by this does an authentic criticism of painters become possible."

13. Benjamin, *Der Begriff der Kunstkritik*, p. 67.

14. A. W. Schlegel, in his lectures on art and literature, does not say anything more than Novalis and Valéry: Poetry is "the summit of science, the interpreter and translator of this celestial revelation, the one the ancients rightly called a language of the gods" (*Die Kunstlehre*, p. 227). See our chapter on A. W. Schlegel.

15. Thus, Gérard Genette tells us, English appears to Mallarmé—as that perfect language "where at a distance all the virtues are projected of

which the own language as real language is deprived. . . . Another language, or rather any *other* language, might just as well have done the job, i.e., the office of 'supreme' language . . . the supreme language being always, for every language, the one across the street" (*Mimologiques* [Paris: Seuil, 1976], p. 273). That is why the German Shakespeare would be better than the English.

16. *Athenäum* fragment no. 297, tr. Firchow, p. 204.

17. That translation should be a "progressive" process, is obvious: it is never definitive and complete, nor can it imagine itself such. Let us say that translations are more mortal than works. And that any work authorizes an infinity of translations. Thus, the act of translating belongs to the space of fragmentary writing which the Romantics seek to define and to legitimate. The theory of the fragment should include a theory of writing in translations.

18. Quoted in George Steiner, *After Babel*, pp. 404–5. [I have provided a *literal* translation of both versions in the right hand column for the benefit of those readers who do not know French and/or German. Needless to say, I claim no *poetic* value for it.—TR.]

19. Novalis, "Blüthenstaub," pp. 439–40.

20. Following which Wilhelm and Caroline Schlegel published a dialogue entitled "The Paintings" in the *Athenäum* in 1799.

21. Novalis, *Fragmente II*, no. 1868, pp. 35–36.

22. Ibid., no. 2100, p. 96. Cf. also fragment no. 1954, "Symbols and Mystifications" (p. 65).

23. Novalis, *Schriften* I, p. 177.

24. Novalis, "Christendom or Europe," in *Hymns to the Night and Other Selected Writings*, tr. Charles A. Passage (Indianapolis: Bobbs-Merrill, 1960), p. 59. The veiled Madonna is also Sophie, the fiancee who died prematurely. The image is linked to death.

25. *Athenäum* fragment no. 235, tr. Firchow, p. 195.

26. Novalis evades the problem in his "Blüthenstaub," saying: "Several names are suitable for an idea." Which indicates a deliberate terminological wavering—making romantic thinking labyrinthine—and shows to what extent language is a relative thing for this thinking. There is no theory here of the "right name!"

27. F. Schlegel, *Dialogue on Poetry*, tr. Behler and Struc, pp. 102–3. These dreamy lines by F. Schlegel may help us understand better what a

mythic translation is: a translation that raises the original to the level—difficult to define, to be sure—of myth. After all, by dint of translations and critiques, *Don Quixote* has really become a myth. And this myth, the so called "Idea" of the work, leaves the actual book far behind itself. This process is a process of destruction of the original. What happens with the "masterworks of universal literature" constitutes the actual side of what the Romantics formulate speculatively: Hyper-translated, hyperknown, they are barely read, and inhabit our world like mythical shadows. It is unnecessary to subscribe to the Romantic dialectic to recognize that, historically speaking, they managed to "mythify" Dante, Cervantes, Petrarch, and Shakespeare. Of their works only the pure Idea, the pure, empty image has remained. The issue for contemporary criticism and translation is to find again, underneath this empty image, the linguistic and empirical density of these works.

But the concept of a "mythical translation," as distant as it may seem from actual translation, may well turn out to be a fertile concept. It alludes to the profound relation of myth, history, and translation intuited, each in their own way, by Rosenzweig and Benjamin. A relation which we should be able to retrieve from speculative thinking.

28. Behind whom German criticism has recognized Gries, translator of these poets and Calderón at the beginning of the nineteenth century. Possibly Brentano also thought of A. W. Schlegel, the most "rationalist" member of the *Athenäum*, as the allusions to the translation of Dante, Shakespeare, and the Italian renaissance poets seem to indicate.

29. Brentano, *Werke* II, p. 258–62.

30. Brentano, *Werke* I, p. 619. Literal translation: "O star and flower, spirit and garb, / Love, suffering and time and eternity."

31. Quoted in Fiesel, p. 40.

Translation as Critical Movement

1. Cf. Beda Allemann, *Ironie und Dichtung* (Pfullingen: Neske, 1969), p. 63.

2. *Athenäum* fragment no. 116, tr. Firchow, p. 175.

3. "Critical" fragment no. 117, tr. Firchow, p. 157.

4. Novalis, *Fragmente II*, no. 1869, p. 36.

5. F. Schlegel, *Kritische Schriften*, pp. 376, 381.

6. Ibid., pp. 424–25. Cf. Mme de Staël, in *De l'Allemagne*: "German literature is perhaps the first to have started with criticism" (p. 130).

7. Benjamin, *Der Begriff der Kunstkritik*, p. 67.

8. *Athenäum* fragment no. 297, tr. Firchow, p. 204.

9. F. Schlegel, "The Essence of Criticism," in *Kristische Friedrich Schlegel Ausgabe*, vol. 2: Charakteristiken und Kritiken, ed. Hans Eichner (Munich: Ferdinand Schöningh, 1975), p. 118.

10. *Athenäum* fragment no. 393, tr. Firchow, p. 226.

11. *Athenäum* fragment no. 287, tr. Firchow, p. 201.

12. This is how F. Schlegel defines the fragment. Cf. *Athenäum* fragment no. 206, tr. Firchow, p. 187.

13. Benjamin, *Der Begriff der Kunstkritik*, p. 119. Cf. Lautréamont: "Judgments on poetry are worth more than poetry. They are the philosophy of poetry. . . . " (*Maldoror and Poems*, tr. Paul Knight [Harmondsworth, England: Penguin, 1978], p. 277).

14. Because the work calls for critical and hermeneutical approaches, is the basis for their necessity, but also escapes from them and destines them to eternal incompletion.

August Schlegel: The Will to Translate Everything

1. Cf. the well-documented and sympathetic article by Marianne Thalmann, "August Wilhelm Schlegel," in *A. W. Schlegel 1767–1967* (Bad Godesberg: Internationes, 1967): "The course of Vienna, which knew three editions between 1809 and 1841, is the most widely read work on literary history. It is translated in all languages . . . and launched movements corresponding to German Romanticism in Northern and Slavic countries. It determined the judgment on the 'classical' and the 'modern' in foreign countries" (p. 20).

2. Cf. Lacoue-Labarthe and Nancy, *The Literary Absolute*, pp. 5–12, and Maurice Blanchot, "The Athenäum," tr. Deborah Esch and Ian Balfour, *Studies in Romanticism* 22 (1983): 163–72.

3. With regard to the Schlegels, Wieland speaks of "exuberant little gods." At the end of his life, Goethe expressed his ill-humor, castigating the *Schlegelei*—by homonymy with *Flegelei*, boorishness—i.e., too much artificiality and versatility in them for the "natural" man he wants to be.

4. Quoted in Thalmann, "Schlegel," p. 13.

5. Who called himself "improving mediator" (ibid., p. 10).

6. Ibid., p. 9.

7. A. W. Schlegel, "Etwas über William Shakespeare bey Gelegenheit Wilhelm Meisters," *Die Horen*, 2, no. 4 (1796), p. 110–12.

8. Ibid. Which entails, for instance, abandoning the alexandrine, which is ill suited for Shakespeare's verses.

9. "My translation has transformed the German theater," he wrote to Tieck on 3 September 1837. "Only compare Schiller's iambs in *Wallenstein* to those in *Don Carlos*, and you will see how much he has been in my school." (Quoted in Frank Jolles, *A. W. Schlegel Sommernachtstraum in der ersten Fassung vom Jahre 1789* [Göttingen: Vandenhoeck and Ruprecht, 1967], p. 34).

10. Quoted in Thalmann, "Schlegel," p. 9.

11. Quoted in M. Thalmann, *Romantiker als Poetologen* (Heidelberg: Lothar Stiehm, 1970), p. 49.

12. A. W. Schlegel, from *Geschichte der klassischen Literatur*, in Lefevere, *Translating Literature*, p. 52.

13. A. W. Schlegel, *Die Kunstlehre*, p. 232.

14. This apology of form grounds the necessity of poetic translation, just like the apology of content motivates Goethe's tolerance in matters of translation.

15. A. W. Schlegel, *Geschichte der klassischen Literatur*, in Lefevere, pp. 52–53.

16. A. W. Schlegel, *Die Kunstlehre*, p. 349.

17. Ibid., p. 349. The text continues with the introduction of the theme of mythology and poetry as the interpreter and translator of the language of the gods. The similarity to Novalis and Valéry is striking. Here, too, translation is translation of translation. Thus, A. W. Schlegel shows himself to be faithful to the Romantic monological principle: Poetry can only be poetry of poetry, translation can only be translation of translation, etc. True, at this stage, A. W. Schlegel allows himself an outright pastiche of his brother. But his own domain as a translator is the *metrical* poetic forms; for his part, F. Schlegel (as a critic) studies the *textual* poetic and literary forms. The former provides a theory of metrics, the latter a theory of genres. The two theories complement each other, and have their "formalism" in common.

18. Hence the correct but indeterminate axiom: "Everything, even the concept of fidelity, is determined according to the nature of the work with which one is dealing and the relation of the two languages" ("Über die Bhagavad-Gita," in Störig, p. 99).

19. "It is clear that the most perfect translation can never equal the text" (A. W. Schlegel, *Geschichte der klassischen Literatur*, in Lefevere, p. 53). Translation is "a thankless task . . . not only because even the best translation is never valued as highly as the original work, but also because the translator, the more his insight increases, the more he must feel the inevitable imperfection of his labor" ("Über die Bhagavad-Gita," p. 98). To be sure, three lines down the tone changes, and the translator becomes "a messenger from nation to nation, a mediator of mutual respect and admiration, where otherwise there was only indifference or even aversion" (ibid.). The eternal balancing of the translator's consciousness between absolute pride and absolute humility, undoubtedly exacerbated by the unstable, and ultimately inferior, status of translation in Romantic thinking.

20. As, for instance, the Greek is for Hölderlin.

21. Novalis, *Schriften* II, ed. Samuel, p. 250.

22. Afterword to Tieck, in *Athenäum*, II, 2, p. 281.

23. As Blanchot says, *Don Quixote* is "the romantic book *par excellence*, in as much as the novel reflects itself and incessantly turns against itself" (*L'Entretien infini*, p. 239). In fact, Cervantes's work has everything to seduce the Romantics. And even more so because it stands in a profound relation to translation, a relation well observed by Marthe Robert in *L' Ancien et le nouveau* (Paris: Grasset, 1963). The story Cervantes proposes to his readers is allegedly a translation from the Arabic (a certain Cid Hamet ben Engeli wrote the original, and Cervantes has to pay someone to translate it). Moreover, Don Quixote and the Canon have a keen interest in the problems translation. A. W. Schlegel quoted the speech Don Quixote held on translation in the printing house in Barcelona at least twice. And a great number of the books that made the hero "mad" are themselves translations. It is not difficult to imagine that under those circumstances the Romantics should have seen in this book a striking example of a "reflexive" work, a "copy of imitation." The fact that Don Quixote should be presented as a translation may count as an ironization, a relativization in the romantic sense. And this is how Marthe Robert interprets it: "Translation, here, is the symptom of a disruption of the unity of language, it marks the dismemberment it is called upon to remedy by an ungrateful labor, destined in the best case to a semi-defeat" (p. 118–19). But in truth, the fact that the greatest novel of

classical *Spanish* literature should be presented by its author as a translation from the *Arabic* could lead to a reflection that moves in an entirely different dimension: that of the mode of affirmation of the Spanish language, culture, and literature that *Don Quixote* represents—a self-affirmation in which, once more, "translation" (though as a fiction) is present. The reflexivity of this work loses its meaning if one makes of it a pure "agile, fantastic, ironic, and brilliant mobility," (Blanchot, *L'Entretien*, p. 239) divorced from any historical soil. Moreover, Cervantes's artifice refers to that category of works which want to present themselves *as translations*. Thus, for that matter, it is more than an artifice: it is *one of the possibilities of interaction of writing and translation*. Or also: the indication that all writing is situated concretely in a space where there is translation and languages. Think, for example, of the works of Tolstoy, T. Mann, or Kafka.

24. *Athenäum* II, 2, p. 281.

25. F. Schlegel also says: "Thus, one must know everything in order to know something" ("Über die Philosophie," p. 73).

26. And yet, the fate of the fragmentary seems to strike him as well in his work as translator: "As such, it goes strangely with this . . . Shakespeare: I can neither abandon him nor proceed to the end," he writes to Tieck in 1809 (quoted in *Weltliteratur*, p. 149). In fact, Tieck and his daughter will continue and finish the great enterprise of the poetic translation of Shakespeare.

27. Who contributes to this program by translating Cervantes, but also by helping A. W. Schlegel finish his translation of Shakespeare. Tieck is close to the Jena group. Since he barely wrote on translation, we do not deal with him in this study. But he is a great Romantic translator: his *Don Quixote* has remained unequalled.

28. By translating the *Bhagavad Gita*, A. W. Schlegel, at bottom, follows the injunction of the *Dialogue on Poetry*: "We must seek the highest romanticism in the Orient" (tr. Behler and Struc, p. 87). And Tieck: "I believe more and more that the Orient and the North are in a close connection and mutually elucidate each other, and that they also elucidate the ancient, and modern times" (in Thalmann, "Schlegel," p. 29).

29. In Thalmann, "Schlegel," p. 24.

30. "The authentically new sprouts only from the old, / The past must ground our future, / The dull present should not retain me." (A. W. Schlegel, dedication to *Blumensträusse italiänischer, spanischer und portugiesischer Poesie*, 1804; quoted in *Weltliteratur*, p. 505).

31. For the German Romantics, French classicism sometimes incarnates this negative. Cf. F. Schlegel, the *Dialogue on Poetry*, tr. Behler and Struc, p. 75:

> *Camilla*. You have hardly mentioned the French at all [in the history of poetry].

> *Andrea*. It happened without particular intention; I found no reason to do so. . . . .

> *Ludoviko*. Through this underhand trick he indirectly anticipated my polemical work on the theory of false poetry.

32. Armand Robin, *Le monde d'une voix* (Paris: Gallimard, 1970), p. 178.

33. Ibid., p. 160.

34. Ibid., p. 93.

35. Ibid., p. 81.

36. Ibid., p. 98. The double movement must be noted by which Robin entitles his translations "Poésie non-traduite" [Untranslated poetry] and otherwise writes a poetry in which the act of translating itself becomes a major poetic theme: translation of poetry and poetry of translation. Armand Robin's relation to poetry, languages, dialects, and translation would warrant an entire study.

37. Cf. Frank Jolles, *Sommernachtstraum*.

38. Erich Emigholz writes, in "Thirty-five times Macbeth:" "The second part of the scene of the porter (II, 3) contains quite coarse obscenities. They are absent in Dorothea Tieck's translation. The reason for this is soon understood, for she translates 'lie' as 'Lüge,' [a lie] and not as what this can and must mean here, namely 'lying with.' The result almost nonsensical. . . . In a certain way, such a mistake (or misunderstanding) is characteristic of the Romantics. Though far from being prudish, they did not like to let obscenities go by in a poet of Shakespeare's level. What is too crude contradicts the poetic sense of romanticism. Which is why Dorothea Tieck substitutes an elevated poetic formula for Shakespeare's direct remark. Moreover, it is not infrequent for the romantic unobtrusiveness to determine the choice of words as well" (in *A. W. Schlegel 1767–1967*, pp. 33–34). One will benefit from Emigholz's brief analysis of Dorothea Tieck's *Macbeth* translation, an analysis in which the limits of romantic translation clearly appear.

39. *Jenaischen Allgemeinen Litteratur-Zeitung*, quoted in Jolles, p. 32.

40. See our Chapter 10.

41. F. Schlegel, *Kritische Schriften*, p. 403.

42. Quoted in Ernest Tonnelat, *Histoire de la littérature allemande* (Paris: Payot, 1952), pp. 165–77.

Schleiermacher and W. von Humboldt: Translation in the Hermeneutical-Linguistic Space

1. Schiller writes to Humboldt in 1796: "In my eyes, you have a nature that would prohibit you from being counted among the speculative and scholarly men of the concept—and a culture that excludes you from the genius sons of nature. Your path is certainly not that of production, but you have the judgment and the patient fervor to accomplish yourself" (quoted in the Introduction to Humboldt's works, tr. Pierre Caussat, Paris: Seuil, 1974, p. 17). The "fervor" and the "judgment" concern the study of language.

2. "The symbolic system is formidably intricate, it is marked by that *Verschlungenheit* [which] designates the linguistic intersection— every isolable linguistic symbol is not only solidary with the whole, but cut through and constituted by a series of affluences, of oppositional overdeterminations that constitute it in several registers at once. Is this system of language, into which our discourse is displaced, not something that infinitely surpasses any intention that we may put in it and that is only momentaneous?" (Jacques Lacan, *Le Séminaire*, vol. I [Paris: Seuil, 1975], p. 65).

3. Cf. Peter Szondi, "Schleiermacher's Hermeneutics Today," in *On Textual Understanding and Other Essays*, tr. Harvey Mendelsohn (Minneapolis: University of Mineapolis Press, 1986).

4. Crudely speaking, theories of understanding postulate that the meaning of its "expressions" is accessible to the subject by virtue of a hermeneutic movement of self-understanding. Theories of interpretation postulate that the subject, in a certain way, does not have access as such to such an understanding. This is the whole conflict between psychoanalysis and phenomenology as it appeared with Merleau-Ponty and Ricœur. Steiner's work on translation is situated in the framework of a theory of understanding, and it is striking that he never once mentions the discoveries of psychoanalysis, though these are of a nature to change our view of interlingual and intralingual processes.

5. In effect, Schleiermacher proposes a reading of oral expressions, i.e., those of "conversation." Cf. Szondi, pp. 98–101.

6. H.-G. Gadamer, *Truth and Method* (New York: Sheed and Ward, 1975), p. 350.

7. Schleiermacher, "On the Different Methods of Translating," in Lefevere, p. 71.

8. Letter to Schiller, quoted by Caussat (tr.), *Introduction*, p. 17.

9. "Latium und Hellas," p. 20.

10. In Lefevere, p. 88.

11. Thus Schleiermacher studies the relations of national languages in conjunction with translation, the case of bi- or multilingualism, the conditions for the access of the mother tongue to the state of "cultivated" language. Translation, then, finds itself in an "intersected" space where the relation to languages can take on a thousand forms. Humboldt studies the relation of languages to their dialects, their communities, etc.

12. This systematic remains in the programmatic stage.

13. In Szondi, p. 99.

14. In Lefevere, p. 82.

15. The same distinction can be found in hermeneutics, where not everything is worth an act of understanding. Cf. Szondi, p. 99.

16. In Lefevere, p. 86.

17. Ibid., p. 71.

18. Foucault, pp. 287–91.

19. In Lefevere, p. 76.

20. Ibid., p. 72.

21. Ibid., p. 74.

22. Ibid., p. 74.

23. Ibid., p. 75.

24. Ibid., p. 74.

25. Ibid., p. 85.

26. Ibid., p. 83.

27. Ibid., pp. 79–80.

28. Ibid., p. 81.

29. Ibid., p. 79.

30. Ibid., p. 79.

31. Ibid., p. 79.

32. Ibid., p. 84. We should not forget that Schleiermacher was talking to the Berlin Academy.

33. Ibid., p. 80.

34. Ibid., pp. 88–89.

35. Humboldt, "Einleitung zu 'Agamemnon'," in Lefevere, p. 41.

36. Ibid., p. 42.

37. Ibid., p. 41.

38. In Caussat (tr.), *Introduction*, p. 22.

39. In Lefevere, p. 41.

40. Ibid., p. 41.

41. Ibid., p. 41.

42. Ibid., p. 42.

43. Ibid., p. 42.

44. Ibid., p. 42.

45. [*Inquiétante-étrangeté* (disturbing strangeness) in the usual French translation of Freud's *Unheimliche*. In English, of course, the usual translation is "the uncanny".—TR.]

46. In the field of translation, the limits of hermeneutical theory—from Schleiermacher to Steiner—seem to be the following: to dissolve the specifity of translating by making it into a special case of the interpretive process, to be unable, as a theory of consciousness, to approach the unconscious dimension in which linguistic processes—and hence, translation—are played out.

Regarding the first point, to assert that translation is an interpretation, an act of "understanding," is a misleading obviousness. That there is interpretation in each translation does not mean that every translation is nothing but interpretation or that it depends essentially on interpretation. The relation to the foreign work and the foreign language played out in translation is *sui generis*, capable of being seized only on the basis of itself. Interpretation always aims at a meaning. Now, translation depends so little on the total capturing of a meaning that, strictly speaking, one should always translate texts one does not entirely "understand." The act of translating produces its own mode of understanding the foreign language and the foreign text, which is different from a hermeneutical-critical understanding. From this it follows that a translation never rests on a preexisting interpretation. For example, the certainty of a philosophical translation does not depend on the critical understanding of the text to be translated, even if, to be sure, some work of interpretation and analysis is indispensable. It might be said that the textual analysis to which the translator has to apply himself— like the charting of the network of fundamental terms and associations in a novel, the "system" of its writing, etc.—is determined *a priori* by the fact that he is going to translate: To read in order to translate is to illumine a text with a light that is not only of the order of hermeneutics, it is to carry out a reading-translation—a *pretranslation*. This pretranslation may appear when one looks at the words, sentences, or segments of sentences that the translator has underlined in the text to be translated *before* starting on the actual translation: not only the words and passages he does not "understand" (which will supposedly be few), but those that, at a first reading, present a problem of translation because of their great distance in relation to the "target language." Those are the skylines of the strangeness of the work, or its line of resistance to translation. And by and large this line coincides with the original system of the work in its language. From this point, a certain reading of the work is possible which may be transformed into a "critical" reading. In this sense, translation is a *knowledge* of the work.

Criticism by translation is a mode of criticism irreducible to interpretive criticism. Hermeneutical theory overlooks this dimension. Logically, it is led to consider the translator as the poor relative of the critic. It does not see the positivity of a translating reading. For hermeneutics, it will always be better to read the work in the original language— translation would be a makeshift solution. But that is not the case: Just as for the work the fact of being translated is an enriching movement, and not an uprooting, the reading of a translation is an original operation for the reader, not only because it concerns a foreign text, but because it is a special type of writing and a special type of text.

We may also point out that the "normal" mode of reading for a foreign text is the reading of its translation. To read a book in its original language will always be an exception, and an operation full of limitations. That is the normal cultural situation, which no learning of languages can or should remedy, because there is nothing negative in it. The issue here is to proceed to a radical reversal of values.

Translation is not a makeshift, but the mode of existence by which a work reaches us as foreign. A good translation retains this strangeness even as it makes the work accessible to us.

In fact, it is always assumed that the one who can read the work in its original language is better equipped to taste and know it than the one who has to settle for a translation. The latter would be to the original what the picture of a woman is to the actual woman. But both readers are dealing with a foreign text, which always remains foreign to them, whether it has been translated or not. This strangeness is irreducible. We French will never read an English poem the way an English reader does. The difference between the two readers is only gradual.

To fight the perennial obfuscation of this situation (which is an historical phenomenon that should be studied, just like studies have begun on what a "bad" translation, culturally speaking, is) is one of the tasks of a theory of translation.

For that matter, that a translation that "smacks" of translation should be considered bad is a contradiction which overlooks that the writing of a translation is an irreducible mode of writing: a writing that welcomes the writing of another language in its own writing, and that cannot, lest it be an imposture, suppress the fact that it is this operation. We should even go further, and say that in all literary writing there is always a trace of such a relation. Just like in our speech, as Bakhtin says, there is always the speech of the other, and just like this this interlacing of two speeches constitutes the dialogic structure of human language. If every writing implies a horizon of translation (and this, in a profound way, is the meaning of Goethe's *Weltliteratur*), it is absurd to demand that a translation appear as a "pure" writing—which is itself a myth. A discipline like comparative literature lives by the obfuscation or the forgetting of this problematic, which we have already mentioned in relation to *Don Quixote*.

Hölderlin: The National and the Foreign

1. Friedrich Beissner, *Hölderlins Übersetzungen aus dem Griechischen* (Stuttgart: Metzler, 1961); W. Schadewaldt, preface to *Sophokles: Tragödien. Deutsch von Friedrich Hölderlin*, ed. W. Schadewaldt (Frankfurt am Main: Fischer, 1957), etc.

2. Benjamin, "The Task of the Translator," pp. 81–82.

3. Jean Laplanche, *Hölderlin et la question du père* (Paris: PUF, 1961), p. 275. Cf. also Louis Wolfson, *Le Schizo et les langues* (Paris: Gallimard, 1970), where this negative relation appears that pushes the schizophrenic toward foreign languages and a sort of mythical language destined to neutralize the language of the "mother."

4. Laplanche: "A poet because he opens schizophrenia as a question, he opens this question because he is a poet" (p. 133).

5. Zuberbühler, p. 18.

6. Ibid., p. 78.

7. Ibid., p. 81

8. Ibid., p. 94.

9. Ibid., p. 101.

10. "I want to speak like your Luther speaks" ("Die Meinige," in *Sämtliche Werke* Bd. I, 1, ed. Friedrich Beissner (Stuttgart: Kohlhammer, 1946), p. 15.

11. "But we are fated / To find no foothold, no rest." Hölderlin, *Poems and Fragments*, tr. Michael Hamburger (New York: Cambridge University Press, 1980), p. 79.

12. Zuberbühler, p. 24, n6. King James version: "For unto you it is given in the behalf of Christ . . . to suffer for his sake."

13. In his article on Shakespeare, A. W. Schlegel writes: "Not all that is old is archaic, and Luther's sententious language is more German even now than many fashionable affectations" (*Die Horen*, p. 112).

14. On the influence of dialects, see Lothar Kempter, *Hölderlin in Hauptwil* (Tübingen: Mohr, 1975).

15. Cf. Gerard Manley Hopkins' poetry; "The mix of Latin and Anglo-Saxon was a historical fact. . . . Nevertheless, one could attempt, if not to exclude Latin entirely, at least to significantly reduce its part . . . by subordinating it to the original Saxon element become dominant. This is what Hopkins did. In search of this new dosage . . . he was led to appropriate words, or meanings, that had become obsolete. . . . Likewise, expressions gathered from a Welsh peasant's lips lose their limited, regional character entirely with him. . . . It is because Hopkins appropriated for himself this local speech, those ancient words, for profound reasons, and because he brings them into play according to the laws" (G. M. Hopkins, *Poèmes*, tr. and intr. Pierre Leyris [Paris: Seuil, 1980], pp. 10–11).

16. Heidegger, *Erläuterungen*, p. 115.

17. Hölderlin, letter no. 236, *Essays and Letters*, pp. 149–50.

18. Hölderlin, "Remarks on 'Antigone'," *Essays and Letters*, p. 114.

19. Ibid.

20. Hölderlin, letter no. 244, in *Sämtliche Werke*, 6, 1, p. 437.

21. Ibid., p. 436.

22. Heidegger, *Erläuterungen*, p. 87.

23. Ibid., p. 90.

24. Friedrich Hölderlin, *Poems and Fragments*, tr. Michael Hamburger, pp. 393–95.

25. Ibid., p. 447.

26. Friedrich Hölderlin, *Hymns and Fragments*, tr. Richard Sieburth (Princeton, NJ: Princeton University Press, 1984), p. 421.

27. Hölderlin, *Poems*, p. 537.

28. Hölderlin, *Hymns*, p. 117–19.

29. *Sämtliche Werke* Bd. 2, 1: p. 163.

30. *Ibid.* 2, 2: p. 608. The "colony," as Heidegger says in his commentary of "Remembrance," "is the foreign country, but the foreign country which simultaneously evokes the home country" (p. 93). "The colony is the daughter country that refers back to the mother country" (ibid.). The appearance in Hölderlin, in a poem that deals with what is foreign and what is one's own, of the notion of "colony," is remarkable. From the poet's perspective, it alludes to the ancient "Greek colonies" (the setting of *Empedokles* is Agrigenta, a colony) which were, in effect like "daughters" to a "mother home country," as well as to the *modern* colonies of the "Indies," mentioned, with Columbus or Vasco da Gamo, in many of Hölderlin's late poems (cf. "The Titans"). Now, those modern colonies, which are established on the "fragrant isles" of Asia and America (the old and the new Indies), maintain a different relation to the "mother home country": The latter is perpetuated in them, but the "daughters," it could be argued, are cross-bred in it: The modern colony is the place in which what is one's own and foreign are united. The daughter has been married to the foreign. And this is something that could not have escaped Hölderlin during his stay in the "colonial" port of Bordeaux.

In this sense, the poet's "Indies" have nothing to do with those of Romanticism: they designate the immense historical space opened by the navigators and the *conquistadores*, who have instituted a new form of "colony," and hence of the relation to the foreign. That this relation has historically been experienced with reference to the Greek colonizers, is borne out by Camoëns's *Lusiades*, which Germany discovered at the time when Hölderlin wrote his poems. A. von Humboldt's voyage to South America is an exploration of the reign of the modern colony.

31. Hölderlin, *Poems*, p. 477.

32. Ibid., p. 557.

33. Hölderlin, *Essays and Letters*, p. 113; our emphasis.

34. Hölderlin, *Sämtliche Werke* 2, 1, p. 325.

35. Hölderlin, *Poems*, p. 559. A confusion for which, perhaps, an example may be found in the following fragment from the Tübingen period:

> Tende Strömfeld Simonetta.
> Teufen Amyclae Aveiro on the river
> Vouga the family Alencstro its
> name therefrom Amalasuntha Antegon
> Anathem Ardinghellus Sorbonne Celestine
> And Innocent interrupted the dis-
> quisition and dubbed it (the Sorbonne)
> the nursery of French bishops—
> Aloisia Sigea *differentiae vitae*
> *urbanae et rusticae Thermodon*
> a river in Cappadocia Val-
> telino Schönberg Scotus Schönberg Tenerife
>
> Sulaco   Venafro
>   Region
> of Olympos Weisbrunn in Lower
> Hungary. Zamora Jacca Baccho
> Imperiali. Genoa Larissa in Syria
> (Hölderlin, *Hymns*, p. 235).

36. Cf. "Remembrance:" "Many a man / Is shy of going to the source" (Hölderlin, *Poems*, p. 491).

37. For his part, Goethe rather wants to keep the language at an equal distance from dialects and foreign languages.

38. "De quoi s'agit-il donc? Quelque propos te tourmente, c'est clair." *Antigone* (Paris: Les Belles Lettres, 1967).

39. "Qu'y a-t-il? Tu sembles broyer un pourpre dessein." Hölderlin, *L'Antigone de Sophocle*, tr. Philippe Lacoue-Labarthe (Paris: Bourgois, 1978).

40. In Zuberbühler, p. 18–21.

41. Hölderlin, letter to Friedrich Wilmans (28 September 1803) in *Sämtliche Werke* 6, 1: p. 434.

42. Beaufret in *Remarques sur Oedipe et Antigone* (Paris: 10/18, 1965), p. 35.

43. Hölderlin, letter to Friedrich Wilmans (2 April 1804) in *Sämtliche Werke* 6, 1: p. 439.

44. Beaufret, p. 37.

45. Ibid., p. 39.

46. Hölderlin, "Remarks on 'Antigone'," in *Essays and Letters*, p. 114. By going back from the figurative to the proper, literal meaning of the Greek verb.

47. Tr. Elizabeth Wyckoff (*The Complete Greek Tragedies*, ed. Grene and Lattimore, vol. III [New York: Modern Library, 1956]). Cf. Beaufret's discussion of this point in his introduction to the *Remarques*, pp. 36–37. Hölderlin himself justifies this divergence, saying: "To bring it [the figure of Danaë] closer to our mode of presentation" (*Essays and Letters*, p. 112).

48. It suffices to think of Nietzsche, Hofmannsthal, or K. Reinhardt's *Sophocles* (tr. Hazel Harvey and David Harvey, Oxford: Basil Blackwell, 1979).

49. Quoted in *Steiner*, p. 346.

50. Hölderlin, "Remarks on 'Oedipus'," p. 107.

51. This modernity should be situated, above all, in the way the essence of poetry is conceived: to open a space of differentiation in the double relation to the "native" and the "foreign." This is by no means particular to Hölderlin, and we suggested that an analogous view may be found in a G. M. Hopkins. Here poetry is conceived as *dialogue* (*Gespräch*), and its element, more than ever, is the *Natursprache*. Now, the space of the *Natursprache* is also that of languages, of Babel. Modern poetry has difficulty living in this space, inasmuch as it is largely connected to Romantic thinking. And poetic translation has the same difficulty.

52. Virgil, *L'Enéide*, tr. P. Klossowski (Paris: Gallimard, 1964).

53. Ibid., tr. Klossowski's introduction, pp. xi–xii.

54. It suffices to think of the growing mass of modern texts, largely overflowing the area of technics or of diplomacy, "edited" in French, Spanish, German, etc., to be sure, but appearing like bad translations from a bad English which is, nevertheless, their *supreme master* and in which, ultimately, they are destined to be retranslated. "Confusion of tongues," genuine "conflagration," in fact the reverse of a cross-breeding. When a language invests the others by virtue of its dominant position, and agrees to transform itself in order to become a "universal

language," a process of generalized destruction emerges. Linguistic cross-breedings, on the other hand, are fertile: Think, in the French domain, of Creole speech, or of the renovated and enriched language that is slowly being elaborated in black Africa.

55. Which would perhaps depend on psychoanalysis and textual analysis. Think of the "corrections" Lacan has brought to Baudelaire's "canonic" translation of Edgar Allan Poe: They clearly show that Baudelaire's translation, wholly within the wake of Romanticism, misses the complex play of signifiers in Poe (*Ecrits* [Paris: Seuil, 1966], p. 33).

56. In "Hölderlin et Sophocle," Karl Reinhardt has excellently laid bare the meaning of Hölderlin's undertaking: "Hölderlin's translations are radically different from all other translations from the Greek, even from all other translations in general. . . . In effect, for the poet translating consists in giving speech to a voice which had hitherto remained mute because of the insufficience of all the successive forms of humanism: baroque, rococo, or classicism . . . " (*Poésie* no. 23 [1982], p. 21). Further, Reinhardt speaks precisely of "the often abrupt and blunt literalism of his translations," of "their enigmatic divergence, no less frequent, from the Greek original" (ibid.). "If, for classical purism, Greek is never Greek enough, Hölderlin's translation, on the other hand, is characterized by its will to strengthen the non-Greek element in the Greek, the 'oriental'" (p. 24). In this respect, and with regard to the "enigmatic divergences," the author mentions "the lack of scruples of the translator, who replaces the Greek names of the gods by denominations forged in his own hymnic language. His Hesperic poetic, conscious of its oriental origin, allows him to cross the intermediary stage of Greek 'national conformism.' Otherwise, Zeus, Persephone, Ares, Eros, etc., would remain prisoners of conventional poetic language, and the Hesperic ear could not be reached by it the way it should be" (ibid.). Thus Hölderlin translates Zeus as "Father of Time" (ibid.). The effacement of the names of the gods, prisoners of "conventional" (humanist) poetic language, in addition to the return to the archaic meanings of the Greek, is another side of the emphasis on the "oriental" element which characterizes Hölderlin's translation of Sophocles first and foremost. Thus, abrupt and blunt literalness on the one hand, and enigmatic divergence on the other, go *in the same direction*. In both cases, it is an *emphasis*. For us, emphasis (in another context, Jacques Derrida said: "A good translation must always 'abuse'") is *the* fundamental principle Hölderlin bequeathed to Western translation. It is emphasis which gives all, and specifically syntactic, literalness its space and which distinguishes it from servile copying. Likewise, emphasis allows divergences of translation that would remain of the order of aesthetic and transtex-

tual variation without it. It is emphasis, equally, which renders null and void the phenomenon of wreckage, which allegedly menaces every translation, and which has motivated its literary and ethical devaluation at all times. It is emphasis which, through its violent house-breaking, brings the original work to our shore in its pure strangeness, and which simultaneously *brings it back to itself*, as Goethe also intuited—for every work on its original soil is distanced from itself in one way or another. That is the danger of the "native." The "experience [*épreuve*] of the foreign" concerns the work as work as well. And the more it is anchored in its "native" element, the richer the promise of translation, both for us and for the work. And, of course, the greater the risk.

But Hölderlin also teaches us to counterbalance this principle of emphasis by the opposite principle of "Western and Junonian sobriety." There can only be abuse, house-breaking, in the space of a sobriety. Sobriety re-veils, so to speak, what emphasis unveils. The balance of these two principles is what makes for the great success of Klossowski's *Enéide*, and which sets it apart from a servile and absurd interlinear.

To deepen these two principles, *emphasis and sobriety*, this is the task of a modern reflection on translation.

Conclusion

1. Matthias Claudius has expressed this effacement of translation almost tragically "Wer übersetzt, der untersetzt"—the one who translates gets swallowed up. Translation is the realm of darkness.

A. W. Schlegel's "manifesto," as we find it in his afterword to Tieck, is incredibly modest in comparison to the literary and critical manifestos of his brother or Novalis.

2. In Störig, p. 369–70.

3. Ibid., p. viii.

4. Clastres, *Le Grand parler* (Paris: Seuil, 1974), p. 15: "To translate the Guarani is to *translate them in the guarani language*. . . Fidelity to the letter in order to conserve its spirit."

5. Roman Jakobson, "On Linguistic Aspects of Translation," in *Selected Writings* II (The Hague: Mouton, 1971), p. 262.

6. Ibid., p. 261. Does this movement by which a sign is being translated by another that "develops it more fully" not remind one of the Romantic "potentiation?" To be sure, modern linguistics considers the poem untranslatable, but could one not reflect on the *positive* aspects of the movement of a translating reformulation, rather than to

perennially underscore its insufficience? Are gain and loss, destruction and "more complete" development situated on the same level here? That is a dimension that should be explored.

7. Ibid., p. 262.

8. Haroldo de Campos, "De la traduction comme création et comme critique," in *Change*, no. 14 (1973), pp. 71–84.

9. To be sure. But national characteristics survive. France remains a cultural sphere in which there is less translation than in Germany, and in which ethnocentric translation, though more and more disparaged, retains solid strongholds.

10. Notably those which seek to express the conditions of a dialogue with other cultures—cultures that are *other*. Think of the works of a Massignon, a Berque, a Clastres, etc. Modern translation must be *dialogic*.

11. "For special languages—and they have always existed—which in earlier times coexisted very well with the common language, now penetrate it well beyond any necessities that could justify it. The word *scholarly* does not so much supplement the proper word than confirm its superfluity: no one has a need to signify properly—to show some *thing*. There is talk of 'new divisions' there where the only concern is the interpretation of the 'real' as 'divisible' into problems that are not even 'new objects'" (E. Martineau, "La langue, création collective," in *Poésie* no. 9 [1979], pp. 99–121). This process, in connection with all the others, establishes vast dimensions of non-translation in cultural life, or rather dimensions in which translation has lost all its meaning.

12. [I have chosen to "not" translate—or to "semi-anglicize"—the French *traductologie* because it is obvious that Berman has something else in mind than the established, though fairly amorphous, body of research and teaching known in the USA as "Translation Studies."—TR.]

13. [Berman refers to the third book in Michel Serres's series "Hermès": *La Traduction* (Paris: Minuit, 1974), from which I translate the opening lines: "We only know things by the transformation systems of the ensembles in which they are incorporated. There are at least four of those systems. Deduction in the logical-mathematical sphere. Induction in the experimental field. Production in the practical domains. Translation [*traduction*] in the textual space. It is not entirely obscure why these should repeat the same word. That there is philosophy only as philosophy of Duction . . . is a state of affairs to the illumination of which one could devote an entire life" (p. 9).—TR.]

14. See, for instance, the work of M. Bakhtin, G. Genette, J. Lambert.

15. Bakhtin: "It could even be said that European novel prose is born and shaped in the process of a free (that is, reformulating) translation of others' works" (*The Dialogic Imagination*, p. 378). "One of the best authorities on medieval parody, Paul Lehmann, states outright that the history of medieval literature and its Latin literature in particular 'is the history of the appropriation, re-working and imitation of someone else's property'" (ibid., p. 69). Bakhtin only scratches the surface of the history of transtextualities and translations.

16. J. L. Borges, "Las versiones homéricas," quoted in *Steiner*, p. 4.

17. P. Valéry: "*To write whatever it may be* . . . is a labor of translation exactly comparable to the one that carries out the transmutation of a text from one language to another" (*Variations sur les Bucoliques*, p. 24).

18. Hence, as W. Benjamin has shown, the translation of a translation is impossible, because it is devoid of meaning.

19. Cf., for the sciences, A. Koyré: "Traduttore-traditore: à propos de Copernic et de Galilée," *Isis* 34 (1943).

20. Quoted in "Comment peut-on traduire Hafiz . . . ou Freud?" by Bernard This and Pierre Thèves, p. 41 of the very important issue of *Meta* (translators' journal) on "Psychoanalysis and Translation," published in Montréal in March 1982, which adduces decisive elements on the relation of psychoanalysis and translation. On the place of the concept of translation itself in Freud's work, see Patrick Mahony's article in the same issue, "Toward the Understanding of Translation in Psychoanalysis," pp. 63–71.

21. Quoted in Meschonnic, *Pour la Poétique II* (Paris: Gallimard, 1973), p. 411–12.

22. The system of deformation can be defined in the first instance by tendencies like rationalisation, illumination, extension, qualitative impoverishment, quantitative impoverishment, homogeneization, destruction of rhythms, of underlying networks of meaning, of systematisms of a text, destruction or exotization of vernacular terms, effacement of overlays of languages, functioning of inadequate literary horizons. For a partial analysis of these tendencies, see our article: "La traduction des œuvres latino-américaines," in *Lendemains* 8 (1982).

23. On this point, cf. J.-R. Ladmiral, *Traduire: théorèmes pour la traduction* (Paris: Payot, 1979).

24. Bernard Catry, "L'édition française face à Babel," *Le Débat* no. 22 (1982), p. 898.

25. Daniel Moskowitz, in Ladmiral, p. 220.

26. During the Third Conference of the International Federation of Translators, Jean Dutourd states: "I think that, since fifteen or twenty years, translation has played a catastrophic role in French literary life, because it has accustomed the public to jargon and contaminated the writers" (quoted in Van der Meerschen, p. 68).

27. Georges Mounin, *Les problèmes théoriques de la traduction* (Paris: Gallimard, 1963), pp. 65–66.

28. Efim Etkind, *Un art en crise: essai de poétique de la traduction poétique*, tr. Wladimir Troubetzkoy (Lausanne: L 'Age d'homme, 1982), p. 99.

29. *After Babel*, p. 365.

Selected Bibliography

1. Primary Sources

Athenäum. 2 vols. Munich: Rowohlt, 1969.

Brentano, Clemens. "Godwi," in *Werke*, ed. Friedhelm Kemp, vol. 2. Munich: Hanser, 1963.

Goethe, Johann Wolfgang von. *Gedenkausgabe der Werke, Briefe und Gespräche*. 25 vols. Ed. Ernst Beutler. Zürich: Artemis, 1948–1960.

————. *The Autobiography of Johann Wolfgang von Goethe*. [*Dichtung und Wahrheit*]. Tr. John Oxenford. Chicago: Chicago University Press, 1974.

————. *Conversations with Eckermann*. Tr. John Oxenford. San Francisco: North Point Press, 1984.

————. *Selected Poems*. Ed. Christopher Middleton. (Goethe-edition, vol. 1) Boston: Suhrkamp/Insel, 1983.

Hamann, Johann Georg. *Schriften zur Sprache*. Frankfurt: Suhrkamp, 1967.

Herder, Johann Gottfried. *Sämtliche Werke*. 33 vols. Ed. B. Suphan, C. Redlich and R. Steig. Berlin: Weidmannsche Buchhandlung, 1877–1913.

Hölderlin, Friedrich. *Essays and Letters on Theory*. Ed. and tr. Thomas Pfau. Albany, NY: State University of New York Press, 1988.

————. *Hymns and Fragments*. Tr. Richard Sieburth. Princeton, NJ: Princeton University Press, 1984.

————. *Poems and Fragments*. Enlarged Edition. Tr. Michael Hamburger. New York: Cambridge University Press, 1980.

————. *Sämtliche Werke* (Große Stuttgarter Ausgabe). 8 vols. Ed. Friedrich Beissner. Stuttgart: Kohlhammer, 1945–1985.

Humboldt, Wilhelm von. *Gesammelte Werke*. Berlin: Reimer, 1841–1852.

———. *Introduction à l'oeuvre sur le kavi et autres essais*. Tr. P. Caussat. Paris: Seuil, 1974.

———. "Einleitung zu 'Agamemnon'." Partial English translation in André Lefevere, *Translating Literature: The German Tradition from Luther to Rosenzweig*. Amsterdam: Van Gorcum, 1977.

Novalis. *Werke Briefe Dokumente*. 4 vols. Ed. Ewald Wasmuth. Heidelberg: Schneider, 1953–57.

———. *Schriften*. 5 vols. Ed. Richard Samuel. Stuttgart: Kohlhammer, 1965–1988.

Schlegel, August Wilhelm. *Kritische Schriften und Briefe*. Ed. Edgar Lohner. Vol. 2: *Die Kunstlehre*, vol. 3: *Geschichte der klassischen Literatur*. Stuttgart: Kohlhammer, 1963–64. [Extracts in Lefevere, *Translating Literature*, pp. 51–54.]

Schlegel, Friedrich. *Dialogue on Poetry and Literary Aphorisms*. Tr. Ernst Behler and Roman Struc. University Park: Pennsylvania State University Press, 1965.

———. *Kritische-Friedrich-Schlegel-Ausgabe*. Vol. 2: *Charakteristiken und Kritiken I (1796–1801)*, ed. Hans Eichner; vol. 8: *Studien zur Philosophie und Theologie*, ed. Ernst Behler and Ursula Struc-Oppenberg. Munich: Ferdinand Schöningh, 1967, 1975.

———. *Kritische Schriften*. Ed. Wolfdietrich Rasch. Munich: Hanser, 1971.

———. *Lucinde and the Fragments*. Tr. Peter Firchow. Minneapolis: University of Minnesota Press, 1971.

Schleiermacher, Friedrich. *Samtliche Werke*. Berlin: Reimer, 1838.

———. "On the Different Methods of Translating." In André Lefevere, *Translating Literature*, pp. 77–89.

2. Texts on German Romanticism

Allemann, Beda. *Ironie und Dichtung*. Pfullingen: Neske, 1969.

Ayrault, Roger. *La Genèse du Romantisme allemand*. 4 vols. Paris: Aubier-Montaigne, 1961–1976.

Benjamin, Walter. *Der Begriff der Kunstkritik in der deutschen Romantik*. In *Gesammelte Schriften* I, 1, ed. Rolf Tiedemann and Hermann Schweppenhäuser. Frankfurt am Main: Suhrkamp, 1974.

Berman, Antoine. "Lettres à Fouad El-Etr sur le Romantisme allemand." In *La Délirante* no. 3 (1968), pp. 85–117.

Blanchot, Maurice. "L' Athenäum." Tr. Deborah Esch and Ian Balfour. *Studies in Romanticism* 22 (1983), pp. 163–72.

Fiesel, Eva. *Die Sprachphilosophie der deutschen Romantik*. Hildesheim and New York: Olms, 1973 (repr. of 1924 ed.).

German Aesthetic and Literary Criticism. Ed. Kathleen M. Wheeler. New York: Cambridge University Press, 1984. [A collection of texts and excerpts from Goethe and the German Romantics, some of them translated here for the first time, including all of Novalis's "Dialogues."—TR.]

German Romantic Criticism. Ed. A. Leslie Wilson. Foreword Ernst Behler. New York: Continuum, 1982 (The German Library, vol. 21). [Another recent anthology, reprinting previously published translations together with hitherto untranslated texts.—TR.]

Guerne, Armel. "Hic et Nunc." In *Le Romantisme allemand*, ed. Albert Béguin. Paris: Cahiers du Sud, 1949.

———. "Novalis." In *La Délirante* no. 4–5 (1972).

Huyssen, Andreas. *Die frühromantische Konzeption von Übersetzung und Aneignung. Studien zur frühromantischen Utopie einer deutschen Weltliteratur*. Zürich: Atlantis, 1969.

Jolles, Frank. *A. W. Schlegel Sommernachttraum in der ersten Fassung vom Jahre 1798*. Göttingen: Vandenhoeck und Ruprecht, 1967.

Lacoue-Labarthe, Philippe and Jean-Luc Nancy. *L' Absolu littéraire. Théorie de la littérature du romantisme allemand*. Paris: Seuil, 1978.

———. *The Literary Absolute: The Theory of Literature in German Romanticism*. Tr. Philip Barnard and Cheryl Lester. Albany, NY: State University of New York Press, 1988.

Staël, Mme. de. *De l'Allemagne*. Paris: Garnier, 1868.

Szondi, Peter. *On Textual Understanding and Other Essays*. Tr. Harvey Mendelsohn. Minneapolis: University of Minnesota Press, 1986.

Thalmann, Marianne. "August Wilhelm Schlegel." In *A. W. Schlegel 1767–1967*. Bad Godesberg: Internationes, 1967.

————. *Romantiker als Poetologen.* Heidelberg: Lothar Stiehm, 1970.

Todorov. Tzvetan. *Theories of the Symbol.* Tr. Catherine Porter. Ithaca, N.Y.: Cornell University Press, 1982.

Weltliteratur. Die Lust am Übersetzen im Jahrhundert Goethes. Ed. Reinhard Tgahrt. Marbach: Deutsche Schillergesellschaft, 1982.

Wilhem, Daniel. *Les Romantiques allemands.* Paris: Seuil, 1980.

3. Works on Goethe, Humboldt, and Schleiermacher

Gadamer, Hans-Georg. *Truth and Method.* New York: Sheed and Ward, 1975 (Schleiermacher).

Meschonnic, Henri. *Le Signe et le Poème.* Paris: Gallimard, 1975 (Humboldt).

Schadewaldt, Wolfgang. *Goethe Studien.* Zürich: Artemis, 1963.

Strich, Fritz. *Goethe und die Weltliteratur.* Zweite, verbesserte und ergänzte Auflage. Bern: Francke, 1957. [English translation of the first edition (1946) in *Goethe and World Literature*, tr. C. A. M. Sym, London: Routledge and Kegan Paul, 1949.]

4. Works on Hölderlin

Beaufret, Jean. "Hölderlin et Sophocle." Preface to *Remarques sur Oedipe et Antigone.* Paris: 10/18, 1965.

Beissner, Friedrich. *Hölderlins Übersetzungen aus dem Griechischen.* Stuttgart: Metzler, 1961.

Bertaux, P. *Hölderlin.* Frankfurt am Main: Suhrkamp, 1978.

Heidegger, Martin. *Erläuterungen zu Hölderlins Dichtung.* (Gesamtausgabe Bd. 4). Frankfurt am Main: Klostermann, 1981.

————. *Approche de Hölderlin.* Tr. Henri Corbin, Michel Deguy, François Fédier, Jean Launay. Nouvelle édition augmentée. Paris: Gallimard, 1973.

Laplanche, Jean. *Hölderlin et la question du père.* Paris: PUF, 1961.

Reinhardt, Karl. "Hölderlin et Sophocle." *Poésie* 23 (1982), pp. 16–31.

Schadewaldt, Wolfgang. Preface to *Sophokles: Tragödien. Deutsch von Friedrich Hölderlin.* Frankfurt am Main: Fischer, 1957.

Zuberbühler, Rolf. *Hölderlins Erneuerung der Sprache aus ihren etymologischen Ursprüngen*. Berlin: Erich Schmidt, 1969.

5. Works on Translation

Benjamin, Walter. "The Task of the Translator." In *Illuminations*, ed. Hannah Arendt, tr. Harry Zohn. New York: Harcourt, Brace and World, 1968.

Blanchot, Maurice. "Traduit de . . . " In *La Part du feu*. Paris: Gallimard, 1949.

————. "Traduire." In *L' Amitié*. Paris: Gallimard, 1967.

De Campos, Haraldo. "De la traduction comme création et comme critique." In *Change* no. 14 (1973), pp. 71–84.

Etkind, Efim. *Un art en crise. Essai de poétique de la traduction poétique*. Tr. Wladimir Troubetzkoy. Lausanne: L'Age d'homme, 1982.

Jakobson, Roman. "On Linguistic Aspects of Translation." In *Selected Writings* II. The Hague: Mouton, 1971.

Koyré, Alexandre. "Traduttore-traditore: à propos de Copernic et de Galilée." In *Isis* 34 (1943).

Ladmiral, J.-R. *Traduire: théorèmes pour la traduction*. Paris: Payot, 1979.

Larbaud, Valery. *Sous l'invocation de saint Jerôme*. Paris: Gallimard, 1946. [Partial English translation in "The Translator's Patron," tr. William Arrowsmith, in *Arion* no. 3 (1975): 314–57.]

Lefevere, André. *Translating Literature: The German Tradition from Luther to Rosenzweig*. Assen/Amsterdam: Van Gorcum, 1977. [I have used extracts from Goethe, A. W. Schlegel, Schleiermacher, and Humboldt collected in this anthology.—TR.]

Leyris, P. "Introduction" to Gerard Manley Hopkins," *Poèmes*. Paris: Seuil, 1980.

————. "Pourquoi retraduire Shakespeare?" Forewerd to Shakespearos *Oeuvres*. Paris: Club du Livre, 1962–1964.

Meschonnic, Henri. *Les Cinq Rouleaux*. Paris: Gallimard, 1970.

————. *Pour la poétique* II. Paris: Gallimard, 1973.

————. *Pour la Poétique* III. Paris: Gallimard, 1973.

————. *Pour la Poétique* V. Paris: Gallimard, 1978.

Meta 27, no. 1 (1982). Special issue on "Psychanalyse et traduction."

Mounin, Georges. *Les belles infidèles*. Paris: Cahiers du sud, 1955.

————. *Les problèmes théoriques de la traduction*. Paris: Gallimard, 1963.

Pannwitz, Rudolf. *Die Krisis der europäischen Kultur*. Nuremberg, 1947.

Paz, Octavio. *Traduccion: literatura y literalidad*. Barcelona: Tusquet, 1971.

Rosenzweig, Franz. "Die Schrift und Luther." In Störig, pp. 194–222.

Schadewaldt, Wolfgang. "Das Problem des Übersetzens." In Störig, pp. 233–41.

Sdun, Winfried. *Probleme und Theorien des Übersetzens in Deutschland vom 18. bis zum 20. Jahrhundert*. Munich: Hueber, 1967.

Steiner, George. *After Babel: Aspects of Language and Translation*. New York: Oxford University Press, 1975.

Störig, Hans Joachim (ed.). *Das Problem des Übersetzens*. Darmstadt: Wissenschaftliche Buchgesellschaft, 1969. (We have often quoted texts on translation by Goethe, A. W. Schlegel, Humboldt, Schleiermacher, Schadewaldt from this excellent anthology).

Valéry, Paul. *Variations sur les Bucoliques*. Paris: Gallimard, 1957.

Van der Meerschen. "La traduction française, problèmes de fidélité et de qualité." *Lectures*, no. 4–5 (1980).

6. Other

Bakhtin, Mikhaïl. *Rabelais and his World*. Tr. Helen Iswolsky. Cambridge, MA.: MIT Press, 1968.

————. *The Dialogic Imagination: Four Essays*. Ed. Michael Holquist, tr. Caryl Emerson and Michael Holquist. Austin, TX: University of Texas Press, 1981.

Benjamin Walter. "Gespräch mit André Gide." In *Gesammelte Schriften* IV, 1, ed. Tillman Rexroth. Frankfurt: Suhrkamp, 1972. ("Conversation avec André Gide." in *Oeuvres I: Mythe et Violence*, tr. Maurice de Gandillac, Paris: Denoël, 1971.)

Berman, Antoine. "L' Amérique latine dans sa littérature." *Cultures* 6 (1979).

———. "Histoire et fiction dans la littérature latino-américaine." *Canal*. Paris, 1980.

———. "La traduction des oeuvres latino-américaines." *Lendemains* 8 (1982).

Catry, B. "L'édition française face à Babel." In *Le Débat* no. 22. (1982).

Du Bellay, Joachim. *Défense et illustration de la langue française*. Paris: Gallimard, 1967.

Forster, Leonard. *The Poet's Tongues: Multilingualism in Literature*. New York: Cambridge University Press, 1970.

Foucault, Michel. *The Order of Things: An Archaeology of the Human Sciences*. New York: Random House, 1970.

Genette, Gérard. *Mimologiques*. Paris: Seuil, 1976.

Hofmannsthal, Hugo von. *Die prosaischen Schriften gesammelt*, vol. II. Berlin: S. Fischer, 1907.

Jaccard, R. "Proust théoricien." In *Le Monde*, August 5, 1982.

Jacottet, Philippe. *Poèmes*. Paris: Gallimard, 1976.

Klossowski, Pierre. *L'Enéide*. Paris: Gallimard, 1964.

Lacan, Jacques. *Le Séminaire*. I. Paris: Seuil, 1975.

———. *Ecrits*. Paris: Seuil, 1966.

Luther, Martin. *Luther's Works*, vol. 35 *Word and Sacrament I*. Ed. Theodore Bachmann. Philadelphia: Muhlenberg Press, 1960.

Martineau, E. "La langue, création collective." *Poësie* no. 9 (1979), pp. 99–121.

Murat, J. *Klopstock*. Paris: Les Belles Lettres, 1959.

Nietzsche, Friedrich. *Beyond Good and Evil*. Tr. Walter Kaufmann. New York: Random House, 1966.

———. *The Gay Science*. Tr. Walter Kaufmann. New York: Vintage Books, 1974.

———. *Twilight of the Idols*. In *The Portable Nietzsche*, ed. and tr. Walter Kaufmann. New York: Viking, 1954.

Robert, Marthe. *L' Ancien et le nouveau*. Paris: Grasset, 1963.

Robin, Armand. *Ma vie sans moi*. Paris: Gallimard, 1970.

Tonnelat, Ernest. *Histoire de la littérature allemande*. Paris: Payot, 1952.

Wolfson, Louis. *Le Schizo et les langues*. Paris: PUF, 1969.

INDEX